The McGraw-Hill
36-Hour
Course in
Finance for
Nonfinancial
Managers

Other Books in The McGraw-Hill 36-Hour Course Series

The McGraw-Hill
36-Hour Course in Finance for Nonfinancial Managers

Robert A. Cooke

McGraw-Hill, Inc.

York San Francisco Washington, D.C. Auckland Bogotá
Caracas Lisbon London Madrid Mexico City Milan
Montreal New Delhi San Juan Singapore
Sydney Tokyo Toronto

Library of Congress Cataloging-in-Publication Data

Cooke, Robert A.
    The McGraw-Hill 36-hour course in finance for nonfinancial
managers / Robert A. Cooke.

        p.   cm.
    Includes index.
    ISBN 0-07-012539-2—ISBN 0-07-012538-4
    1. Budget in business.   2. Financial statements.   3. Business
enterprises—Finance.   4. Corporations—Finance.   I. Title.
II. Title: McGraw-Hill thirty-six-hour course in finance for
nonfinancial managers.
HG4028.B8C663   1993
658.15—dc20
                                        92-31306
                                        CIP

        4 5 6 7 8 9 10 DOC/DOC 9 0 3 2 1 0 9

ISBN 0-07-012539-2 {HC}
ISBN 0-07-012538-4 {PBK}
        11 12 13 14 15 DOC/DOC   0 3 2

*The sponsoring editor for this book was Betsy N. Brown, and the production
supervisor was Donald F. Schmidt. It was composed in Baskerville by North Market
Street Graphics.*

Printed and bound by R. R. Donnelley & Sons Company.

*This book is printed on recycled, acid-free paper containing a minimum of
50% recycled de-inked paper.*

This book is dedicated to my wife, Cay, who was not only a constant source of encouragement and support, but spent endless hours correcting the manuscript; and to Gwynn Kelley who provided much help in "keeping it simple."

Contents

8. Ownership and Equity   117

9. Budgeting/Planning   136

Final Examination (follows Index)   **1**

Preface

My friend, Ralph, went to college and majored in history (and extra-curricular activities). With sheepskin in hand, he applied for many chairman-of-the-board positions and wound up in a slot selling copy machines. The social amenities learned in college helped, and the eventual responsibilities of one-and-a-half children ensured that he became a heavy hitter in the sales representative roster. He became a field supervisor/trainer; and eventually, when the third child was within two months of arriving, he was appointed Southeast Regional Sales Manager.

The euphoria of the private office, first-class travel, secretary, and impending large bonuses was short-lived. Ralph moved into the high-powered job on September first. On October first there arrived the memo from the national sales manager: "Regional sales budgets for next year are due by October 31."

Ralph had heard of budgets, but he wondered, "How do you make a budget?" Partying 101 and the related advanced courses did not include anything about budgeting. He looked at last year's budget. Where do the numbers come from? What do they mean? He was desperate. With embarrassment he went to the corporate controller and asked for help. Judy, a young staff accountant just out of college, was assigned to help him. From her, Ralph heard words such as *capitalized, prepaid, deferred, depreciation,* and others. Definitions? Judy was a technician. She knew what the terms meant, but brief explanations of them were not her forte. Accounting majors do not receive much exposure to the communications, journalism, or English departments.

At the executive budget meetings, each executive was to discuss the impact of other department budgets on his own budget. Ralph muddled through, but it was plain to everyone that he was not only deficient in understanding the budgeting process, he was terrified by it.

Yes, a budget for the Southeast region was produced. Was it meaningful? Was it a useful management tool? In despair, Judy and Ralph had taken last year's budget and added 10 percent. But Ralph's predecessor had already won approval for one additional sales person in the region. Fax machines were to be added to the line in January. There would be fax kick-off displays and meetings in Charlotte, Atlanta, and Miami, but Ralph's budget made no provision for that added expense nor for the additional sales that would be generated.

By April, the national sales manager, the vice-president of sales and marketing, the president, and the board of directors all knew that Ralph's budget was useless. "Ralph," the president told him, "finance is the language of business. You would be well advised to learn it."

For self-preservation, Ralph enrolled in Accounting 101 at a junior college. His summer evenings and weekends were filled with learning about debits, credits, journals, ledgers, and all the details that qualify one to keep books—a skill that Ralph did not need. What he did need was knowledge of how to use what an accountant puts together—financial statements, operating reports, and budgets of a complex operation such as a manufacturer and distributor of office equipment. That information, Ralph found, did not come until the second semester of the second year of accounting.

Ralph needed a viable way to short-circuit the details and find answers to questions such as: "If I authorized an expenditure, why does it not show up on my operating report until weeks later? How do I prove that purchase of a new piece of equipment is justified? How can I get my budget to change during the year to reflect changes in business conditions? How do I make sense out of the company's annual financial statements?"

As Ralph found, the taking of accounting courses would eventually provide answers to these questions, but that route is extremely time-consuming and entails the absorption of much extraneous information. For accounting involves not only the theories of presenting financial information, but the nuts-and-bolts procedures and the rationale behind the theories. The sales managers, the production managers, and all nonfinancial managers can learn to use the product of accountants efficiently without being proficient in the processes by which accountants generate the numbers. In other words, Ralph could function very well without knowledge of debits, credits, "T" accounts, journals, ledgers, trial balances, etc.

I wrote this book to meet the needs of all the Ralphs, Shirleys, Toms, Nancys, and everyone who is not a finance expert or an accountant, but who has to deal with finance, financial concepts, and budgets in the daily course of work. I have conducted workshops across the country with the same purpose. I found that almost every company, nonprofit organization, and government entity has a little bit different procedure in their accounting ways and, therefore, different expectations of input from their nonfinancial managers. So, you probably will not find every question about your company's procedure answered here, but you should find the basic concepts and buzzwords that will allow you to ask intelligent questions of your finance and accounting personnel and understand their answers.

If you own a small business, you're probably aware of the importance of minding the numbers, but are frustrated by blocks to communicating with your bookkeeper and accountant. This book should improve that communication.

And, if you invest, or would like to invest in stocks, this book should give you the knowledge to cut through the sales hype or the hot tip and understand what, exactly, you are buying when you buy stock in a particular company.

You can read this book casually to gain some basic background in finance. However, if you treat it as it is constructed—that is, as a *course*—your retention will be greater. The questions and case study questions at the end of each chapter (lesson) are designed to test your understanding of the concepts covered in the chapter. The answers follow the appendixes at the back of the book, and where it seemed appropriate, I have included an explanation of the answers—to reinforce the explanations in the chapters. Although the chapters vary in length and complexity, the average time devoted to each should be about 3 hours, for a total of 36 hours of study.

Certainly, you should take advantage of the final exam at the end of the book. You make the choice whether it is to be open book or closed book. Be sure to send your completed answers to McGraw-Hill for grading and a handsome certificate if you pass. The details are at the beginning of the exam.

I have tried to keep what I have to say simple. Where there are major exceptions to a concept or definition, I have mentioned them. Where such details are small, and it is unlikely most readers will run into them, I have omitted any comment about them. My purpose in writing this book is to help you learn the language of finance so you can communicate with financial people and ask about any details that you, in your specific situation, need to know.

Good luck. I hope this book speeds you toward your financial success.

Robert A. Cooke

1

Numbers, Numbers, Numbers: The Why and the How

Statistics and Numbers That Confound Us

My attitude toward numbers was strongly influenced by having Miss Ball for Algebra in the 10th grade. She was most successful—in turning off any interest I had in numbers! She stated her philosophy as: "Don't try to understand why. Just do it!" Most of us have run into such a figure at some time in our youth. If we ever thought that there isn't much fun in numbers, Miss Ball made sure we forever believed it. To be fair, there were other, kinder teachers who explained reasons and tried to tie mathematics to popular applications. But they were hampered by being required to use textbooks that asked questions such as:

> Mary had twice as many apples in her basket as John had chickens in a number of boxes, and the number of boxes was the square root of Alice's age. Alice was twice as old as Mary and half of John's age. How many wings did the chickens have and should they be fried or broiled?

Who cares?

This attitude carries over to our adult lives. We hear statistics about the gross national product, the unemployment rate, stock price averages, the national debt, and our employer's productivity gains. We know that all of these things are important, but the basketball game or the latest movie on HBO is usually more appealing.

Scores: Numbers We Enjoy

Yes, these experiences made most of us averse to numbers, particularly when they appear formally on tax returns, financial reports, bank statements, etc. But note that we still find numbers to be friendly in informal areas such as the point spread in the Super Bowl, a golf handicap, or tennis score. Those of us who have been to Las Vegas or Atlantic City know all the combinations of numbers that add up to 21, although we would rather we had never become acquainted with the combinations that add up to 22 or more.

Years after my experience with Miss Ball, I became comfortable with numbers and spent much of my time involved with them. How? I took the easy step from sports and other leisure activities to business. I say it's an easy step, for business has been described as "sports, but for real." Business is competitive. If you commit a foul, the judge will penalize you, and score is kept in dollars. So, if you need or want to be more comfortable with financial reports and the like, think of them as scorecards. If your company, division, or other area of responsibility has made more profit or reduced expenses, you have won. The prize is more income, a promotion, or both. For example:

> You manage a restaurant for the G-Spoon Eatery chain. Compared to last year, sales have increased by $500,000. Net profit has increased by $100,000, and net income as a percentage of sales is 17 percent, compared to 5 percent last year. It sounds good, but it's still a bunch of numbers—pretty dry stuff. However, if you make some more computations, you find that, because of the increase in sales and profits, your bonus will be $35,000. Now the numbers become much more interesting. And if you want to equate that $35,000 to being able to turn in your old Chevrolet for a Porsche, the numbers become extremely interesting.

So, as you read on in this chapter, think of the numbers as a scorecard. Just as a tennis book will explain the intricacies of tennis scorekeeping, this and the following chapters will explain the intricacies of business scorekeeping. Or think of it this way: Most of us like to talk (remember all those bull sessions as a teenager?); in other words, we are social animals who like to communicate with each other. When we communicate about boyfriends, girlfriends, spouses, war, peace, or Uncle Lem, words are the language of communication. When we communicate about business, we use numbers as well as words, for financial numbers are the basic language of business. So, when you study financial numbers, you are merely adding to your vocabulary.

Simplicity Makes It Easier

In most of the examples and case studies in this book, you will find numbers rounded to the nearest hundreds or thousands of dollars because that makes it easier to understand the concepts. You can do the same with your own numbers. If you are dealing in millions of dollars, round off the numbers you are working with to the nearest thousand. If you are dealing in thousands, round off to the nearest hundred, and so on. Of course, pennies should almost always be disregarded (unless you are dealing with costs per each item, as discussed in the next paragraph). After all, if sales are actually $8,573,425.76, and you round it off to $8,573,000 you have introduced an error of only 0.005 of 1 percent—hardly enough to alter any decisions made based upon the report.

Accountants call this concept *materiality*. A *material error* is one which is large enough to cause people to make a decision that is different from a decision they would make if they had the correct figures.

For instance, let's say you are the president of the Pointless Pencil Company. Your accounting department has a clerk who, after rounding off too many numbers and making several errors, computes that each pencil costs $0.01 to manufacture. You and your chief accountant decide, therefore, that you can sell the pencils, in jobber lots, at $0.013 each. You do so, and after several months find that the company checkbook has a zero balance and many bills remain unpaid. Your accountant reviews the clerk's figures and finds that he rounded the cost from the actual figure of $0.014 per pencil to $0.01. Of course, had you known that the pencils really cost you $0.014, you would not have run the company into bankruptcy by selling them for only $0.013 each. The error the clerk made was a whopping 29 percent ($0.004 ÷ $0.014) and was obviously material, for it caused an incorrect decision. The moral: Round off whenever it will not be material (as the 0.005 percent error in the first example), but be careful. Sometimes even a fraction of a penny can be material.

Going Into Business
(Our Novel)

Business schools use the case study method of instruction. Why should we be different? What follows is a story of a company that starts in simple fashion as a retailer. The evolution of this company will serve to illustrate many basic concepts. In later chapters, the company expands into service, contracting, and manufacturing, so nearly all types of businesses are illustrated.

You did know that accountants are frustrated novelists, didn't you? That is why, woven through the figures in this book, you will find the story of Rosie Rouse and how she started and ran the Spouse House Company. What's a Spouse House? Until recent times, disgraced or out-of-favor spouses were banished to the dog house in the backyard. Poor Rover, displaced from his home, had to do the best he could under the porch or in the bushes. Now, with the emerging support for animal rights, Rover can no longer be evicted from his dog house. The disgraced spouse must find shelter elsewhere. Here is a new need, a new market—shelter for discredited spouses.

Rosie is the first to see this new market, and the first to fill it. She decides to sell Spouse Houses—buildings that are much larger than dog houses but small enough to fit in backyards. These buildings include amenities such as recliner, carpet, and insulation. She starts into business by making arrangements with Fred's Sheds, a manufacturer of Dutch colonial garden storage sheds. To fill Rosie's orders, Fred will modify sheds into Spouse Houses by adding the amenities.

Rosie rents a small office, has a telephone installed, and places some advertising in the newspaper. She also has some stationery and business cards printed, and leases (for one year) the automobile in which she will make sales calls. During January, her first month, the following occurs:

- Rosie sells three Spouse Houses at $1500 each, for cash.

- She purchases the three Spouse Houses from Fred's Sheds for $900 each. She pays him for two of the Spouse Houses ($1,800) and promises to pay him for the third one on February 5.

- She pays $800 for her office ($400 for January rent and $400 as a security deposit).

- She pays $150 to purchase a telephone, and $30 for service during January.

- She buys newspaper advertising for $300.

- On February 5, she receives an electric bill for electricity used during January. It totals $100.

- She charges the January rent of the automobile ($280) to her credit card, which she does not pay until February 15.

Now, because you are reading this book, Rosie has selected you to be her accountant. She asks for a report on her January business. There are a couple of ways you can prepare it for her.

Basic Concept
(Cash Accounting
and Accrual Accounting)

Report Version 1

Cash receipts and cash disbursements (what went into or out of Rosie's checkbook and/or pocket):

January Report

Cash receipts:

For sale of 3 Spouse Houses		$4,500

Cash disbursements:

Purchase of 2 Spouse Houses	$1,800	
Office deposit and rent	800	
Telephone purchase	150	
Telephone service	30	
Advertising	300	
Total cash disbursements		3,080
Excess of receipts over disbursements		$1,420

For clarification, let's define the headings of "cash receipts" and "cash disbursements." *Cash receipts* are all the checks, money orders, and cash received in a given period of time. *Cash disbursements* are all the checks written (and mailed) or cash paid out in a given period of time.

Report Version 2

Income and expense (what was earned and what were the costs and expenses related to the earnings):

January Report

Revenue:

Sales, 3 Spouse Houses		$4,500
Subtract: Cost of goods sold (3 Spouse Houses @ $900)		2,700
Gross profit		1,800

Expenses:

Office rent	$400	
Telephone service	30	
Automobile rent	280	
Electricity	100	
Advertising	300	
Total expenses		1,110
Net income		$ 690

There's a difference between the two reports. Just looking at Rosie's checkbook as reflected in Report 1 indicates she is ahead by $1420, but in Report 2, she has a net income of only $690. Why the difference? While the differences may look obvious, let's review them in detail, for they are simple examples of what is forever confusing about sophisticated financial reports and budgets.

Report 1 is just a reflection of Rosie's checkbook, but Report 2 is based on what accountants call the *matching principle*. If three Spouse Houses are sold during January, the offsetting cost of those sales, which is the cost of three Spouse Houses, should be recorded as the January cost that matches the January sales. So, the cost (at $900 each) of the three Spouse Houses sold in January (at $1,500 each) of $2,700 is displayed as the "cost of goods sold," even though the third house was not paid for as of January 31. In other words, the *matching principle* requires that expenses be deducted from related revenues in the periods in which they occur.

Similarly, Report 2 for January reflects the expense of car rental of $280, even though Rosie does not write a check for it until February 15. We cannot tie the car rental expense to a particular product sale, as we could tie the cost of the third Spouse House to its sale. However, we can tie it to a time period—the month of January, in this case. Because January has come and gone, the related automobile rental expense has occurred; it is *matched* with January, and therefore is listed as a January expense, regardless of when payment is made.

This process of recording transactions when they happen (not when they are paid for) to meet the matching principle, is called *accrual* accounting. It is the basis on which all publicly held companies* report their earnings, and it reflects better the true results of a company's operations. For instance, the Spouse House Report 1 suggests that Rosie may have $1,420 to spend as she pleases. Of course, she doesn't, partly because she owes Fred's Sheds $900 of that cash, she owes the credit card company $280 for the car rental, and she owes the electric company $100.

There are two other differences between Reports 1 and 2, or between cash and accrual accounting. Report 1 records the $800 as paid for the office rent and deposit. In the accrual Report 2, it is listed as only $400, the rent for January. The $400 deposit is not an expense of January. In fact, it is never an expense, for some day Rosie (or one of her heirs) will close the office and receive a refund of the $400. In the same way, the purchase of the telephone is not an expense of January, but an expense of all the years during which it may last and be used by the company. Actually, a very small part of that cost of the telephone is January expense, but it is so small that we can ignore it for now. In Chap. 5 we will cover this item and its computation, which is known as *depreciation*.

---

* The concept of *publicly held* companies is more fully discussed in Chaps. 8 and 11. Briefly, it refers to companies whose stock is owned by many people and actively traded, as on a stock exchange.

When to Use and Not Use Cash Accounting

One of the accounting rules is that, with few exceptions, reports of the income of a business should be prepared on the accrual basis. You may ask, "If accrual accounting is preferred, why even discuss cash basis accounting?" The answer is that the cash basis is very simple, and for small service companies that sell for cash and pay their bills on time, it may be adequate. If you are on a cash basis, you have only to take your checkbook to your accountant in order to have a tax return prepared. (The Internal Revenue Service does accept cash basis reporting from some small businesses.)

A Few Basic Terms

There are some terms in Report 2 that will be with us not only for the rest of this book, but for the rest of our lives:

Sales refers to what is charged to customers for goods or services. The term is used almost synonymously with *revenue.*

Revenue refers to the income that flows to an enterprise before deduction for any costs or expenses. In a business, the term is used almost synonymously with *sales.* In governments and nonprofit organizations, it includes taxes and grants.

Cost of goods sold means the cost, to the company, of the merchandise that was sold to customers.

Gross profit is what's left after you subtract cost of goods sold from sales. (*Gross margin* means about the same thing.)

While on the subject of margin, let's go over the distinction between two related terms: Profit margin percentage and markup percentage. *Profit margin percentage* is the difference between the selling price and the cost price of a product, divided by the *selling* price. *Markup percentage* is that same difference (between selling price and cost price) divided by the *cost* price. We can apply this to Spouse Houses. The facts are as follows:

Selling price, each Spouse House	$1,500
Subtract cost of each Spouse House	900
Gross profit (margin), one Spouse House	$ 600
Gross profit (margin) percentage = $600 ÷ $1,500 =	40%
Markup percentage = $600 ÷ $900 =	67%

Expenses are other costs that are not matched with sales as part of cost of goods sold, but are matched with a specific time period, as, for example, the Spouse House Company's rent of $400 per month.

Net income, also called *net profit* or *earnings,* is what's left after you sub-tract expenses from cost of goods sold. The "net" part does not refer to basketball or tennis, but it might relate to fishing in that the "fish left in the net" are what is left of sales after all the costs and expenses have drained out. This net income is often referred to as *the bottom line.* You will hear accountants use *net* as a verb, saying that a minus figure was *netted* to a positive figure. They mean that, for example, if −3 is netted to +5, the result is 2.

In hard times, net income can be negative, in which case it is called a *loss.* That occurs when cost of goods sold and expenses are larger than sales.

Financial Statements and Reports

Up to this point we have referred to our display of operating numbers as reports. For much of this book we will talk about reports, but at times we will talk about financial statements, which are documents that look just like some reports. What's the difference?

What are reports? If you call or write one of the companies listed on a stock exchange and ask for their *annual report,* you will receive a glossy booklet full of prose that extols the company's success, along with some pages full of numbers. When your boss asks for a report of your production last week, he or she probably wants a list of numbers, such as sales made or paperweights produced. The boss probably does not want a report full of prose, which might better be labeled "excuses." While a report can contain anything from a fifth grade exposition of the causes of Mackenzie's Rebellion to a quarterly report of earnings of General Motors Corporation, this book will be concerned mainly with financial reports.

A *financial report* is anything that the management of an enterprise wants prepared. It could be a cash register tape of today's sales, a summary report of all the financial transactions for a year, and many things in between.

Financial statements are financial reports in a special, prescribed format. They should be put together in a format that meets the rules of Generally Accepted Accounting Principles (explained in the next section). I suppose they are called financial statements because they make a statement about operations and financial condition. Generally, they are suitable for distri-bution to creditors, bankers, investors, etc. A set of financial statements contains several displays of numbers in specific formats. We will be talking about them throughout this book and wind up with complete coverage in Chap. 12.

Generally Accepted Accounting Principles (GAAP)

Why should financial statements be prepared according to Generally Accepted Accounting Principles if they are to be given to people outside of the company management? The idea is to have every company's financial statements prepared in the same way so that, for instance, a banker could compare two similar companies and decide which one was in better shape and deserving of his or her loan services. Does it work? Only "sort of." Every company is different, so every company puts its financial statements together a little differently, but still within the framework of Generally Accepted Accounting Principles. Throughout this book we will find instances where the rules provide a company with alternatives of more than one way to report a given transaction.*

Generally Accepted Accounting Principles is a mouthful of a phrase if it has to be repeated several times. Accountants, not being given to verbosity, therefore shorten it to GAAP. When you hear these number-crunchers talking about "gap," they are not talking about a pass through the Blue Ridge Mountains. They are referring to Generally Accepted Accounting Principles.

Who Makes the Rules? Who Defines GAAP?

What are those principles, and who makes them up? Until 1973, the accountants, through the American Institute of Certified Public Accountants, made up their own rules. (That's nice work, if you can get it.) They called them "Generally Accepted Accounting Principles," and that phrase still sticks around. But other people, such as bankers, stockbrokers, etc., wanted a say in what was in financial statements. They convinced the accountants to let them in on the deal and together they formed the Financial Accounting Standards Board, which, since the early 1970s, has been churning out rules almost (but not quite) as fast as the Internal Revenue Service. Here again, accountants abbreviate and create new words. They call the Financial Accounting Standards Board the *FASB* and pronounce it "fazz-be."

A concise definition of GAAP is somewhat elusive if it is to avoid several technical accounting terms, but here is an attempt: *Generally Accepted Accounting Principles* is a broad set of rules, developed by tradition over centuries, and now codified by the Financial Accounting Standards

---

* A good example of different, but acceptable, ways of preparing financial statements is in inventory valuation. See Chap. 3.

Board, that delineate how various transactions will be reported on financial statements.

Finance and accounting people often refer to financial statements as external or internal. *External financial statements* refer to those that are put together, according to the rules of GAAP, for people outside of the company, such as bankers, other creditors, and investors. *Internal financial statements* are for use within the management of the company. There is no law that requires the latter to be assembled according to any rules. Management people can have them put together in any form that will best help them manage.

Do the examples in this book follow GAAP? If they are labeled "financial statements," they essentially do, except they may be incomplete. If the examples are labeled "operating reports" or "management reports," they may or may not be according to GAAP.

My earlier mention of the Internal Revenue Service brings up the final point of this rule discussion. The IRS makes rules for preparation of tax reporting. In many instances, the rules for financial statements, as set forth by the FASB, are much different. In this book, we will be concerned with accounting (communication) rules promulgated by the FASB, rather than with reporting taxes to the IRS.

In our discussion of the accounting rules and the various examples, we will sometimes ignore some of the details of the rules. After all, our purpose here is to cover the basic concepts. So, if your friendly neighborhood CPA tries to mire you in confusing and detailed rules, explain that you are after the basics. When you run into a situation in which you need to know what the nit-picking details of a rule are, you can ask for the accountant's help in that area at that time. (This book should provide you with the words and enough skill to be able to ask the question and understand the reply.)

Perhaps it appears that we are getting too far away from finance when we discuss the intricacies of accounting rules. After all, this is a book on finance, not a book designed to make you into an accountant. As I mentioned at the beginning of this chapter, the financial numbers are the language of business. To understand what the numbers mean and where they came from, we need to have some familiarity with the rules by which accountants put the numbers together. We will, though, omit any substantial discussion of the detailed process by which accountants accumulate, total, and then transfer the numbers to the reports with which we are dealing.

Summary

Think of numbers as a scorecard for your business or department. Think in terms of the concept—what the numbers represent: sales, expenses, new equipment, etc. After you have visualized the concept, attach the numbers (rounded).

Activities of a business can be reported on a cash or accrual basis of accounting. Generally, accrual gives a more accurate picture of a company's operations during a given period. The accounting principles and rules are made up by the Financial Accounting Standards Board, not the Internal Revenue Service.

Review Questions

1. Fill in the blank: Financial numbers are the _____ of business.

2. Numbers should always be rounded off to nearest thousands.　　　　T　　F

3. Accrual basis reflects only the cash flow (money received and money disbursed).　　　　T　　F

4. Matching principle requires that expenses be deducted from related revenues in the periods in which they occur.　　　　T　　F

5. The Financial Accounting Standards Board makes up the rules that the Internal Revenue Service enforces.　　　　T　　F

Case Study Question _____

Wally's Wallpaper Company sells wallpaper, installed on the customer's wall. Wally does not stock the wallpaper, but buys it after the customer has made a selection. During April, his company picked up 500 rolls of wallpaper from the wholesale house and installed all 500 rolls, charging the customers $10 per roll, installed. At the end of the month, he had collected for all of his sales except for the sale to one customer (Uncle George), who still owed him for 25 rolls.

Wally has a charge account at the wholesale house, which charges him $4 per roll. He has paid for 350 of those wallpaper rolls and still owes the wholesaler for 150 rolls. During April, Wally's company also has these transactions:

- The company pays April rent of $300 for its small office.
- The company receives a telephone bill for $120 but does not pay it until May 5.
- Hot weather is coming, so Wally signs up for a drinking-water service. He writes a company check for $175. Of that, $50 is for a bottle of water, and $125 is a deposit on the cooler that holds the bottle of water. (When and if the cooler is returned to the water company, the deposit will be refunded to Wally's company.)
- Wally has one helper, Jack. Jack started with the company in late March and earned $300 in March and $800 in April. The company pays Jack on the first day of the month for all the work performed

the previous month. In this computation, pretend the year is 1928—there is no social security or income tax withheld. Jack is paid his entire salary, with no deductions. (Remember, this is pretend, to make it simple. Do not pay your employees this way in these modern, IRS-afflicted times.)

Your assignment: Make up two reports for Wally's Wallpaper Company: (1) A cash receipts and disbursements report for April and (2) an accrual basis income and expense report for April.

2
Keeping Score: Sales

What Is a Sale?

What is a sale? In the vernacular of our everyday life we tend to equate selling with the art of persuading others to part with their money in exchange for some goods or services.

But, in this book, we are dealing with terms as they are used in the finance area and in the financial reports put together by accountants—and accountants live in a rather precise world. That is as it should be, for people who use financial reports want to know that an accounting term always means the same thing, whether it is used in McDonald's annual report or in the statement the local paint store submits to its banker. Also, the reports that accountants produce all too often end up as documents in court proceedings, and that has required accountants to lean heavily on the lawyers' terms, and even to create some terms used by lawyers.

Therefore, in the field of finance, *sales* is not the art of persuasion, but the transfer of ownership of (title to) property or the rendering of service. Also, sales does not refer to those who sell what they don't own (and I refer to both my Uncle Roscoe, who sold the Brooklyn Bridge several times, and to individuals such as stock brokers and real estate agents who legally sell property belonging to others). Sales does refer to selling what you do own—your house, your car, or the pottery you make on Saturdays. It also refers to providing services to others, whether it is washing cars for your neighbors for $15 each, or a whole year of services to the Amalgamated Consolidated Corporation for $40,000, $100,000, or whatever you can get.

Types of Sales

Cash Sale

When Rosie Rouse started the Spouse House Company, she put a ready-made Spouse House on a flat-bed trailer, off-loaded it in the customer's backyard, collected the money, and left. This was clearly a sale—she traded money for merchandise.

Credit Sale (Sale on Account)

In March, Rosie sold her tenth Spouse House to her Uncle Harry. He was a rather wealthy individual, and part of his wealth accumulation came about because he never parted with money until he absolutely had to. This had two results germane to our story: he needed the Spouse House because his stinginess kept him in trouble with his spouse, Aunt Matilda; and he did not pay Rosie for the Spouse House until June. Was the sale made in March, when the Spouse House was delivered, or in June, when Uncle Harry finally wrote the check? The accountants' (and the lawyers') rule is that the sale happened when Rosie delivered the Spouse House to Uncle Harry. In technical terms, *the sale occurred when ownership of (title to) the property was transferred.*

When does transfer of ownership really occur? When Rosie delivered Uncle Harry's Spouse House on the company truck and Uncle Harry signed the delivery ticket, ownership transferred and the sale was made. However, when she sold a Spouse House to Uncle Oscar, who lived 2,000 miles away in East Barrel Stave, she had a truck line pick it up and deliver it to Uncle Oscar. He had agreed to pay the truck charges, so the shipping terms on Rosie's invoice were FOB shipping point. The acronym *FOB* stands for *free on board* or *freight on board,* both of which mean the same thing. It specifies the point to which the shipper will pay freight charges, and that point is normally the point at which ownership changes. Had Rosie agreed to pay the truck charges, the shipping terms would have read FOB destination. Ownership would not have changed, nor would the sale have occurred, until the Spouse House arrived at Uncle Oscar's yard.

Is this important? No, if delivery takes place in a few hours and there are no transportation company complications. But if delivery takes days or weeks there can be complications.

Years later, the Spouse House Company had expanded into manufacturing Spouse Houses and shipping them to distributors. Rosie shipped a container of 10 Spouse Houses to her distributor in China, FOB the pier in China. As the crane on the ship was off-loading the container, it dropped the container in the water before the container and the Spouse Houses ever landed on the pier. As the market for salt-water-soaked Spouse Houses is extremely limited, there was a loss of about $9,000. Who pays? Was there a sale made? When did ownership of the Spouse Houses transfer to the distributor?

As the shipping terms were FOB the pier, the important question became: "Had the Spouse Houses ever been on or over the pier before they went swimming?" The lawyers are still arguing. Rosie, fortunately, had insurance that covered this mishap, but only for the cost of the Spouse Houses. The insurance proceeds did not represent a sale, but only a reimbursement of her costs. The sale was made when she shipped 10 more Spouse Houses to China and they were landed successfully on the pier.

There are exceptions to considering a sale made when title transfers. For instance, my former client, Frank, was a dealer in large yachts priced at $250,000 and up. He owed the bank over $2 million (secured by his inventory of yachts). To keep the bank from demanding full payment of the $2 million, he had to provide the bank with reports that proved he was making a profit. It was December, and the year had not been good. He needed one more sale of a large yacht for his profit and loss report to show a profit. What did he do? He enlisted the aid of his brother-in-law, Charlie. Charlie bought a $360,000 yacht from Frank, taking delivery on December 28 when he gave Frank a promissory note for $360,000, payable on January 10. Frank considered title to have been transferred and recorded it on his records as a sale in December, creating enough profit to satisfy the bank.

On January 3, Charlie applied for a bank loan so he could pay off the note he gave Frank for the boat. When, on the same day, he was turned down for financing on the yacht, he returned it to Frank, who tore up the note, but included the transaction in sales on his December operating report. Then he listed a $360,000 return of merchandise on his January report. Yet, when Frank sold the yacht in December, he was fully aware that Charlie had not worked in 18 months and was on welfare and food stamps.

Was there a genuine sale of that yacht in December? Of course not. There has to be a reasonable expectation that the buyer is financially capable of completing the deal. In this case, not only was there not a sale, but the transaction, and its later cancellation, appears to have been a sham.

Consignment (Sale?)

Back to Rosie Rouse's Spouse Houses: As the company grew, it became involved in manufacturing Spouse Houses and distributing them through a countrywide dealer network. Generally, the dealers arranged financing of their Spouse House inventory and paid, at the wholesale price, when the Spouse Houses were delivered. But Rosie treated her brother, Ronald, a little differently. When he became a dealer in the town of Knowhere, he was unable to procure bank financing, so Rosie sent him three Spouse Houses on consignment.

The arrangement works like this: The Spouse House Company continues to own the houses. When Ronald sells a Spouse House, he is immediately to send the payment for the wholesale price of the house to Rosie.

When should Rosie record the sale of the three Spouse Houses to Ronald? As we have already discussed, the accountant's definition of a sale is, "A sale occurs when title transfers, regardless of when and how payment is made." Therefore, Rosie does not have a sale of a Spouse House to Ronald until she transfers title (ownership) to him or to his customer. As she elects not to transfer title until Ronald remits the money, she cannot report the sale of three Spouse Houses when she ships them to him. She must wait until he sells a Spouse House and can send her the money. In other words, she does not have a sale until he has a sale. Until that time, she considers the three Spouse Houses to be in the company's inventory of goods held for sale. In fact, if Ronald does not sell them, she will have to have them shipped back to her warehouse.

This *consignment* can be defined as a delayed sale, in that the shipper of the merchandise (in this case, Rosie's Spouse House Company) retains title to the merchandise until the retailer (Ronald) finds a customer to buy the merchandise. As each consigned item is sold, there is a simultaneous sale from the shipper to the retailer and from the retailer to the customer.*

Why would Rosie ship the houses to Ronald on this consignment arrangement? Would not her financial report be more likely to impress her banker if she could report the shipment of the three Spouse Houses as an immediate sale? She could accept his promissory note as payment.†
The immediate sale would be more impressive, so why does Rosie ship on consignment?

From the fact that Ronald cannot obtain bank financing, Rosie can surmise that his financial condition is weak. If financial disaster (as in bankruptcy) hits Ronald, Rosie still owns the houses and can pick them up. If she had transferred ownership to Ronald when she shipped the houses, and then financial disaster hit him, a court might sell the Spouse Houses and use the proceeds to pay other suppliers. There may be no funds left with which to pay off the note to Rosie, so she would be out the wholesale price of the Spouse Houses.

---

* Our lawyer friends would find technical errors in this definition. I overlooked them in order to define how the consignment sale appears to flow in most of these arrangements with retail stores. See the glossary for a more technically correct definition.

† This is not the same situation as the sale (in exchange for a note) by Frank, the yacht broker. In Rosie's case, she would expect that Ronald would pay the note from the proceeds of selling the Spouse Houses.

Secured Sale

If it is important to Rosie that the Spouse House Company reports the shipment of the houses to Ronald as an immediate sale, she could immediately transfer ownership to him and have him sign a promissory note and documents that give her company a security interest (similar to a mortgage or a lien on a car) in the houses. If Ronald became insolvent, the security interest should enable her to repossess the houses before the other creditors. However, this generally involves court procedures and legal expenses that consignment can avoid. Rosie has to decide, "Is the benefit of recording an immediate sale worth the risk of future hassle?"

Floor Plan Sale

This can be the best of several worlds for the seller, because the accountants allow it to be considered an immediate sale. If the seller assumes any credit risk, he or she is protected by a security interest in the merchandise, and most important, the seller is immediately paid.

For example, although Rosie is afraid Ronald may go broke, Clementine, who owns the local bank in Knowhere, thinks better of Ronald—although not enough better to lend him money without security or collateral. This is the *floor plan* arrangement Rosie, Ronald, and Clementine worked out:

Ronald orders the three Spouse Houses from the Spouse House Company. The company ships the Spouse Houses to Ronald, but *invoices the bank* for the $2,700 wholesale price. Ronald, in effect, borrows the $2,700 from the bank by signing a promissory note, but he never sees the money. (Instead, he sees the Spouse Houses in his warehouse.) The bank sends the money directly to the Spouse House Company. Also, Ronald gives the bank a security interest in the Spouse Houses as collateral, and the Spouse House Company guarantees Ronald's promissory note to the bank.

The note is due as the houses are sold, or at the latest, 24 months from the date the note is signed, whichever comes sooner. If Ronald does not sell the houses within 24 months, he is in trouble—he has to find other funds with which to pay the note. If Ronald doesn't pay, the bank has *recourse* to the Spouse House Company (i.e., the bank can demand payment from the Spouse House Company because it guaranteed Ronald's note).* However, if the company has to pay off Ronald's debt to the bank, it would then take over the bank's security interest in the Spouse Houses. That is, Rosie could repossess the Spouse Houses from Ronald.

---

* Sometimes (very rarely) a bank will offer floor plan financing without a guarantee by the manufacturer or distributor. In such cases, the bank would not be able to force someone such as Rosie to take the Spouse Houses back.

This floor plan arrangement has several advantages over the Spouse House Company's keeping title to the houses physically at Ronald's store, as in a consignment arrangement. Foremost, of course, is that Rosie is paid on delivery for the original sale and it is immediately a bona fide sale. If Ronald defaults on the note, the bank is geared to collection and repossession procedures and can effect them easier than can Rosie. A *floor plan sale* to a dealer can be defined as a sale accompanied with a guarantee by the manufacturer (or distributor) of the dealer's debt incurred to purchase the merchandise.

Sale of Services

As business grew for the Spouse House Company, Rosie added various services for her customers. They could sign up for weekly cleaning of their Spouse Houses, repairs to the plumbing and electric service, and/or daily restocking of the refrigerator in the Spouse House. (The latter service was useful for those spouses in chronic disgrace.) In providing service, there is no tangible product on which title can transfer, so we have to have another instant at which the sale occurs. And for service, it's simple: the sale occurs when the service is rendered. So if, on Monday, Rosie sends the plumber to fix a leak and he or she does so in an hour, the sale is made and recorded on Monday. What if the job is to replace the roof, and that takes three days and is completed on Wednesday? The sale is recorded on the day it is completed—Wednesday. Again, it makes no difference when the customer pays for the service. The sale is made on the day it is rendered. Obviously, a service cannot be returned for refund after it is performed, so there can be no consignment of or security interest in a service.

Long-Term Contracts

What if Rosie expands, or rather, her company expands into building 100-story office buildings that take three years to complete? Is there no sale until the last door trim on the 100th floor is finally painted? Now it is more complicated. The short and incomplete answer is that, in recording "long-term" contracts, part of the sales income, and part of the cost of the construction, is reported in each of the 36 months. The long answer is in Chap. 11 of this book.

Reduction of Sales

Bad Debts

Bad debts are amounts owed by customers who are insolvent, bankrupt, or who have disappeared. Payment will never be collected.

For example, five years after opening, the Spouse House Company's sales were over $2.5 million per year. In June, Rosie sold a Spouse House to her old math teacher, Miss Ball, on open account. The price of $1,800 was to be paid in 30 days. Miss Ball bought a Spouse House because she was to be married to George Square the following Saturday, and she wanted to be prepared for all eventualities of married life. However, when George saw the Spouse House, in Miss Ball's backyard, he panicked—breaking off the engagement and cancelling the wedding. Miss Ball, brokenhearted, left town—along with the Spouse House, which she had apparently put in the back of her pickup truck before disappearing.

Rosie hired a collection agency to try to track down Miss Ball and collect the $1,800. After six months, they reported that they were unsuccessful. Miss Ball had completely vanished and the collection agency was giving up. Rosie had a bona fide bad debt.

To be accurate and true to the materiality principle, Rosie could thumb through the file of monthly reports, find June's report, and correct it by reducing sales to reflect the $1,800 that was not really a sale. At least it was not the type of sale anyone wants—an exchange of merchandise or service for an account receivable that is never paid. Rosie would also have to change other numbers for items that are related to that sale, such as the wholesale cost of the shed that became the Spouse House.

If this were an isolated incident of a bad debt and such happened only once every five years or so, it might be feasible to correct a monthly or yearly report in this fashion. However, most companies frequently encounter customers who do not pay.* Revising previous reports for each bad debt would be a time-consuming task. In addition, there would be a herculean task of correcting the accounting books that underlie the reports. (Fortunately, details of "keeping the books" are not included in this book. Just take my word for it, the task would be huge.) The expeditious course is for Rosie to list, on the December report, a "bad debt expense" of $1,800. Sure, it is an error in "matching," but on sales averaging $250,000 per month, an item of $1,800 is only $\%_0$ of 1 percent of one month's sales, which is hardly material.

However, in her sixth year of business, Rosie eyes new markets. She finds that it is not only spouses in the United States who become disgraced, but that spouses in most foreign countries are a market for Spouse Houses. She looks for distributors in other countries and locates many, among whom is the merchandising firm of Adolf & Saddam in Upper Slipovia. The president of that country, who happens to be Adolf's cousin, assures Rosie

---

* In fact, marketing experts state that if a company does not suffer some bad debts, its credit policy is too strict. See the discussion in the Appendix.

that Adolf & Saddam is an old, respected company that always fulfills its obligations. Based on that recommendation, and assured by Adolf that Spouse Houses would be a hot item in Upper Slipovia, Rosie ships 500 Spouse Houses to Adolf & Saddam. That company was to pay $450,000 to Rosie's company within 30 days.

This meant that Rosie would have to buy the materials and pay the production people to manufacture these Spouse Houses before she would receive money from Adolf & Saddam. For this, she had to borrow $300,000 by giving the bank second mortgages on the factory, her house, and her Jaguar.

The 500 houses were shipped in October. On November 24, her shipping agent notified her that the houses had been off-loaded in Upper Slipovia and trucked to Adolph & Saddam's warehouse. On November 26, the television news told Rosie that there had been a coup in Upper Slipovia. Was she concerned? Of course. She tried to call Adolf & Saddam and received a recording that the telephone had been disconnected. Efforts to contact that distributor through the State Department, the Upper Slipovian embassy, and a private investigator turned up no sign of Adolf, Saddam, their company, or the houses. By March of the next year, Rosie knew there was no hope. She was out the $450,000!*

Rosie had to renegotiate the bank loan, paying it off in monthly installments. She survived, but this episode had a major impact on her financial picture.

How should this be recorded on her books and in her operating statements? Let's look at the basic accounting rules that apply.

A sale is a sale when title transfers. Rosie shipped these houses FOB the dock in Upper Slipovia, at which point Adolph & Saddam owned the houses. The sale had taken place and should have been recorded as a sale in November. A bad debt becomes a bad debt when the chances of payment become so small as to be nonexistent, which was in March of the following year.

As in the case of the small Miss Ball debt, going back to the November report and removing the $450,000 from sales would be a laborious task. Not only that, it would leave the problem of what to call the cost of the Spouse Houses that were shipped. Besides, the sale was legally made in November. There was a sale made, as Rosie honestly expected to be paid. The noncollection is a result of her erroneous judgment. Also, by March, when it is obviously a bad debt, not only has the report for November been completed, but the year-end financial statements and tax returns have been

* Do not let this episode discourage you or your company from selling in foreign markets. There are ways to protect against this calamity, such as a letter of credit or banker's acceptance. Rosie should have sought competent advice in international commerce.

completed. Accountants are reluctant to change financial statements they have already issued, for it indicates that someone did not know what he or she was doing—not the best way to impress the company's banker or its owners.

Another alternative would be to record this traumatic event as a bad debt in March. Look what it would do to the March report: sales of approximately $250,000 and a bad debt expense of $450,000. Without considering the cost of the houses and the administrative expense, the company has already lost $200,000 in March. Realistic? Of course not. But does it matter that it is not realistic? This unusual item can be explained as a footnote to the financial reports.

It does matter. Rosie has her vice presidents on an incentive program. Their monthly bonuses are computed on the improvement of that month's profit over the same month of the previous year. If the sale was made in year 6, the bad debt is recorded in March of year 7, and there is no such catastrophe in March of year 8, the profit for March of year 8 would be several hundred thousand dollars greater than the "negative profit" (loss) in year 7. The resulting bonuses, computed on that large an improvement, would be another financial calamity for Rosie.

What should Rosie do? She should do what the accounting rules say to do. (Eventually, we will always get back to those rules.) The Spouse House Company, you, I, and everyone else who do our accounting according to GAAP, should level out the bad debt expense by using an *allowance for bad debts* system.

Jeff, her accountant, set this procedure up for her in her first year in business: Because Rosie anticipated she would be shipping to marginal credit risks, such as her brother Ronald, she and Jeff decided to assume that bad debts might run 4 percent of sales. So, on each monthly and annual report, there was a subtraction from income of an item called *bad debt expense* that was 4 percent of sales. Did Rosie write a check to someone called "Bad Debt"? No. Remember, Jeff is preparing the company financial statements on an accrual basis. Expenses are subtracted from income when they are incurred (when they happen). If the expectation is that 4 percent of sales will never be paid for by customers, then we can assume that the 4 percent bad debt expense has happened when the sale is made.

The matching principle can be followed by anticipating that expense and deducting it from the current sales. We can look at each $100 of sales as including $4 that will never be paid. For the first year of the Spouse House Company's operation, Jeff might prepare a report that looked like this:

Sales	$250,000
Subtract bad debt expense (4%)	10,000
Sales for which company eventually will be paid	$240,000

But there is something different here! For every other expense we have looked at, a check is written. It may be paid before or after the expense is incurred and listed on the report, but a check is written at some time. However, the bad debt expense is just listed on the report. A check for the $20,000 will never be written. (You wouldn't write a check to someone who owes you money and will never pay you, would you?) Is it just a figure that is stuck in the report and then forgotten?

Not really. Jeff keeps track of the total of all the bad debt expense figures that have been listed on the reports. From that total he subtracts the bad debts that have actually happened. The result is a running total of where the company stands—bad debts expected versus actual bad debts. For the Spouse House Company, the record for the first seven years looks like this:

Year	Sales	Expense	Bad debts incurred	Accumulated allowance for bad debts
1	$ 250,000	$ 10,000		$ 10,000
2	650,000	26,000		36,000
3	1,500,000	60,000	$ 1,800	94,200
4	2,000,000	80,000		174,200
5	2,500,000	100,000	3,600*	270,600
6	3,500,000	140,000		410,000
7	4,000,000	160,000	450,000	120,600

So, when the Spouse House Company was beaten out of $450,000 by Adolph & Saddam in year 7, it was not an expense of $450,000 in year 7. It just reduced the accumulation of expenses that had been subtracted from income every year since year 1.

Now let's convert this to the jargon of accountants. The running balance shown in the table is called *allowance for bad debts.*† It can be defined as the accumulation of amounts subtracted from sales as future bad debt expense, reduced by amounts that become known bad debts. The actual event of someone beating you out of money that is owed to you we labeled "bad debts incurred." Accountants call this *bad debts written off.* The term means that the money that will never be collected is "written off" or subtracted from the ongoing balance of the allowance for bad debts. As for what we called "bad

---

* The $3,600 bad debt that was incurred in year 5 was another customer that we have not discussed.

† You may also hear the term *reserve for bad debts.* This is an obsolete term. The reason: many people interpreted the term "reserve" to be akin to such as "oil reserves"; i.e., "reserve" meant there was money in the bank to cover losses from deadbeat customers just as surely as there is oil in the ground to provide future needs. As we have discussed, that is not the case.

debt expense" in the example, the accountants also, amazingly, call it *bad debt expense*. It can be defined as the amount that is subtracted from sales revenue for the portion of sales that will probably become bad debts.

Before we leave the unpleasant subject of bad debts, let's consider the admonition: "One should never say 'never.' " In the ninth year of the Spouse House Company's existence, who should show up at the front door? Miss Ball, whose debt of $1,800 had been deemed to be uncollectible and had been "written off" six years previously. She still had the Spouse House (now needing a coat of paint) on a trailer. She apologized to Rosie and told her stories of her nomadic life, traveling and living in the Spouse House. She paid Rosie the $1,800 and left to spend the next year in Calgary.

How should Rosie handle the bookkeeping of this "found" money? I hear some of you readers saying, "It's found money. Take it to Vegas or Atlantic City and have a good time!" Inasmuch as Rosie owns the company, I suppose she could do that. (She also would have to ignore some IRS concerns in this area.) So let me rephrase the question: suppose Rosie gives the $1,800 to Jeff, her accountant, and he goes to Vegas and spends it. Rosie doubtless does not think that is a satisfactory accounting solution. What Jeff is supposed to do is put the money in the bank and account for it by increasing the allowance for bad debts by the $1,800. Accountants would say that he *reverses* the bookkeeping entry that reduced the allowance for bad debts when Miss Ball disappeared. Notice that this *recovery of bad debts* does not change the sales figures or the profit figures for the year in which Miss Ball brought back the $1,800. It only changes the balance in the allowance for bad debts record and the bank balance.

We've discussed bad debts at some length. Are they that important? It depends on how extensive bad debts are in the company's history. The foregoing discussion provides a good example of the concept of setting up allowances for future expenses. There are many business situations to which the same concept can be applied, and a discussion of some of them follows.

Sales Returns

During February of the fourth year, Rosie sold 50 Spouse Houses. The fifth one was to a man named George. He had it delivered to his house, which was on Mosquito Lane, down by the swamp. Because of the mushy condition of George's land, Rosie sold him on having a contractor drive piles on which to set the Spouse House. When the second piling went down, up oozed a black liquid—oil! Lucky George, as he became known, insisted that Rosie take back the little standard Spouse House. Rosie agreed, inasmuch as George had decided to order instead a deluxe model Spouse House, complete with hot tub, sauna, and swimming pool to go with his new beachfront mansion.

George had already paid Rosie for the regular model Spouse House. When she took it back, she did not refund his money, but kept it as a deposit on the custom model that George ordered. What will appear on which month's operating report?

When Rosie delivered the standard "plain vanilla" Spouse House in February, the title (ownership) of the house transferred to George. That was a sale. When she accepted its return three days later, that was what is called a *sales return*. It would appear on the report for February as follows:

February Sales Report

Sales (50 houses)	$75,000
Less sales return	1,500
Net sales	$73,500

In effect, Rosie really sold only 49 houses during February. Why not just cancel the sale to George and show it on the report as 49 Spouse Houses at $1,500 each for total sales of $73,500? You could. However, most managers want to know what fraction of sales is returned. It's a means of measuring customer satisfaction. Also, if George had bought the house in February, but did not return it until March, the sales return would be on the March report, not the February report. So, by listing the return separately, we are letting the reader of the report know that the returned item(s) *may not* be the item(s) sold during that month.

"Aha," you say to me, "if the March return is for something sold in February, you have just violated the matching principle! How could you?" You are right. It is a violation. However, most businesses have a limit on how long a customer can keep a product and still return it.

Let's suppose you retail automatic light bulb screwer-inners by allowing customers to return them in 40 days if not satisfied. Over the year you find that 5 percent of the buyers return the machines in an average of 30 days after purchase. If that is the picture month after month, then, *on the average,* 5 percent of January's sales are returned in February, 5 percent of February's sales are returned in March, and so on. You have not materially distorted any month's net sales simply by listing the returns in the month they happen.

However, let's say you sell electric flyswatters on a slightly different guarantee. The customer may buy them anytime through July 31 and, if not satisfied, return them by August 31 for a complete refund. Sales figures from April through July will be accompanied by almost no sales returns, while August will be hit with all the returns. Is this a material violation of the matching principle? Yes, unless there are virtually no returns. And there is another accounting principle that is violated: *conservatism.*

What is the conservatism principle? Does it mean that accountants must wear dark three-piece suits, white shirts, and gray ties? Not necessarily. (I am wearing blue jeans and an orange T-shirt as I write this.)

Conservatism simply means that the financial reports do not report any operating results as being rosier than they are. For instance, if your report for June lists sales of the electric flyswatters as $100,000, is that a conservative figure for June sales? Remember, you expect 5 percent to be returned, so the conservative (or realistic) figure for June sales would be $100,000 less the $5,000 expected returns, or $95,000. You could handle this by setting up an *allowance for sales returns,* in just the same method that Rosie set up an allowance for bad debts. In other words, 5 percent of sales would be shown as sales return expense each month and the dollar amount would be added to the allowance for sales returns. The amount of actual returns, as the merchandise is received from customers, would decrease the allowance for sales returns.

As for the deluxe model Spouse House that George ordered, it will not be delivered until May, when title (ownership) will be transferred from the company to George. By definition, then, the sale will be recorded in May. Even though Rosie kept the money George paid for the regular house as a deposit, the sale of the deluxe Spouse House will not be a sale until delivery in May.

Sales Allowances

Rosie sold a Spouse House to Sheila, who lived in East Old Galoshes, three miles off the paved highway. Delivery was a real hassle, but the truck made it. However, in trucking it through the country lane, some overhanging tree branches scratched the paint on the side of the Spouse House, and Sheila complained about the scratches. It would have cost Rosie $200 to send out a painter to cover the scratches. Instead, she offered to lower the price of the Spouse House by $50 if Sheila would accept the Spouse House as is and do the paint touch-up herself. Sheila accepted the offer.

Rosie had made a *sales allowance* and that is what it would be called on the Spouse House Company operating report. For most companies, if such allowances are granted, they are usually granted at the same time the product is delivered, so the matching principle is followed. (The allowance occurs in the same period as the sale to which it pertains.)

Warranties

Rosie provides a one-year warranty with each Spouse House. The warranty covers all manufacturing defects, but it does not cover damage the aggrieved spouse may inflict on the building when trying to reach the occupant of the house. Six months after delivering a Spouse House to Sam, he calls to tell her that the door to the Spouse House will no longer close. It has apparently swelled up. Rosie sends her carpenter to fix it. After arriving, the carpenter calls Rosie to tell her that the door appears to have been beaten upon with a baseball bat. Although it was probably the beating that caused the door to no longer fit the doorway, Rosie decides to avoid argument by having the carpenter plane it down to fit anyway. The cost will be treated as a repair required under the warranty.

Notice the difference between the sales allowance and the warranty repair. The sales allowance is granted at almost the same time as the sale is made. The warranty may come up months later, or years later for some products (as automobile recalls). Now, to make the matching principle work, Rosie has to use the same concept as she did for bad debts. In other words, Jeff sets up an *allowance for warranty claims*. Rosie estimates that such claims will, over time, average 4 percent of sales. Therefore, each month 4 percent of sales is subtracted from sales as a *warranty expense* and the same amount is added to the allowance for warranty claims. Amounts actually paid for warranty repairs are deducted from the allowance for warranty claims. The concept is the same as for the allowance for bad debts.

This procedure of estimating an expense, subtracting it from income, and keeping track of it in a running "allowance for . . ." balance can be used for any type of expense you know will occur sometime in the future. Of course, you have to be able somehow to estimate the amount of the expense.

Cash Discounts
(Also Called Sales Discounts)

After the Adolf & Saddam episode* in year 6, Rosie was much more particular about choosing distributors to whom she extended credit terms. But even those who were financially strong often delayed payment for 30 to 60 days. To encourage them to pay sooner, the Spouse House Company offered a cash discount on terms *2/10 net 30*. The distributor could deduct 2 percent from the invoice amount if he or she paid the invoice within 10 days from the date the invoice was mailed. The distributor could take up to 30 days to pay, but then he or she would not be eligible to take the discount.

Of course, many distributors tried to pay in 15 to 20 days and still take the discount. In order to maintain goodwill with the distributor, Rosie usually allowed the discount if payment was received within 20 days after invoicing. When it was allowed, she did not receive the wholesale price of $900 per Spouse House, but $900 less 2 percent ($18), or $882.

---

* See the discussion of bad debts earlier in this chapter.

On October 25, she ships four Spouse Houses to Mary, her distributor in Upper Overshoe. The invoice to Mary of $3,600 is dated and mailed October 26, so Mary has until November 5 to take the discount, paying only $3,528. On November 1, Jeff makes up the operating report for October. How should he reflect the sale to Mary? Neither he nor Rosie know whether Mary will pay $3,528 in the next four days or $3,600 later, so Jeff does not know what the net amount of the sale is. There are at least two solutions:

1. Jeff could record the sale in October at $3,528. If Mary pays $3,600 after the ten days, the extra $72 would be listed as *other income* in November. The rationale here is that Mary, by not paying until 30 days after receipt of the invoice, has effectively borrowed $3,600 from the Spouse Company for 30 days. The additional $72 that Mary pays is not for the Spouse Houses, but for the use of the money (i.e., interest income).

   Again, we have run into a minor violation of the matching principle. The November *other income* should be matched with the October sale. However, the error is only 2 percent of sales and is self-correcting within 30 days, so it is *immaterial* and ignored.

2. Jeff could record the sale as $3,600 in October. If, as just mentioned, Mary pays $3,600 after the 10-day discount period, there is no other item to put in the report. If Mary pays $3,528 before the 10 days are up, the $72 shortfall in the payment will have to be listed as a subtraction from sales in November. That subtraction is usually called *cash discounts allowed.* The rationale for this method is that cash discount is an expense of collecting the money as quickly as possible. You can think of it as in the nature of interest expense, although it is generally not called that, but "cash discounts allowed."

Which method is preferable? It depends on company policy. Method 1 will state sales at 98 percent of the amount that would be stated by method 2. That could have some effect on sales commissions and other management computations. Whichever method a company elects, it should be consistently followed year to year.

Now we have slid into another accounting principle: *consistency.* When GAAP allows more than one way to present the results of transactions, the company should select one method and follow it every year. The reason: one of the tools of a financial analyst (covered in Chap. 12) is the comparison of one year's financial report to the previous year's. For instance, we want to compare sales this year to sales last year. If, at the beginning of this year, we had changed from method 2 to method 1 to handle the display of sales and cash discounts, we would have built in a fictional 2 percent decrease in sales.

The *consistency principle,* then, is that the same accounting methods and procedures should be followed every year.

You may come across other cash discount terms, such as *1% 10th prox/ net 30* (10 percent discount allowed if paid by the 10th of the following month; otherwise, due in 30 days). The business world is full of various discount terms. If you find some you do not understand, the best source of explanation is a telephone call to the company that put them on its invoice.

Volume discounts and other concessions to customers are not handled in the same way as these cash discounts. They are generally just deductions on each invoice. When Rosie Rouse started manufacturing her own sheds and setting up distributors, she instituted a policy of allowing a 10 percent volume discount to distributors who purchase more than 12 Spouse Houses at a time. So a sale to a distributor for 20 Spouse Houses would be computed as follows:

20 Spouse Houses @ $900 each	$18,000
Subtract volume discount	1,800
To be included in "sales" line of report	$16,200

Reports

After discussing several types of sales and various reductions in sales, we need to consider how to put these items on a report. The first line would be sales, and would include all the sales we discussed, with the caution that consignments are not recorded as sales until the merchandise is delivered to the consumer. Sales returns, allowances, and cash discounts are usually subtracted directly from sales to create a *net sales* number. Bad debts and warranties are usually subtracted from gross profit under headings of selling expense or administrative expense, although management of a company can classify these items any way it chooses. There is more on classification of expenses in Chap. 4.

Summary

A sale happens when ownership of property is transferred from one person to another, or when service is rendered by one person for another. (Corporations are persons for this purpose.) The date of payment is generally not a factor in determining sale date, for it is the date of delivery of the goods and/or services to the customer that determines sale date. When goods are shipped, the freight terms determine delivery date and place.

If the credit rating of the buyer is inadequate, the seller could keep title to goods in the buyer's hands by delivering the goods to the buyer on consignment. The seller can also protect himself or herself by taking a security interest in the goods or invoicing to the provider of floor plan financing.

Sales of services happen when services are delivered.

Long-term contracting is a special case and is discussed in later chapters.

Sales of products involve certain items that may materialize in the future, and when they do they will represent reductions in sales. If they are material, there should be some deduction from sales to account for the probability that not all sales will remain bona fide sales without a reduction for bad debts, returns, allowances, warranties, and cash discounts.

Review Questions

1. A sale of goods is recorded as such and can be included in "sales" in a report when _____ .

2. A sale of services is recorded when _____ .

3. When terms are "FOB Destination," the sale happens when _____ .

4. Dishonest management may fool its accountants into creating fraudulent financial statements.   T   F

5. Shipping your product to a dealer but retaining title to the product is called a _____ sale.

6. "Bad debts" are something that just happen and there is no need to make any provision for them.   T   F

7. If an "allowance for bad debts" system is properly set up, a recovery of a bad debt that was never expected to be collected should be considered as "other income" or found money.   T   F

8. A customer who buys in extra-large quantities is granted an extra 5 percent discount. This should be handled as if it were a cash discount for prompt payment.   T   F

Case Study Question _____

As of October, Wally's Wallpaper Company has the following transactions relating to sales and bad debts during the year (total sales for the year were $72,000, broken down as shown in the accompanying schedule):

- Wally estimates his bad debts will be 2 percent of sales and maintains an allowance for bad debts based on that assumption.
- In May, a customer who owed him $500 files for bankruptcy, so Wally will never collect that debt.
- In October, a customer (who was renting the house in which Wally hung some wallpaper) skips out of town. No one can find him, so Wally assumes he will never collect that debt, which is $800.

Your assignment: Make up a schedule of sales, the resulting increases in the allowance for bad debts, and the write-off of bad debts. (I've started the format for you.)

Month	Sales	Bad debt expense	Bad debts incurred	Accumulated allowance for bad debts
Beginning balance				$ 600
January	$ 4,000			
February	6,000			
March	5,000			
April	7,000			
May	9,000			
June	5,000			
July	3,000			
August	4,000			
September	8,000			
October	10,000			
November	9,000			
December	2,000			
Totals	$72,000			

3

Keeping Score: Cost of Sales

Looking for a business that will allow you to put every dollar of sales in your pocket? So am I. I doubt that either of us will find one. A business that sells products must buy or manufacture those products. As discussed in Chap. 1, that expense is called *cost of goods sold*. An enterprise that provides services will find that the people it hires to perform the services expect to be paid for their efforts. That labor usually is called *cost of sales* or *cost of services*.

Cost of Goods Sold

In Chap. 1, the Spouse House Company started in business by buying garden sheds from Fred's Sheds for $900 and selling them to buyers for $1,500. The $900 that the company paid for each shed was the *cost of goods sold*. Simple, isn't it. But life is never as simple as it appeared in Chap. 1, for into the life of Rosie and the Spouse House Company crept *inventory*.

Inventory

The simple definition of inventory is that *inventory* is a stock of items. As an example, most of us would think of something like the bottles of aspirin sitting on the local druggist's shelf, but the term can cover many things, such as a stack of paper that has not been gobbled up by the office copier. Inventory also comes with challenges as to how much it is worth while sitting on a shelf. Let's look at the following example:

By June of the Spouse House Company's first year, business was booming. Rosie lost two sales because, by the time Fred modified a shed to her specifications, the customers had reconciled their differences and decided they no longer needed a Spouse House. Her sales would be significantly increased if she could deliver a house as soon as it was ordered. She therefore ordered 12 extra finished Spouse Houses from Fred's Sheds and rented some warehouse space in which to keep them. The 12 extra Spouse Houses were completed and delivered to Rosie's warehouse on July 10.

During July, the Spouse House Company sales were:

Delivery of 7 Houses ordered by customers in June @ $1500 each	$10,500
Delivery of 4 Houses ordered by customers in July @ $1500 each	6,000
Total sales (11 Spouse Houses)	$16,500

During July, the Spouse House Company purchased from Fred's Sheds:

7 Houses that were ordered by the Spouse House Company in June and received in July	$ 6,300
12 Houses ordered and received by the Spouse House Company in July	10,800
Total purchases in July (19 Spouse Houses)	$17,100

So, now it looks like sales of $16,500 less purchases of $17,100 results in a loss of $600. On July 31, Rosie lay awake until 4:00 A.M. wondering how, if she sold the houses for more than they cost her, she could have lost $600. She called Jeff immediately for an explanation. (Yes, people do call accountants in the middle of the night!) Jeff, after some muttering, offered the following:

"The Spouse Houses left in the warehouse are *inventory*—goods that are held ready for sale or use at a later date. They are not included in cost of goods sold because they have not been sold yet. We can describe it on the monthly operating report like this," and he explained the following report:

July Report

Sales of 11 Spouse Houses @ $1,500		$16,500
Subtract cost of goods sold:		
Purchase of 19 Spouse Houses	$17,100	
Subtract 8 Spouse Houses remaining in inventory at end of month	7,200	
Cost of Spouse Houses sold		9,900
Gross profit		$ 6,600

Notice that sales are displayed at the price the customer pays for the Spouse Houses, while the purchases and inventory prices are what the company pays for the houses. The profit (or loss), of course, is the difference.

For August and succeeding months, there are two more lines to add to the report. In August, the Spouse House Company sold seven Spouse

Houses. Rosie had previously ordered 10 more Spouse Houses for inventory (and immediate sales) and they were delivered in early August. The additional two lines take into account the eight Spouse Houses that were left in the warehouse at the end of July, as follows:

August Report

Sales of 6 Spouse Houses @ $1,500		$9,000
Subtract cost of goods sold:		
Inventory at end of July/beginning of August (8 houses)	$ 7,200	
Purchase of 10 Spouse Houses	9,000	
Houses available for sale (18)	16,200	
Subtract 12 Spouse Houses remaining in inventory at end of month	10,800	
Cost of Spouse Houses sold		5,400
Gross profit		$3,600

Jeff hung up the phone, thought of retiring to Bongo Bongo, and tried for more sleep.

In this example, computation of the inventory is fairly simple. In order to be sure the report is accurate as to inventory, Rosie should physically count the houses left in the warehouse at the end of the month. If there were only 11 Spouse Houses there at the end of August, it would mean that either there was a mistake in computation or someone stole one.

Consider, however, the inventory problems of Uncle Harry, who owned a hardware store. He could keep an index card for every item he had in the store—tools, fertilizer, various sizes of nuts and bolts, and thousands of other items. He could keep track of every item received from his supplier and every item sold, do the addition and subtraction on each index card to find a balance, add up the balances on all the index cards and arrive at a total inventory to subtract from the "goods available for sale" line. This system is called a *perpetual inventory system.* It can be defined as a continuous record of items added to (purchased) and subtracted from (sold) inventory. As I have watched people keeping manual records of inventory pluses and minuses, I have often thought that it was called "perpetual" because the record-keeping work went on forever—it was perpetual.

As an alternative, Uncle Harry could just count and price (at cost) everything in the store at the end of the month and use that as his "remaining inventory at end of month." In actual practice, most hardware store owners on this system will estimate (wild guess)* the monthly inventory and physically count the inventory only at the end of the year.

---

* The "wild guess" term may be a little unfair. The estimate is usually computed by determining cost of goods sold as a percentage of sales and working backwards to determine inventory. This method defeats the purpose of determining an inventory figure—to compute cost of goods sold and gross profit. However, it is a little better than an outright wild guess.

Until recently, the second Uncle Harry method was most often used by small businesses. The inventory at the end of a period was not computed from adding and subtracting purchases and sales, but from a physical count, and the result was deducted from total beginning inventory and purchases to arrive at cost of goods sold. This method is called *periodic inventory method*. We can define it as a method of determining inventory by physically counting and pricing the items in the inventory.

The first Uncle Harry method (perpetual inventory), with the tedious and labor-intensive card system, was too expensive for most small businesses. Large companies did maintain such perpetual inventory systems with batteries of clerks busy posting purchases and sales on inventory cards. However, since the late 1970s, the availability of reasonably priced computers and software has made the maintenance of perpetual inventories feasible for almost every business. The advantage: the accountants can compute what the inventory should be; then other people can count the inventory to determine what is really there. If there is a large discrepancy, it calls for auditing and investigation procedures that are better left to professional accountants and investigators.

Inventory Value (FIFO/LIFO)

Sorry, we are not through with inventory yet. We would be if, for every item a company purchased for inventory, prices always stayed the same, but such is not the real world.

In October, Fred of Fred's Sheds explained to Rosie that his price of $900 per shed did not cover his costs for the basic shed and the modifications she required. He would have to raise his price to $1,000. Rosie was not happy, but she continued to use Fred as her supplier, as he was reliable and did quality work.

Several prospective customers had indicated they intended to buy a Spouse House for the Christmas season. (Office parties generate disgraced spouses.) Rosie therefore ordered 15 Spouse Houses from Fred for delivery in November. The facts were as follows:

- Inventory of houses in inventory on November 1: four, purchased at $900 each.

- Purchase of houses during November (recorded as purchase at time of delivery): 15 at $1,000 each.

- Sales (at time of delivery) during November: 10 at $1,500 each.

At the end of November, Rosie is astonished when Jeff asks her, "Do you want to go for high income to show the bank or low income to show the IRS?"

"I have a choice, legally?" Rosie asks.

"Yes, while your company is starting, you can make a choice between FIFO and LIFO inventory, but whichever election you make, it will be binding almost forever," Jeff spouted with a professional air.

Rosie eyeballed him. "Explain yourself, please!" Here is Jeff's explanation:

You can treat inventory as if you always sell the oldest items first. That is the way a grocery store sells gallons of milk. The oldest is placed at the front of the cooler, so it will be sold first. The reason, of course, is to reduce spoilage. The method is called *first in, first out,* or by the initials FIFO.

Or, you can assume that you always sell the newest items, the items you just purchased from the supplier, first. A good example is the coal yard that great-great-grandfather Ebenezer started in 1895. The coal that Ebenezer V sells today is the coal that was delivered yesterday. The first few tons of coal the railroad dropped in the coal yard in 1895 are still there. There have been tons of coal added and taken away, but the first lot is still there, at the bottom of the pile of coal. This is called *last in, first out,* or LIFO.

Applying this to November at the Spouse House Company, the option as to inventory method would result in two different reports:

November—First In, First Out (FIFO)

Sales of 10 Spouse Houses @ $1,500		$15,000
Subtract cost of goods sold:		
Inventory at beginning of November		
(4 houses @ $900 each)	$ 3,600	
Purchase 15 houses @ $1,000 each	15,000	
19 houses available for sale	18,600	
Subtract remaining inventory:		
9 houses (purchased in November)		
@ $1,000 each	9,000	
Cost of Spouse Houses sold		9,600
Gross profit		$ 5,400

November—Last In, First Out (LIFO)

Sales of 10 Spouse Houses @ $1500			$15,000
Subtract cost of goods sold:			
Inventory at beginning of November			
(4 houses @ $900 each)		$ 3,600	
Purchase 15 houses @ $1,000 each		15,000	
19 houses available for sale		18,600	
Subtract ending inventory:			
5 houses @ $1,000	5,000		
4 houses @ $900	3,600		
Total remaining inventory		8,600	
Cost of Spouse Houses sold			10,000
Gross profit			$ 5,000

There is a difference in the profit, and the reason is logical. If Rosie sells the Spouse Houses that cost more, she will make less profit on the sales. This concept is displayed in Fig. 3.1. Notice also that the choice of methods makes a difference in the value of the remaining inventory.

Does the type of inventory determine which method a business must use? That is, does a grocery store have to use first in, first out and a coal yard have to use last in, first out? No. You can make the assumption that the flow is FIFO or LIFO regardless of the actual physical movement of items in the inventory.

Why is there an option? Most businesses would sell their products on a first in, first out flow in order to prevent deterioration of the products. Is not last in, first out just artificial? Well, the theory that justifies the last in, first out concept is that it matches the current cost of an inventory item with its current selling price (the matching principle again!). For instance:

Angus owned and ran a bagpipe and tartan store in the mountains of North Carolina. During his first year in business he imported 100 bagpipes from Scotland at a cost of $300 each and sold 75 of them at retail for $400 each, leaving 25 in his inventory. At the beginning of his second year the exchange rate between the British pound and the U.S. dollar changed drastically, so that bagpipes would then cost him $450 each. Angus decided to order only 25 more bagpipes at this high price and hope the exchange rate would improve before he needed more. He borrowed the $11,250 ($450 × 25) he needed to pay for these pipes.

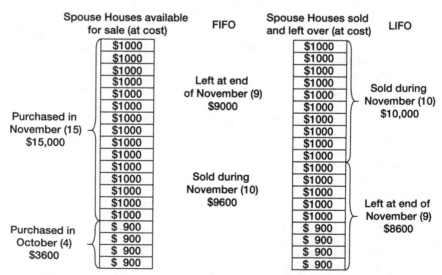

Figure 3.1 Valuing inventory and computing cost of goods sold by FIFO vs. LIFO, month of November—Spouse House Company.

Angus valued his inventory using the FIFO method. That meant he assumed he was selling bagpipes out of the inventory he had left over from last year, so he could assume they cost him only $300 each. He therefore sold them for last year's retail price of $400. He intended to raise his retail price to $600 when he started selling the bagpipes for which he had paid $450.

By April, he had sold all 25 of the pipes left from last year, and his loan at the bank was due. He went to write a check to the bank.

Oops. Look what happened to his cash flow:

Sold 25 pipes (last year's) @ $400 each	$10,000
Bought 25 pipes @ $450 each	11,250
He went in the hole	($ 1,250)

In other words, he did not generate enough cash to replace his inventory. He did not match his *current* costs of bagpipes with his sales price. Had he been using LIFO, he would have viewed his cost of goods sold as $450 each and would have raised his price to $600 right away.

Angus learned his lesson well. Now he says, "FIFO, LIFO—I dinna ken aither one. But if they raise their price, I raise my price." Any savvy businessperson should do the same.

But the biggest reason for using last in, first out is to cut down the income tax bite. When prices are generally rising, which seems to be most of the time, LIFO will reduce profit (as in the Spouse House example of LIFO shown earlier) and therefore reduce income tax.

Inventory Value (Average Cost)

This is another concept that has become practical for many businesses only since computers became available for all. It consists of averaging the cost of beginning inventory with purchases to arrive at an average cost for each item sold. For instance, the Spouse House Company's report for November would look like this if an averaging system were used:

November—Average Cost Method

Sales of 10 Spouse Houses @ $1,500		$15,000
Subtract cost of goods sold:		
Inventory at beginning of November:		
4 houses @ $900 each	$ 3,600	
Purchase 15 houses @ $1,000 each	15,000	
19 houses available for sale	18,600	
Subtract remaining inventory:		
9 houses @ $979*	8,811	
Cost of Spouse Houses sold		9,789
Gross profit		$ 5,211

* Average cost = $18,600 ÷ 19 = $979 each.

If cost prices are constantly changing, the average cost of inventory will change as often as it is recomputed. It could actually be recomputed after each purchase and each sale. If that were the method, the results would be different from the above example.

Lower of Cost or Market

Remember the conservative accountant? He's really shown up here. Regardless of whether you use the FIFO, LIFO, Average Inventory, Wild Guess (not recommended), or Phases of the Moon (again, not recommended) to value your inventory, you should not value it above market value. What is *market value?* It's what it would cost you to replace the inventory in today's marketplace. (It could be less if it has deteriorated.)

Let's visit Angus again. After he bought the 25 bagpipes at $450 each, the exchange rate changed for the better and he could then purchase the same pipes for $375. The conservatism principle dictates that he should now value his inventory at $375 each. In effect, because of changing market conditions, he has lost $75 on each bagpipe in inventory. That loss should be shown on his operating report as a separate item: *loss on valuation of inventory.*

What if exchange conditions became worse? What if it now would cost $500 per bagpipe to replace his inventory? Can he change his inventory value to $500 each? No. That would not be a conservative approach. The accountants' rule is: *Losses are reflected on reports immediately. Gains are not reflected until they are confirmed by a sale of the property on which there is a gain.* So, Angus would not report any gain on the increased value of the inventory.

Freight on Purchases

In July of the second year of business, Rosie learned that Fred would no longer be able to supply her with Spouse Houses. He had become so wealthy from her orders that he decided to close his shed business, buy a 50-foot sailboat, and enter the BOC—the round-the-world-single-handed sailboat race. Rosie desperately needed a new supplier who could make immediate shipment, and the only one she could find on such short notice was Red's Sheds. Red agreed to the old $900 price, FOB his factory, but he was 3,000 miles away. Rosie would have to pay substantial freight charges, which could be displayed in the operating reports in one of two ways:

First, the easy way. The operating report lists these freight costs as another line under purchases. The subtraction for the remaining inventory is for the invoice price of the merchandise only, so the *freight-in* charges are deducted in the month in which they are incurred. (The "-in" is added to "freight" to distinguish it from *freight-out,* the cost of shipping to customers.) Let's use the same numbers as in the July report on page 32.

July Report (with Freight-In)

Sales of 11 Spouse Houses @ $1,500		$16,500
Subtract cost of goods sold:		
Purchase of 19 Spouse Houses	$17,100	
Freight-in	1,000	
Total purchases	18,100	
Less 8 Spouse Houses remaining in inventory at end of month	7,200	
Cost of Spouse Houses sold		10,900
Profit		$ 5,600

Compare this report to the July report on page 32. The entire $1,000 of freight-in expense has ended up reducing the profit by $1,000. What tenet have we violated? You guessed it—the *matching principle.* Some of those freight costs really should be attached to the remaining inventory. How much can be computed by dividing the freight charges among the Spouse Houses shipped in. For this example it would be $1,000 divided by 19 Spouse Houses, or $53 each. By this method, the July report would appear as:

July Report (with Freight-In Allocated)

Sales of 11 Spouse Houses @ $1,500		$16,500
Subtract cost of goods sold:		
Purchase of 19 Spouse Houses	$17,100	
Freight-in	1,000	
Total purchases	18,100	
Less 8 Spouse Houses remaining in inventory at end of month @ $900 + $53 freight each	7,624	
Cost of 11 Spouse Houses sold		10,476
Profit		$ 6,024

We can check this computation by multiplying the 11 houses sold by the cost plus the freight:

$$11 \times (\$900 + 53) = \$10,483$$

The answer is approximately the same as the $10,476 shown in the report. The $7 difference is due to rounding off the pennies in the computation. Don't worry about it; it's not material.

Comparing the two methods of subtracting freight expense from income appear as:

	Profit
Method 2, allocating freight expense	$6,024
Method 1, deducting all freight expense immediately	5,600
Difference	$ 424

Which method is preferable? Where the allocation is simple, as in this example, the allocation would probably be better. After all, the $424 difference is 7½ percent of the method 1 profit, and that may be material. However, freight could consist of a steady stream of bills for import duties, ocean freight, land freight, and other freight costs. Allocation may be an expensive chore. If both the flow of the product and the freight charges are fairly constant month to month, the chore of allocation may result in little difference in the bottom line (profit) figures and may not be worth the hassle.*

Other costs of sales, such as import duties, are handled the same way as freight. They should stay with the item that incurred the cost, whether that item ends up in cost of goods sold or in inventory.

Discounts on Goods Purchased

Discounts, as offered by the vendors of merchandise or services, can come in several "flavors." For financial reporting, they can be classified into three categories: trade discount, volume discount, and purchase discount.

Trade Discount

If you or I, as individuals, had tried to buy a shed from Fred's Sheds, we would have found that Fred sold them at retail for $1,200 each. However, he sold them to the Spouse House Company with a trade discount of $300, as the company was a reseller, or retailer, of the sheds. In other words, a *trade discount* is a discount offered to someone in the "trade" of selling the product. The net price, arrived at by subtracting the trade discount from the retail price, is called the *wholesale price.*

The rationale of the discount is, I suppose, that when Fred sells a shed to a consumer, such as you or me, he will have to take time to point out the features and the quality of construction. He also will have to bear the risk that if I set my shed on quicksand and it sinks, I will be back, pounding on his desk, demanding to know why the shed was not built to float. When he sells at wholesale to Rosie Rouse and her Spouse House Company, she has to

---

* The income tax rules may require some companies to allocate such items as freight to inventory. Check with your accountant as to IRS' full absorption rules.

take the time to sell (point out features and quality) and deal with the wrath of the unhappy consumer.

Volume Discount

Later in this book, Fred offers an additional 5 percent discount to Rosie and the Spouse House Company if she would buy 100 sheds at one time. That arrangement is usually called a *volume discount* or *quantity discount.* It is a discount offered if the buyer will buy in large quantities.

Both of these discounts could be treated as separate items in a report, but they aren't. Accountants view them as the vendor's adjustment of price, so the cost of purchases is computed by using the net price on the vendor's invoice.

Purchase Discount

Please refer to the discussion of cash discounts, relative to sales, in Chap. 2. A *purchase discount,* which is a cash discount taken on a purchase, is the opposite side of the picture. As the buyer, the Spouse House Company can take a 2 percent cash discount that Fred offers if it pays within 10 days. The discount can be treated as a reduction in the cost of goods purchased, or it can be treated as other income earned by good money management. Rosie, at Jeff's suggestion, chose the latter method for the Spouse House Company. That is, Rosie looked at the discount for prompt payment as a type of interest income. That discount was earned because she had the money available to quickly pay the invoice from Fred's Sheds.

To sum up the discussion of discounts, let's look at how Jeff handled the numbers on an invoice received from Fred's Sheds for the 100 Spouse Houses bought at one time. It read like this:

100 Sheds @ $1,200 each	$120,000
Less trade discount of 25%	30,000
Subtotal	90,000
Less volume discount for 100-shed lot (5%)	4,500
Net amount due	$ 85,500

Terms are 2/10 net 30. If invoice is paid within 10 days deduct cash discount of $1,710.

Jeff treated the invoice this way. He divided the "net amount due" of $85,500 by the quantity of 100, for a cost per shed of $855. As the Spouse House Company paid the invoice within 10 days, the additional cash discount was listed on the report as *other income.*

Cost of Services

During the second year of the Spouse House Company's existence, Rosie set up a separate service division that provided a weekly cleaning of a Spouse House for $50 per week. Initially, she was able to sell only four cleaning contracts to the customers who had purchased Spouse Houses. Rather than hire an employee to provide this small amount of service, she subcontracted with Cleo, who had an office-cleaning business. Cleo was happy to have the additional work, which could be accomplished during daytime hours, and charged the Spouse House Company only $35 for each Spouse House cleaned. The company's weekly report of the cleaning service looked like this:

Sales of service (4 Spouse House cleanings @ $50 each)	$200
Subtract cost of service (4 @ $35 each)	140
Gross income from service	$ 60

Simple, wasn't it? Unfortunately, Cleo was able to sell her services to several night clubs at high rates, so she notified Rosie that she could no longer contract with the Spouse House Company at the subcontract rates. Rosie thought of doing the cleaning herself, but wisely decided her time was better spent in selling Spouse Houses. At the same time, Rosie found that the carpenters were running behind in erecting the sold Spouse Houses. They no longer had time to load the houses on the truck and deliver them, so Rosie would have to hire a truck driver. The trouble was that there was not enough truck driving to keep one person busy 40 hours a week. But Rosie was lucky because one of the applicants for the driving job was Eggbert, who had experience not only in truck driving but in operation of a mop and a vacuum cleaner. She hired Eggbert and put him to work driving the truck, cleaning the customers' Spouse Houses, and also cleaning the company's office and warehouse.

At Jeff's urging, Rosie decided to keep her accounting reasonably accurate by insisting that Eggbert fill in a time report each week. For his first week, his report looked like this:

Cleaning Spouse Houses	12 hours
Driving truck	24 hours
Cleaning office and warehouse	4 hours

In his accounting records, Jeff changed the hours into dollar amounts by multiplying the hours times the $10 per hour that Eggbert was paid, so the report now looked like this:

	Hours	Dollars
Cleaning Spouse Houses	12	$120
Driving truck	24	240
Cleaning office and warehouse	4	40
Totals	40	$400

The part of Eggbert's labor that was involved in cleaning the Spouse Houses now becomes part of the *cost of service,* along with the cost of cleaning supplies such as soap, rags, etc.

Sales of service (4 Spouse House cleanings @ $50 each)		$200
Subtract cost of service:		
Labor	$120	
Soap, rags, etc. (supplies)	10	
Total cost		130
Gross income from cleaning		$ 70

The dollar amount of Eggbert's truck driving became part of the *freight out* or *delivery expense* of the sales of Spouse Houses. That part of his labor spent in cleaning the office and warehouse became part of the expenses covered in Chap. 4.

Summary

Cost of goods sold involves not just the cost of goods purchased, but the conception of what goods are added to inventory and what goods are withdrawn from inventory for sale to customers. *Purchase of goods* can be modified by costs, such as freight, and reductions, such as trade and volume discounts. *Purchase discounts* (cash discounts on purchases) may or may not reduce cost of goods sold, depending on management's philosophy about what the discount really represents.

The most significant part of *cost of services* is usually labor, but it also includes supplies and other items that are used in providing that service.

Review Questions

1. The dollar amount of goods purchased for resale is just one of several ingredients of the computation of *cost of goods sold.*   T   F

2. When computing *gross profit* for a retail store, cost of goods sold should be listed at retail prices.   T   F

3. A *perpetual inventory system* keeps track of every item that is purchased and put in inventory and every item that is sold or taken out of inventory.   T   F

4. A *physical inventory* pertains to a medical practice. (How many physicals did the doctor do last month?)   T   F

5. If prices are rising, a LIFO inventory will result in a lower gross profit.   T   F

6. A business such as a coal yard *must* use LIFO inventory because that is the nature of its inventory. (The last coal dumped by the railroad goes on top of older coal and therefore will be sold first.)   T   F

7. If competition will permit, a business, in order to protect its cash, should raise its selling prices as soon as its supplier raises prices.   T   F

8. The cost of freight on merchandise that is received from suppliers should *eventually* end up in cost of goods sold.   T   F

Case Study Question

In September, Wally's Wallpaper Company had the following transactions relating to sales and cost of goods sold:

- Wally sold 500 rolls of wallpaper at $10 each. All of the wallpaper sold was of one design.
- Inventory on the first of September was 100 rolls of wallpaper at $3 each.
- On September 3, Wally bought 300 rolls of wallpaper wholesale, at $4 each.
- On September 18, he found that the wholesale price of the wallpaper had gone up to $5 each, but he had to have some, so he bought 250 rolls at $5 each.
- Inventory at the end of the month was 150 rolls of wallpaper. (Wally values his inventory on a first in, first out basis.)

Your assignment: Make up an accrual basis report of sales and cost of goods sold, similar to those for the Spouse House Company in this chapter. Use the following form:

Wally's Wallpaper Company
September Report

Net sales   _____

Minus cost of goods sold:

   Beginning inventory   _____

   Add purchases   _____

    Goods available for sale   _____

   Subtract ending inventory   _____

   Cost of goods sold   _____

    Net income   _____

4
Keeping Score: Expenses

Expenses, What Are They?
How Are They Reported?

This seems like a silly question, doesn't it? Expenses . . . we all have too many of the darn things—food, clothing, house payments, etc. Anyone who has made it through the first grade understands expenses for lunch, candy, and so on. If you're the neat and orderly type, you probably keep track of your expenses by categories—housing, food, clothing, entertainment, etc. If, like so many of us, you are not the orderly type, you probably keep track of expenses by watching them soak up the money. When it's all gone, there are no more expenses. (That ignores credit cards.)

Accountants define expenses a little more precisely: *Expenses* are costs that contribute toward the creation of revenue. The rent for your shoe store is an expense. If you take money out of the till to buy steaks for the family dinner, that is not a business expense.

It is virtually mandated that business expenses be categorized one way or another. That mandate comes from the banker from whom you want to borrow money; Uncle Elmo, who you want to invest in your business; your suppliers, from whom you need payment terms; and, of course, the Internal Revenue Service. These people want to know how much you spent on necessities, such as rent, and how much went for the managers' meeting in St. Thomas. They also have a variety of other questions that can only be answered by sorting the expenses into categories. And most important, you need to know how much was spent for what if you are going to effectively manage your business or department.

Expense Classification, in General

As to classification of expenses and the order in which to list them, there is no prescribed method. Some companies' reports will list expenses in alphabetical order, some in the order of dollar amount (with the highest at the top—where did the money go?). However, there are more sophisticated ways of classifying expenses, particularly for internal company use. (The sophistication is not just so accountants can create job security by making financial reports complex. It is to provide better information to management.)

This chapter covers the more common ways of classifying costs and expenses, and it includes examples of reports that utilize those classification methods. Note that the following examples omit the lines for purchases and beginning and ending inventory, and display only the result as *cost of goods sold*. This not only simplifies these examples, but it is a common and acceptable procedure.

No doubt, you will notice that the cost price of sheds is back to $900 each. In December, Rosie located a company, the Leaky Shed Company, which would sell her sheds at $900 and pay the freight charges. Faced with that competition, Fred reduced his price to his original $900 per shed.

The GAAP recommendation is that income taxes should be stated separately. The theory is that management has no control over that expense, except for the effects of programs such as pension plan structure and election of LIFO inventory. Incidentally, in these examples I have used 25 percent of net income as the income tax rate.* Unfortunately, such a simple computation of income tax is not realistic, but this is not a book on income taxation, so this oversimplification of income tax computation will be used throughout the examples.

The numbers in these examples have been rounded to the nearest 10, which seems insignificant, but it is as far as the rounding I preached of in Chap. 1 can go with these small numbers. Let's look at some of the ways expenses can be classified and displayed.

Alphabetical or Size Order

Listing expenses in alphabetical order, as in Fig. 4.1, is a common procedure for small retailers or service companies. As an alternative, the business

---

* This also assumes the business is operated as a regular corporation. If the business is a sole proprietorship, partnership, or an S-corporation, there would be no line for income tax expense, as the income tax is not assessed on the business, but on the owner of the business. More about the structure of business organizations is in Chap. 8.

```
                    Spouse House Company
                      Operating Report
                    February of Second Year

Sales of 30 Spouse Houses @ $1,500 each                    $45,000
Subtract cost of goods sold (what was withdrawn from
  inventory)                                                27,000

    Gross profit                                            18,000

Expenses:
  Advertising                          $2,000
  Automobile expenses                     430
  Bad debt expense                      1,800
  Delivery of Spouse Houses             1,500
  Insurance                               550
  Rent                                  1,000
  Supplies                                170
  Salaries, wages, and commissions      7,750
  Taxes (other than income)              910
  Telephone                               150
  Warranty expense                        900

    Total expenses                                          17,160

    Net income before income tax                              840

Subtract income tax                                            210

    Net income                                          $    630
```

Figure 4.1   Operating report—Spouse House Company.

owner might list them in descending-size order. For a small operation, this format of an income statement may satisfy the needs of the bank and other creditors.

Does such a report provide all the management information it could? Probably not. For instance, insurance of $700 per month seems high. Rosie can wonder why, but she won't find the answer in this report. She will have to ask Jeff, he will have to dig up the information for her, and Rosie will have to pay for his time.

Detailed, by Department or Division

Figure 4.2 breaks down the line items of Fig. 4.1 into several subcategories. Note that the net income is still $630. Had Jeff prepared a report such as

Spouse House Company
Operating Report—Classified by Department
February of Second Year

Sales of 30 Spouse Houses @ $1,500 each		$45,000
Subtract cost of goods sold (what was withdrawn from inventory)		27,000
Gross profit		18,000

Expenses:
  Selling expenses:

Advertising	$2,000	
Sales commissions	2,250	
Bad debt expense	1,800	
Warranty expense	900	
Total selling expense		$6,950

  Warehouse expense:

Wages	2,000	
Rent	600	
Delivery	1,500	
Supplies	140	
Total warehouse expense		4,240

General, administrative expenses:

Executive salary		2,000
Administrative salary		1,500
Automobile expenses:		
Automobile rental	280	
Gas, oil, repairs	150	
Total automobile expense		430
Insurance expenses:		
Worker's compensation	110	
Fire and other casualty	100	
General liability	110	
Product liability	230	
Total insurance expense		550
Rent, office		400
Supplies, office		30
Taxes:		
Payroll taxes	550	
Business license	230	
Property taxes	130	
Total taxes		910
Telephone		150
Total expenses		17,160
Net income (loss) before income tax		840
Income tax		210
Net income		$ 630

Figure 4.2 Operating report, classified by department—Spouse House Company.

Fig. 4.2 in the first place, Rosie would have the information about insurance that she needed, without having to ask Jeff to dig through his records for it. It is now obvious that the largest insurance item is for product liability, which is coverage of claims that customers might have for damages from a Spouse House. Perhaps Rosie should spend some time trying to convince the insurance company that a Spouse House is completely safe. The roof cannot collapse on the occupant, no matter how much the other spouse batters the Spouse House.

In this format of the report, we can see that even though Rosie owns the company, she has the company pay her a salary of only $2,000 per month. While that is not a get-rich-quick income for her, it does make the executive expense appear on the reports and financial statements. If she did not manage the company herself, she would have to pay someone to do it, so why should she not pay herself? I have seen many entrepreneurs think they are doing well because their company shows a net income, but have made no payment of salary to themselves. It was a disheartening chore to point out that the profit from the business was not much different from what they would have earned as a salaried employee for someone else—without the risk of entrepreneurship.

Like any good manager, Rosie looks ahead to the years when sales will be several million dollars per year, and she will have an executive staff, including a sales manager and a warehouse manager. As they will be responsible for expenses in their respective areas, this operating report in Fig. 4.2 breaks down expenses into sales, warehouse, and administrative expenses.

This assigning of expenses to departments could be detailed even further. For instance, payroll taxes could be allocated to sales, warehouse, and administrative areas. Remember, though, this entails extra bookkeeping effort, and the result has to justify the expense of the effort. In other words, is it worth it?

Fine-Tuning a Departmentalized Report

Remember Angus, the bagpipe dealer? Angus' customers have a problem not unlike Rosie's customers have. Spouses usually forbid bagpipe playing inside the house, and neighborhood standards forbid playing the pipes outside. Therefore, a good bagpiper, and especially a not-so-good bagpiper, needs his or her own practice house. It was almost natural, therefore, that Angus should set up a division of his company to be a dealer for Spouse Houses. His company's name became Angus' Great Pipes and Wee House Mart.

Angus hired Margaret to manage the Spouse House dealership division of his company and promised her a small salary plus 25 percent of the net income of that division. Margaret and the Spouse House division started on January 1, and the net income was to be computed at the end of each quarter, when Margaret would be paid her percentage.

In April, Angus asked his accountant, Gertrude, to prepare a report *by division* for the first quarter, which ended March 31. She prepared the report in Fig. 4.3. As you can see, it broke down sales, cost of goods sold, and sales expenses into divisions, but it lumped all the general and administrative expenses together. Gertrude was unaware that Margaret's compensation was based upon *net* income. When Angus explained that Margaret and he needed a *net* income for each division, Gertrude said: "Sure, I'll be glad to fix up a report like that, but you will have to tell me how to split up

	Bagpipe division	Spouse House division	Total
Angus' Great Pipes and Wee House Mart Operating Report, by Divisions First Quarter of the Year			
Sales	$36,000	$18,000	$54,000
Cost of sales	27,000	12,000	39,000
Gross profit	9,000	6,000	15,000
Selling and delivery expenses:			
Commissions	1,800	900	2,700
Delivery	0	600	600
Total selling and delivery expense	1,800	1,500	3,300
Operating profit	7,200	4,500	11,700
General and administrative expenses:			
Salaries			6,000
Advertising			1,000
Insurance			600
Rent			2,400
Supplies			150
Taxes and licenses			200
Telephone			150
Total general and administrative expense			10,500
Net income before income tax			1,200
Income tax			300
Net income			$ 900

Figure 4.3 Operating report by division—Angus' Great Pipes and Wee House Mart.

the administrative expenses. For instance, how many hours did the receptionist spend answering the telephone for the bagpipe division and how
many hours for the Spouse House division? I will need a breakdown on
every item of general and administrative expense."

Angus and Margaret had a problem. There was no way to answer
Gertrude's question with any accuracy. They would just have to arbitrarily
assign, or allocate, a percentage of these expenses to each division. How to do
it? Angus thought that, because a Spouse House is much larger and weighs
hundreds of pounds more than a set of bagpipes, most of the expenses
should be allocated to the Spouse House division. Margaret contended, however, that because the bagpipe division was well established and the Spouse
House division was brand new and still struggling, most of the expenses
should be allocated to the bagpipe division. Who was right? Maybe the question could have been answered simply by saying that Angus is the boss. . . .

Actually, Angus wanted to keep Margaret satisfied enough to stay on with
his company. He therefore asked Gertrude for her opinion, and reluctant
as she was to play arbitrator, she suggested allocating the expenses on the
basis of sales of each division. Fair? Who knows. This is an interminable discussion within the management of every company that has more than one
product line or one area of sales. At any rate, Margaret and Angus accepted
Gertrude's suggestion, and she produced the report in Fig. 4.4.

The bagpipe division's sales were \$36,000 out of a company total of
\$54,000, or 66.7 percent. Therefore, 66.7 percent of the general and
administrative expense, or \$7,000 was allocated to the bagpipe division.
Similarly, the Spouse House division's sales were 33.3 percent of the company total, so the allocation of general and administrative expense to this
division was \$3,500 (\$10,500 × 0.333).

The apportionment could be done on some other basis, such as the
number of units sold by each division, the number of employees, etc.
Also, each item in the list of general and administrative expenses could be
allocated by a different formula. For instance, rent could be allocated by
the proportion of floor space used by each division, with administrative salaries allocated by sales percentages as outlined earlier. Again,
don't let the tail wag the dog. Don't get so fancy in the allocation of
expenses that the accounting expense far outweighs the benefits of the
resulting reports.

Controllable and
Uncontrollable Expenses

These terms could almost, but not quite, be synonymous with the prior section on classification by department and division. The words *controllable*

Angus' Great Pipes and Wee House Mart
Operating Report, by Divisions
With Allocation of G&A Expense
First Quarter of the Year

	Bagpipe division	Spouse House division	Total
Sales	$36,000	$18,000	$54,000
Cost of sales	27,000	12,000	39,000
Gross profit	9,000	6,000	15,000
Selling and delivery expenses:			
Commissions	1,800	900	2,700
Delivery	0	600	600
Total selling and delivery expense	1,800	1,500	3,300
Operating profit	7,200	4,500	11,700
Expenses:			
Allocation of general and administrative expenses in proportion to total sales	7,000	3,500	10,500
Net income before income tax	200	1,000	1,200
Income tax	50	250	300
Net income	$ 150	$ 750	$ 900

Figure 4.4 Operating report, by division, with G&A expense allocated—Angus' Great Pipes and Wee House Mart.

and *uncontrollable expense* mean just what they say in everyday English. Controllable costs and expenses can be changed by the action of a manager. Uncontrollable costs and expenses cannot be affected by a manager's actions. Whether an expense is controllable or uncontrollable will change with the level of management.

The expense of eating dinner tonight is obviously a controllable expense. Instead of spending $85 for the Maine lobster and French champagne, you could open a 79-cent can of beans at home. You can control the outgo for food.

Is your monthly mortgage payment controllable? Obviously not. It is uncontrollable, with exceptions. It was controllable up to the date you originally agreed to buy your house. You could have controlled the expense by not buying the house. Similarly, you could control the mortgage payments by selling the house, which would end them. However, it can take months to sell a house, so within a period of a few months, it is an uncontrollable expense.

Applying this concept to a business, we can say that Rosie Rouse, as owner and general manager, has complete control over all the expenses of the Spouse House Company—if the period is long enough. She can control today's automobile expense by not driving the car. She can control rent expense only when the lease term expires.

For Lem, the warehouse manager, controllable expenses are not the same as they are for Rosie. He can, of course, control the supplies expense by careful use of the supplies. Rent expense, though, is uncontrollable to Lem. What buildings to buy, build, or rent is normally a decision by, and therefore controllable only by, top management. So, there is a difference between classifying expenses as to department and classifying them as to whether they are controllable. In Lem's case, the rent for the warehouse is clearly an expense of his department, but it is not controllable by him. This difference can be the cause of many disagreements over budget performance. We'll address that further in Chap. 10.

Summary Reports (Just the Essentials)

The formats of income statements or operating reports we have looked at so far are fairly detailed—what a company prepares for its management or for submission to a private investor or banker. The statements found in annual reports of large, publicly traded companies are more likely to look like Fig. 4.5.

This is an overly summarized report, and is inadequate for company management decision making or, frankly, for most other purposes.

Spouse House Company
Operating Report—Summary
February of Second Year

Sales of 30 Spouse Houses @ $1,500 each	$45,000
Subtract cost of goods sold (what was withdrawn from inventory)	27,000
Gross profit	18,000
Selling warehouse, general, and administrative expenses	17,160
Net income before income tax	840
Income tax	210
Net income	$ 630

Figure 4.5 Operating report, summary format—Spouse House Company.

Fortunately, there are other sources of information on large companies, and some of those sources are listed in App. C.

You often will find that accountants prepare income statements for small companies in this format. However, they will also prepare schedules of expenses that provide the detail needed for analysis by management and creditors.

Variable and Fixed Expenses, Breakeven Point

It was March, and Rosie knew that as the income tax deadline approached, there would be more spousal conflicts (over who did not have enough withheld, or who gets to spend the refund). The market for Spouse Houses would grow. How aggressively should she try to capture that market by spending more money on advertising? How much, for example, would a 33 percent increase in sales increase profits and net income? Would it be enough to justify the additional advertising expense?

In her next thought, Rosie pictured prospective customers trying to scrape together enough money to appease the folks at the IRS. Would they have enough left with which to purchase a Spouse House? What would happen to the company's bottom line if sales fell off 33 percent?

To answer those questions, Jeff prepared a report in a substantially different format. It was based on the concept of variable and fixed expenses.

Variable expenses are those expenses that go up and down with the ups and downs of sales. The most obvious example is the cost of goods sold. If the Spouse House Company's sales increase from 30 to 40 houses a month, the dollar amount of sales will increase (at $1,500 per house) from $45,000 to $60,000. The cost of goods sold (at $1,000 per house) will increase from $30,000 to $40,000—in exact proportion to the increase in sales. Similarly, other expenses will increase proportionately to sales. For the Spouse House Company, they are: sales commissions, delivery, liability insurance (the premium is billed at 0.25 percent of sales), product liability insurance (billed as 0.5 percent of sales), warehouse supplies, and the city business license (computed as a percentage of sales).

Other expenses are "fixed." *Fixed expenses* will remain the same, regardless of whether sales increase, decrease, or stay the same. For instance, rent of the office and warehouse will not change with an increase (or decrease) in sales. It will total $1,000 per month whether 20, 30, or 40 Spouse Houses are sold in March. The other fixed expenses are executive (Rosie's) salary, administrative salaries, warehouse salaries, advertising, automobile, office supplies, property taxes, and telephone.

I hear rumblings from some readers: "If sales went up to 1,000 houses per month, the rent and several other 'fixed' expenses would have to change. Rosie could not do that volume from a small office and warehouse with just one administrative person and one warehouse person." You are correct. Fixed expenses stay fixed only up to a certain point. The accountant's definition is, "Fixed expenses are fixed within a relevant range." For practical purposes, though, there is no way Rosie will sell 1,000 houses a month in the near future. She will have accomplished her goal if she sells just 40, so, realistically, we can view the "fixed" expenses as *fixed*.

There is one other class of expenses that, to keep things simple, is not in these examples: *semivariable* (sometimes called *semifixed*). For instance, in these examples we have assumed that the sales commissions are not subject to payroll taxes.* If the commissions were subject to payroll taxes, those taxes would be semivariable. The portion of payroll taxes on executive, administrative, and warehouse salaries would be fixed, as those salaries are fixed expenses. But the portion levied on the commissions would be variable, as the commissions are variable expenses.

Back to Rosie's questions: How much, for instance, would a 33 percent increase or a 33 percent decrease in sales change net income? To answer that question, Jeff first analyzed what was known—the operating report for February. He divided the expenses into *variable* and *fixed* as in Fig. 4.6. (Note that the net income is still the same $630 as in Figs. 4.1 and 4.2.) Then he took a step that, to accountants, is a formidable risk—he made an assumption! He assumed that if sales in March were the *same* as in February, the expenses would also be the same, and he copied the numbers from the February report in Fig. 4.6 to a *projection* of March operating results. From those numbers he rather easily computed what could be expected if sales contracted to 20 Spouse Houses or increased to 40 in March. The result of his efforts is the completed projection in Fig. 4.7.

As I outlined previously, the middle column is just a copy of the February report with expenses classified as *variable* or *fixed*. Projecting the fixed expenses to sales of 20 or 40 houses (columns 1 or 3) was easy—he just copied them. Projecting the variable expenses was not much more difficult, although it took some time. For example, he projected the variable expense of cost of goods sold at the 20-house-sales level by these computations:

First, he determined the cost of goods sold for one house. He divided the total cost of goods sold for the 30 Spouse Houses by the 30 houses sold.

$$\$27,000 \div 30 \text{ houses} = \$900 \text{ per house}$$

---

* In real life, that may be a dangerous assumption. If the salespersons don't meet some stringent IRS rules to qualify as independent contractors, their commissions would be subject to payroll taxes.

Spouse House Company
Operating Report
Classified by Variable/Fixed Expenses
February of Second Year

Sales of Spouse Houses	$45,000
Variable expenses:	
Cost of goods sold	27,000
Sales commissions	2,250
Delivery	1,500
Bad debt expense	1,800
Warranty expense	900
Liability insurance	110
Product liability insurance	230
Supplies, warehouse	140
Business license	230
Total variable expense	34,160
Fixed expenses:	
Executive salary	2,000
Administrative salaries	1,500
Warehouse & repair salaries	2,000
Advertising	2,000
Automobile	430
Worker's compensation insurance	110
Fire and casualty insurance	100
Rent	1,000
Supplies, office	30
Property taxes	130
Payroll taxes	550
Telephone	150
Total fixed expense	10,000
Total expense	44,160
Net income before income tax	840
Income tax	210
Net income	$ 630

Figure 4.6 Operating report, classified by variable/fixed expenses—Spouse House Company.

57

Spouse House Company Projection of Operating Report March of Second Year	Projected March 20 Houses	Projected March 30 Houses	Projected March 40 Houses
Sales of Spouse Houses	$30,000	$45,000	$60,000
Variable expenses:			
Cost of goods sold	18,000	27,000	36,000
Sales commissions	1,500	2,250	3,000
Delivery	1,000	1,500	2,000
Bad debt expense	1,200	1,800	2,400
Warranty expense	600	900	1,200
Liability insurance	80	110	150
Product liability insurance	150	230	300
Supplies, warehouse	90	140	180
Business license	150	230	300
Total variable expense	22,770	34,160	45,530
Fixed expenses:			
Executive salary	2,000	2,000	2,000
Administrative salaries	1,500	1,500	1,500
Warehouse & repair salaries	2,000	2,000	2,000
Advertising	2,000	2,000	2,000
Automobile	430	430	430
Worker's compensation insurance	110	110	110
Fire and casualty insurance	100	100	100
Rent	1,000	1,000	1,000
Supplies, office	30	30	30
Property taxes	130	130	130
Payroll taxes	550	550	550
Telephone	150	150	150
Total fixed expense	10,000	10,000	10,000
Total expense	32,770	44,160	55,530
Net income (loss) before income tax	(2,770)	840	4,470
Income tax	0	210	1,120
Net income (loss)	($ 2,700)	$ 630	$ 3,350

Figure 4.7   Projection of March operating report—Spouse House Company.

Then he multiplied the cost of goods sold for each house by the 20 houses for which he wanted total cost of goods sold in column 1.

$$\$900 \times 20 \text{ houses} = \$18,000$$

By making the same computation for each item of variable expense, he was able to determine the total expenses at the 20-house and 40-house levels and complete the projection in Fig. 4.7.

While Rosie liked the idea of a $3,350 net income from sales of 40 Spouse Houses, she realized the critical number is that volume of sales that she *must* reach to be sure she does not have a loss. That is called the *breakeven point*. It is defined as that level of sales at which there is neither income nor loss. Obviously, that point is somewhere between 20 and 30 sales per month, but Rosie asks Jeff: "Just where is it?"

Jeff could compute that by trial and error. He could do a projected report similar to Fig. 4.7 for March sales of 21 houses, 22 houses, 23 houses, and so on. For the Spouse House company, one could do such a computation. But for larger operations it would be far too time-consuming. What Rosie and Jeff can do is to plot the changes in expenses and sales volume on a graph.

The first step is to set up the graph as in Fig. 4.8. Horizontally, along the bottom, are the number of houses sold in a month. Vertically, along the left edge, the scale is in thousands of dollars. The first line to plot is for fixed expenses, which are $10,000 for any number of houses sold, so the fixed expense line will start at the left, at $10,000, and be drawn horizontally across the graph, always at the $10,000 level. The area under that line

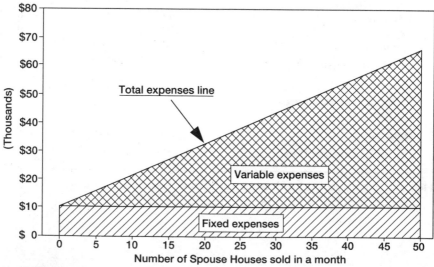

Figure 4.8   Fixed and variable expenses—Spouse House Company.

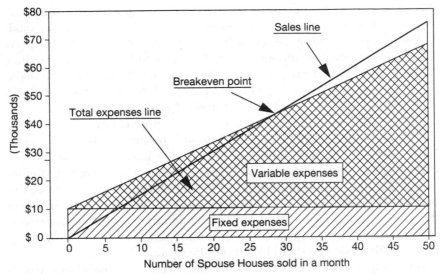

Figure 4.9   Breakeven point—Spouse House Company.

represents the fixed expenses. The next line drawn reflects the *addition* of variable expenses to fixed expenses. Where should it start? At zero sales, there will be no variable expenses, but there are fixed expenses, so the addition of variable expenses will start at the zero sales point but at the $10,000 expense level. As sales increase, variable expenses will increase in addition to the fixed expenses, so the line that slopes up from the $10,000 point is actually a line that represents *total* fixed and variable expenses. The area between it and the *fixed expenses* represents *variable expenses.*

The next step is to plot the sales on the graph. It will, of course, start at zero, where the number of houses sold is zero, and slope up as sales increase. It has been added to the expenses graph in Fig. 4.9.

Now jump back to our reason for making this graph—Rosie wants to know at what point there is no income or loss. If the net income line on the report is to be zero, then sales will have to exactly equal total expenses. On our graph, that will be the point at which the sales line crosses the total costs line. After finding that point, we can drop vertically down to the sales scale at the bottom and find that this breakeven point is 28 house sales per month. Now Rosie knows that she must sell at least 28 per month in order to avoid going broke.

Contribution Margin

What's that you say? It's time-consuming to draw graphs, and you're not that accurate with a pencil and graph paper? Fear not. If you want to know the breakeven point for any enterprise, you can also compute it by a process that involves the concept of *contribution margin*. It is the portion of the selling price of an item that remains after *variable* costs and expenses are paid.

Assume your monthly personal fixed expenses of mortgage, property taxes, utilities, and food amount to $2,000 per month. Then your daughter signs up for a profitable paper route and contributes $100 per month to the family fixed expenses. Now you have to cover only $1,900 of those monthly fixed expenses. Obviously, if you are tired of working and trying to cover the family expenses, the solution is to have 19 more children, each with a paper route and contributing $100 a month toward the fixed expenses. With $2,000 (20 × $100) of contributions, you have covered your fixed expenses. You are at your personal breakeven point and can retire. (Before you get carried away, please be advised that my experience indicates this won't work, because [1] If the kids are sick, Mom and Dad have to deliver 20 paper routes and [2] with each additional child—particularly teenagers—the food expense becomes not fixed but extremely variable. However, this example should illustrate the idea.)

Rosie applies this concept to her business. Each Spouse House that is sold contributes something toward fixed expenses. How much? Each house sells for $1,500. With each house that is sold the company incurs a variable cost of the wholesale cost of the house *plus* all the other variable expenses. In Fig. 4.10 she computes the variable expenses per house sold, using the numbers from Fig. 4.7. As you might expect, the variable expenses *per house sold* remains constant at $1,140 (rounded). Therefore, she can extend this to the following concept:

Each house sells for	$1,500
Subtract the variable expenses of each house	1,140
What's left (the *contribution* that each sale makes toward paying for fixed expenses)	$ 360

Spouse House Company
Projection of Variable Expenses per Spouse House
March of Second Year

	Projected March 20 Houses	Projected March 30 Houses	Projected March 40 Houses
Total variable expenses	$22,770	$34,160	$45,530
Variable expense per house sold (variable expenses divided by number sold)	$ 1,140	$ 1,140	$ 1,140

Figure 4.10 Projection of variable expenses per unit sold—Spouse House Company.

To summarize: The Spouse House Company's fixed expenses are $10,000 per month. From the sale of each house, there will be a contribution toward fixed expenses of $360. Therefore, the number of sales necessary to cover fixed expenses with the contributions can be computed by dividing fixed expenses by contribution per sale. For the company, that is:

$$\$10,000 \div \$360 = 27.8 \text{ houses sold}$$

And that equals the breakeven point. (Of course, Rosie is not going to saw a house into fractional sections, so the practicable breakeven is 28 houses.)

You can prove that 28 is the breakeven point by constructing a graph, or you can make a computation using the same expense percentages and figures as in Fig. 4.7. It works out as follows:

Sales (28 Spouse Houses @ $1,500)	$42,000
Variable expenses (28 @ $1,140)	$31,920
Fixed expenses	10,000
Total expenses	$41,920

The small difference between total sales and total expenses is due to the fact that Rosie does not sell ²⁄₁₀ of a house.

Besides being a method of computing breakeven point, the contribution margin concept can help in some decision making. For instance, Rosie would like to lease a computer and hire a computer operator for her bookkeeping and sales-prospect tracking. The monthly computer rent would be $250 and the salary and payroll taxes for the operator would be $1,500, for a total of $1,750. If Rosie divides that by the contribution margin of $360, she will find that she needs to sell five ($1,750 ÷ $360) additional Spouse Houses each month to pay the expense of the computer and operator. If she is sure she can sell the additional five houses, should she go ahead and rent the computer and hire the operator? Would that decision making could be so simple. Are there other benefits to having the computer? Will the prospect tracking substantially increase sales? Will the bookkeeping capability cut down on the need for an outside bookkeeping service? If sales do increase by five houses per month, could she use that additional $1,750 more effectively somewhere else (by buying her own delivery truck, for instance)? Definite answers come very seldom, but concepts such as contribution margin, and some others we will discuss later, can help make decisions.

Direct and Indirect Expenses

These terms of classification originally arose in manufacturing, which will be covered more thoroughly in Chap. 11. However, the terms have crept into use in nonmanufacturing areas, so a short definition is appropriate here: *Direct expenses or costs* are those items and labor that become part of a manufactured product. *Indirect costs or expenses* are those items and labor that assist in manufacturing the product.

To the literal-minded, those definitions might sound as if the worker who performs direct labor becomes glued to the frames of a shed in the Fred's Sheds factory. It really does not mean that. Let this example clarify it:

In the shed factory, the two-by-fours that become the frame are direct materials; the paint brushes are indirect materials. The people who beat the nails into the wood produce direct labor, the floor sweeper is indirect labor.

When these terms migrate into merchandising and service industries, they take on different meanings that will vary with the industry and with the company. For instance, they may mean the same thing as controllable and uncontrollable expenses. You are not labeling yourself as uninformed if you ask an accountant to define *direct* and *indirect,* as he or she is using those terms. Often, the distinction is murky.

In some cases, I'm afraid, this obfuscation of terms is intentional. Many government contracts are written so that the contractors will receive payment based upon their ability to allocate general and indirect expenses to the contract. This leaves the same room for controversy that we found in Angus' Great Pipes and Wee House Mart. So, it is to a contractor's advantage to play a "confuse-the-government-auditor" game. Being vague about *overhead, indirect, direct,* and other terms can help allocate more expenses to a contract or product—until one day the Pentagon ends up paying $800 for a toilet seat!

Summary

The format for income statements (for use by those outside the company) is quite flexible, and formats for operating reports for use by company managers are completely flexible, as management can make its own rules and procedures for generating these reports.

Classification of expenses can range from an alphabetical list of broad categories to detailed breakdown of each classification. Expenses also can be listed, by department, as variable and fixed, or in any other way that makes it easier to analyze operations.

Reports that classify expenses as variable and fixed can be very useful for determining breakeven points and determining sales goals. The result of subtracting variable expenses from sales is the contribution margin. This concept also can help determine sales goals and the point at which fixed costs can be increased, as in acquiring new or larger equipment.

Direct and *indirect expenses* are frequently used terms that can have different shades of meaning to different accountants and companies. One should ask for a definition.

Review Questions

1. An expenditure for a business is an expense only if it is meant to contribute to the earning of income.   T   F

2. All of the same information that is in reports prepared for management is suitable for financial statements to be given to creditors and the public.   T   F

3. The main reason for reporting expenses grouped by responsibility area is to keep the IRS happy.   T   F

4. A report that separates expenses into variable and fixed expenses is the conventional way to create reports to submit to your banker or investors.   T   F

5. Breakeven is the point at which total sales equal total expenses.   T   F

6. Drawing a graph is the only way to compute the breakeven point.   T   F

7. A contribution margin is computed by subtracting variable costs per unit of sales from the sales price of each unit.   T   F

Case Study Question ──────────────

Charlene Ripper and Tonya Upper own and run the Ripper-Upper Carpet Cleaning Company. They charge $100 for each carpet cleaning job. Their expenses are:

- Sales commission: 20 percent ($20 for each job sold)
- Operator (the individual who actually pushes the equipment over the carpets: $30 per carpet cleaning job)
- Gas for truck: average $5 per cleaning job
- Soap: $2 per job
- Maintenance of cleaning machine: overhaul of machine costs $300 and has to be done after every 100 jobs (Hint: Divide the $300 overhaul costs by the 100 jobs to find the overhaul cost per job)
- Rent, office and warehouse: $500 per month
- Salaries to Charlene and Tonya total $2,250 per month
- Receptionist: $1,200 per month
- Insurance: $100 per month
- Utilities and telephone: $150 per month

(Note: All figures for commissions, salaries, and wages include payroll tax expense.)

Your assignment: Separate the expenses into two lists:

1. *Variable expenses.*   List these with the dollar amount of cost per cleaning job.
2. *Fixed expenses.*   List these with the dollar amount of the expense per month.

Compute the contribution margin by subtracting variable expenses per job from the sales price of a job. Compute the breakeven point by dividing total fixed expenses by the contribution margin. Use the following form. It should help.

Variable expenses:

_____   _____

_____   _____

_____   _____

_____   _____

_____   _____

   Total variable expenses
                                                         ═══════════════
Fixed expenses:

_____   _____

_____   _____

_____   _____

_____   _____

_____   _____

Computation of contribution margin:

   Sales price of cleaning job $100
   Subtract variable expenses per job (above) ___
      Contribution margin $__

Breakeven point:

   Total fixed expenses divided by contribution margin

= $_____ ÷ $_____ = _____ cleaning jobs per month.

5

Equipment and Other Things That Will Be Around for Years

Depreciation: How Much Does It Cost to Have the Stuff Around?

Some things you buy and they are gone, used up, tomorrow. Around my house it's chocolate chip cookies. At the office it's ball point pens. Some things last forever (almost). We still have a bottle of cod liver oil my grandmother purchased in 1937.

However, accountants don't talk in terms of chocolate chip cookies and cod liver oil. They talk in terms of benefit. In other words, does what you bought benefit you, or your company, in this year only, or is the benefit spread over several years?

Rosie Rouse conducted a survey and found that many of her customers were unhappy with the fact that the sheds she sold as Spouse Houses had no windows. She hired two carpenters and kept them busy cutting holes in the Spouse Houses and putting in windows. However, the labor was expensive, and by a process we will cover in Chap. 6, Rosie determined that the company should buy an Automatic Window Machine. This machine cuts out the holes for windows, cuts the lumber and glass to make them, installs them, paints the trim, and washes the windows. It costs $55,000. Rosie expects the machine will last five years, and at the end of that time, she will be able to sell it for $5,000. So the benefit of the machine will be spread over the five years that the Spouse House Company owns the machine.

Compare that to the purchase of a dozen typewriter ribbons that will be used up in less than a year, or to buying a one-year fire insurance policy. The benefit of the $30 spent for the typewriter ribbons or the $500 spent for the fire insurance policy will not last more than one year. A year from now, Rosie will have to buy more typewriter ribbons and contract for a renewal of the fire insurance policy. So the $30 and the $500 are expenses of doing business this year. However, the Automatic Window Machine will last, and benefit the company, more than one year. Can we say, then, that the whole $55,000 for the machine is an expense of the first year the company owns it? Of course not. However, Rosie can make this computation:

Machine cost	$55,000
Less sale value in 5 years (we hope)	5,000
Cost to be spread over 5 years	50,000
Divide $50,000 by number of years (5) to determine	
annual expense of owning the machine	$10,000

In other words, we have spread the cost of the Automatic Window Machine over the five-year life of the machine. Now, let's translate that into accounting terms. Here are the same figures labeled with some technical terminology.

Machine cost	$55,000
Less *salvage* value	5,000
Cost to be *depreciated* over 5 years	50,000
Divide $50,000 by the *useful life* (5 years) to	
determine *depreciation* expense each year	$10,000

Definitions of these technical terms are: *Useful life* is how long management of the company expects the equipment to be in operation (useful) for the company. *Salvage value* is what management guesses the equipment will be worth at the end of its useful life. *Depreciation* is the spreading out, or allocation, of the cost of the equipment over the useful life of the equipment.

If, for each year, the Spouse House Company operating reports and income statements show a depreciation expense of $10,000, then each monthly operating report will show an expense of $10,000 divided by 12 months, or $833. Now Rosie has an accounting situation that is similar to the bad debt situation in Chap. 2. She has an expense for which she did not write a check or say "charge it." Again, Jeff will keep a tally of how much depreciation expense for the Automatic Window Machine he has listed on the reports over the months and years. At any given time, he can subtract this total of *accumulated* depreciation from the original cost of the machine. For instance, at the end of the second year of using the machine, his computation would look like this:

Equipment (Automatic Window Machine), original cost		$55,000
Subtract accumulated depreciation:		
Depreciation first year	$10,000	
Depreciation, second year	10,000	
Total accumulated depreciation		20,000
Remaining (??)		$35,000

What is this "remaining" number? Is it:

(*a*) The remaining value of the machine, or

(*b*) The remaining cost of the machine?

Suppose, for a minute, that instead of an Automatic Window Machine, these same numbers applied to the company's purchase of a brand new Chromium Super 16 automobile. Remember the last shiny new car you bought? Is it realistic to suppose that Rosie could sell a $55,000 automobile for $35,000 after using it for two years? Maybe, if she is lucky, she could get $25,000 for it. So, for an automobile, answer (*a*) would be wrong. The $35,000 is *not* remaining value, but remaining cost.

I have researched the market for used Automatic Window Machines and find the same situation applies. Used window machines sell at low prices, just as do automobiles. So the above $35,000 is remaining cost, not a market value.

If, for some piece of equipment at a given time, the remaining value equals the remaining cost, it is only coincidence. *Depreciation records are concerned with cost, not value.*

In automobile showrooms, family rooms, and bowling alleys, we talk about how much an automobile or other equipment "depreciates" as soon as it is taken out of a showroom. In that context, we are describing the loss of value. However, in financial reports and statements, depreciation has nothing to do with current value, except for the original purchase price (cost) and the "guesstimate" of remaining salvage value. It is simply a method of spreading the original cost of equipment over the useful life of the equipment. The "remaining" number ($35,000 in this example) is called the *book value* of the equipment. That is a misnomer, for it is not a "value" in the sense of market value, but really a "remainder."

This finance term of *book value* has no relation to the "book value" terms that are bantered around in automobile showrooms and on boat dealers' docks. Those businesses have publications that list the current *market* prices of used cars and boats. They provide handy numbers, but they are not the numbers that generally appear in financial reporting. Other terms you may hear in this area are *basis* and *remaining basis*. These are tax terms developed by the IRS. When used in a nontax context, they usually mean the same as *cost* and *book value*.

Over the five years that Rosie expects to use the Automatic Window Machine, Jeff's depreciation record would look like this:

	Annual depreciation expense	Remaining cost of machine (book value) at end of year
Purchase		$55,000
First year	$10,000	45,000
Second year	10,000	35,000
Third year	10,000	25,000
Fourth year	10,000	15,000
Fifth year	10,000	5,000

Notice that he ends up with a remaining book value of $5,000—the amount he and Rosie estimated the machine would be worth at the end of five years. Of course, this is no guarantee that she will be able to sell it for $5,000. Later in the chapter, we will talk about what to do with the difference between the remaining book value and the actual proceeds of selling the old equipment.

Which Way to Compute Depreciation?

After Rosie ordered the machine, she lay awake, worrying about the expenses from the machine that would show up on her operating report and financial statements. She was particularly worried about the income statement that she would be presenting to her banker four or five years down the road.

"There are," she thought, "5,287 moving parts in the machine. By the fifth year, they will be wearing out and I will be spending a fortune for repairs. At the same time, my income statement will show a depreciation expense of $10,000 per year, so my total machine expense will be extra high. And that fifth year is when I may want to borrow substantial money from the bank, for by then I should be expanding to the European and Japanese markets."

Again, Jeff received a telephone call at 2:00 A.M. Rosie repeated her concern to him and added: "How can I cut down on the depreciation expense as the repair expense goes up in later years?"

Jeff had become a little more adept at handling middle-of-the-night phone calls. "That's easy to do. I'll draw you a picture in the morning," he replied.

In the morning, he explained: "We'll set up *accelerated* depreciation. That means there will be much more depreciation expense in the early years of the life of the equipment than in the later years. Thus, when there are few repairs, there will be lots of depreciation expense. When depreciation expense is low in later years, there will be more repairs, so the total of depreciation and repairs will be about the same in each of the five years."

Then, true to his word, Jeff drew a picture for Rosie. Like most accountants, when Jeff draws a picture, it comes out looking like a graph, and that bar graph is shown in Fig. 5.1. The part of each bar representing accelerated depreciation becomes smaller each year, while the part of the bar representing maintenance becomes larger as the equipment becomes older. The total of both the depreciation and the maintenance sections of the bars stays almost the same for all five years.

There are various methods of computing accelerated depreciation, and they all result in about the same picture—more depreciation in the early years. The actual computations are usually performed by the accounting department or by outside accountants, for these people have software that does it quickly. In other words, there is no need to be overly concerned with or try to remember how accelerated depreciation is computed. Our need is to see the effect of the methods on depreciation expense. (How fast do you want your accelerated depreciation to be?) Here are brief descriptions and graphic displays of the more common methods.

For simplicity, these examples assume that the Spouse House Company purchases the Automatic Window Machine on January 1. If the equipment is purchased later in the year, the depreciation computed for the first year would be proportionately less. For ease of computation, some accountants assume that all equipment purchased during the year was put into service

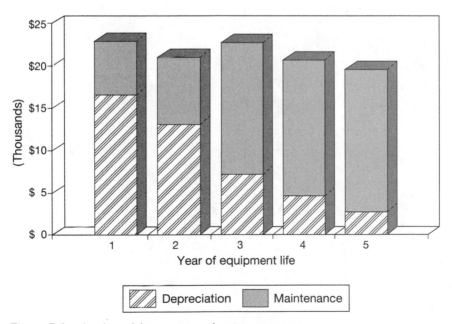

Figure 5.1   Accelerated depreciation and maintenance expenses.

on July 1. The depreciation for the first year will be one-half of a full year's depreciation. (This procedure is called a *half-year convention,* which is an IRS term that has spilled over to financial reporting.) However, to keep this example simple, we'll assume Rosie bought the machine on January 1 and Jeff computes a full year of depreciation for the first year.

Straight-Line Depreciation

This is the method we have been looking at in this chapter: the cost of the machine, less salvage value, is divided by the number of years of useful life. The result is that the depreciation expense is the same each year, as in Fig. 5.2.

200 Percent (or Double) Declining Balance Depreciation

In this method the total cost (without any deduction for salvage value) is divided by the useful life. For the first year, that number is doubled for the annual depreciation expense. Then the *book value* (cost less depreciation expense to date) remaining at the end of the first year is divided by the useful life to determine the second year depreciation, and so on. Figure 5.3 illustrates the result graphically.

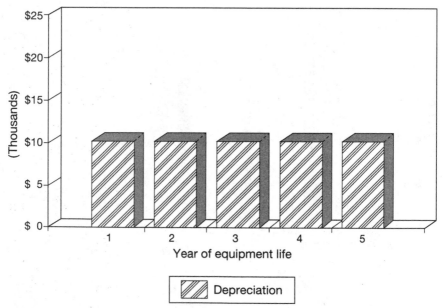

Figure 5.2   Straight-line depreciation.

150 Percent Declining Balance Depreciation

This method is very similar to the 200 percent method just mentioned, except that instead of doubling the figure first computed, it is multiplied by 1½. Figure 5.4 depicts the results, showing a little slower acceleration than the 200 percent in Fig. 5.3.

Other Declining Balance Methods

The number resulting from dividing cost by useful life can be multiplied by any percentage over 100 percent to generate some type of accelerated depreciation.

Sum-of-the-Years Digit Method

This method is covered in most accounting textbooks, but I have never found anyone who uses it. However, in the event you do run into it, I have included a graph of the results in Fig. 5.5. The underlying calculations are somewhat complicated, so I have banished them to a footnote.* (Information in footnotes is not on the exam!)

Units of Production Depreciation

This is appropriate for any production machinery, such as the Window Machine. Again, we subtract the salvage value of $5,000 from the $55,000 cost and have $50,000 to allocate to depreciation. The equipment dealer tells Rosie that, on the average, a machine will cut out and install 5,000 windows before it will need to be replaced. If Rosie divides the $50,000 by the 5,000 windows (units-of-production), she will find that the depreciation per

* If you *have* to know, it is computed by adding the digits of the useful life and then, for each year, multiplying the cost (less salvage value) by a fraction, the numerator of which is the year, in reverse order, over the sum computed above. For the Window Machine, it is:

Denominator of fraction = 1 + 2 + 3 + 4 + 5 = 15
Cost of Window Machine $55,000
Subtract salvage value   5,000
  To be depreciated $50,000
First year = 5/15 × $50,000 = $16,667
Second year = 4/15 × $50,000 =   13,333
Third year = 3/15 × $50,000 =   10,000
Fourth year = 2/15 × $50,000 =   6,667
Fifth year = 1/15 × $50,000 =   3,333
  Total depreciation $50,000

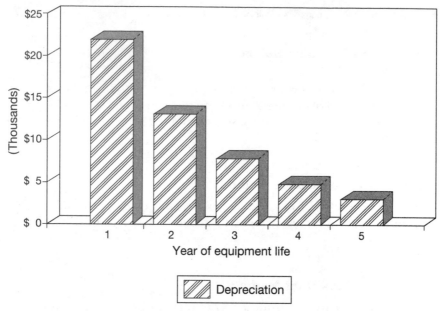

Figure 5.3   200 percent declining balance depreciation.

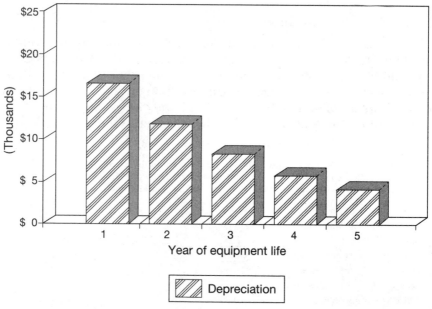

Figure 5.4   150 percent declining balance depreciation.

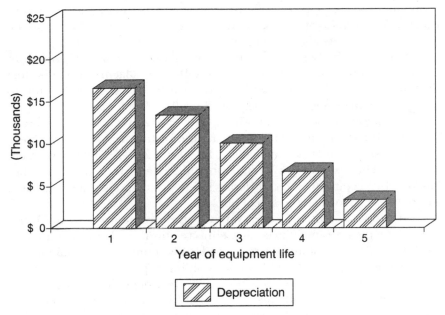

Figure 5.5   Sum-of-the-years' digits depreciation.

window is $10. Therefore, if during March, the machine installs 20 windows, the depreciation expense would be 20 × $10 depreciation, or $200. (Actually, this can get more complicated if the Spouse Houses in which the windows were installed remain in inventory instead of being sold during March. We will cover that situation in Chap. 11.) I didn't include a graph of this, for it would just be a squiggly line—up and down, depending on the production volume.

Group Depreciation

Often, accountants will group various equipment together and compute depreciation on the group, as if it were one piece of equipment. The same methods already discussed can be applied to these groups. The reason the accountants do this is to make the record keeping a little simpler.

Tax Depreciation vs. Financial Depreciation

You're right. I promised not to bring IRS and the tax rules into this book. However, sometimes the tax rules affect financial reports, and depreciation is one of those areas. Technically, there is no requirement that the deduction for depreciation on a business income tax return be the same as on the financial statements of the company.

For instance, the IRS rules might allow the Spouse House Company to compute its depreciation of the Automatic Window Machine using double declining balance depreciation with a five-year life. That would amount to a tax deduction during the first year of $22,000 ($55,000 ÷ 5 years × 200 percent). However, if the machine will actually last 20 years and the salvage value is still $5,000, the annual depreciation for financial report purposes could be computed as only ($55,000 − $5,000) ÷ 20 = $2,500 per year. So, Rosie could increase the profit on her income statement (that she gives her banker) by keeping two sets of depreciation calculations. This is an area where it *is* legal to keep two sets of books!

For the Spouse House Company, that extra income may be significant. However, if the investment in equipment is relatively small, the amount that the financial statement income could be legally "pumped up" would not be large enough to justify the added bookkeeping expense. So, many companies just follow the IRS rules in maintaining their depreciation records.

After Jeff explained all this, Rosie considered using an accelerated method of depreciation. However, she was also aware that complicated accounting can be expensive. So she decided to use the *straight-line* method of depreciation, resulting in a depreciation expense of $10,000 per year on the window machine.

Small Bits and Pieces of Equipment

Soon after moving into her office, Rosie found that the light bulb in the ceiling fixture had burned out. She could not reach the fixture, so she bought a small stepladder for $20. The stepladder will probably be around for 20 years, so Rosie should depreciate it at $1 per year for 20 years, right? Wrong! We would all go nuts and need a room full of accountants if we are going to do all the record keeping necessary to keep depreciation records on $20 stepladders, $8 pencil sharpeners, $40 drills, and other small pieces of equipment.

Therefore, all companies should have a dollar level of the cost of a piece of equipment, below which the whole purchase is treated as an expense in the year of purchase. It's called "keep it simple." Rosie decided that any purchase of under $500 would be treated as an expense rather than setting up depreciation records for the equipment. For larger companies, this cut-off level may be substantially higher. One international oil company uses a cut-off of $40,000. Accountants call setting this cut-off level a *capitalization pol-*

icy. It can be defined as a dollar figure below which equipment cost will not be depreciated but will be considered an expense in the year the equipment is acquired.

Be aware of some improper English that accountants use: they make a verb out of the noun "expense." You may hear one say, "We are going to expense the purchase of the $495 computer printer." All he or she means is that, though the printer may last five or more years, the whole cost of $495 will be treated as an expense of the current year.

Reserve for Depreciation

Back when accountants wore green eyeshades to ward off the glare from candlelight, *accumulated depreciation* was called *reserve for depreciation*. You may still hear some old-timers call it that. (The IRS still calls it reserve for depreciation, but the IRS is an old-timer—it's been around a long time, perhaps too long!) Accountants dropped the term because *reserve* carries an implication that there is something in reserve for an emergency or future use. For example, I used to have a Volkswagen with a "reserve" gas tank. There was extra gas in it for those times when the regular tank ran out. (The trouble was, there was no second reserve tank to use when I ran the reserve tank dry.)

Because of this connotation of "reserve," many people thought that a "reserve for depreciation" was actually a wad of cash, stuffed in a mattress or in a bank account, that was there to buy a new machine when the old machine wore out. It was no such thing. As the modern term, *accumulated depreciation,* indicates, it is just a total of depreciation expense over the years.

Rosie could have tried to provide for cash with which to buy a new machine by taking $10,000 each year out of the company checking account and putting it in a savings account. This would not have been any type of expense. It would just be a movement of cash from one bank account to another. Realistically, because of our ever-present inflation, she would really need to sock away something like $11,000 or $12,000 per year. If you find some business following this procedure, it might be called a *funded* reserve. Because it is funded, the use of the term *reserve* would be appropriate, but note that it is a *cash* reserve and has nothing to do with *accumulated depreciation.*

Actually, Rosie did not elect to set up such a funded reserve, as she could make more by using that cash in her business than she could on the interest from a savings account. For instance, she could receive an additional discount from her supplier, Fred's Sheds, by using the cash to buy sheds (future Spouse Houses) in volume.

When the Equipment Is Sold,
Lost, Junked, or Stolen

Accountants have a catch-all word for any of these events. They talk about the *disposition* of equipment. This does not refer to how the equipment feels today (mean equipment/happy equipment). It refers to the *disposal* of old equipment.

At the end of the third year of the Spouse House Company's existence, Sam, the equipment salesperson, showed Rosie the latest model of an Automatic Window Machine. This one not only cut out the window, installed the sash, and painted it, but it also installed the front door and put the roof vents in place. Rosie did some computations, similar to those we will discuss in Chap. 6, and decided that purchasing the new machine would be justified *if* she could sell the old one. After diligent advertising and negotiation, she found a builder who would pay her $15,000 for the old machine.

Please look back to the record of depreciation, on p. 68, which Jeff kept. At the end of the third year, the old machine had a remaining cost (*book value*) of $25,000. When Rosie sells the machine for only $15,000, it leaves a difference of $10,000. This is the part of the cost of the machine that has not been eaten up by depreciation expense or recovered by sale of the used machine. The accounting rules do not let us ignore the ten grand. It does not just float away, but is a *loss on sale of equipment*. It will show up, on the Spouse House Company income statement, as a separate line, usually near the bottom of the statement.

One attribute of accountants is that they are good at making up rules and then breaking them. For instance, one accounting rule we discussed is that expenses should be listed on reports in the period in which they occur. When did the loss on the old window machine occur? The day it was sold?

Alternatively, you might say that it happened because Rosie and Jeff incorrectly estimated how long the company would keep the machine (the *useful life*) and how much it would be worth when it was sold. (Don't be too hard on Rosie and Jeff—they did not have the advantage of hindsight as we do.)

You might argue either way, but probably the more logical answer is that it occurred over the three years that the company owned the machine. Theoretically, to adhere to the accountants' *matching* rules, Jeff should go back over every income report during the last three years and increase the depreciation expense for the window machine. But he doesn't. Practicality reigns (thank goodness) and he displays the loss on the income statement for the period in which the machine is sold. Note that it is termed a *loss* rather than an expense. Why? We could get into a lot of unnecessary theory, but for purposes of this book, it's easier to say, "because we have always done it that way—called it a loss."

If Rosie had been lucky enough to sell the used window machine for *more* than its book value, the result would have been some extra money in the till—an item of income. On financial statements it may be called *income from sale of equipment,* or the IRS term of *gain from sale of equipment* might be used.

Trade-Ins

If you trade in your old clunker on a new Chromium 16 automobile, you may be amazed to find that it is worth far more than you thought it was. Of course, the price of the new car may also be pumped up to cover the "generous" trade-in value the dealer is allowing you. As you are probably aware, this is not a situation that applies solely to automobiles. It can appear in the sale of any type of equipment. So, how do you compute the income or loss when trade-ins are involved? There are two sets of rules: those of the FASB and those of the IRS.

The FASB rule states that the price of the new equipment should be reflected at the true *market* value. Then the trade-in allowance should be computed from that, and the income or loss on the old equipment should be displayed on the income statement, as an accountant would do for an outright sale of old equipment.

For example, if, at the end of the third year, Sam offered Rosie a trade-in deal like this:

New machine (list price)	$100,000
Subtract trade-in	35,000
Difference (write check or finance)	$ 65,000

Rosie knows, from previous conversations with Sam, that he will discount his equipment 20 percent. She also knows that there is no way the old machine is worth $35,000. Therefore, the true market value of the new machine is $100,000 minus 20 percent, or $80,000. Then, to reflect the same $65,000 cash difference between the new machine and the trade-in, the trade-in must have a real value of $15,000. If Rosie accepts the deal, the figures that go into the accounting records should be:

New machine	$80,000
Check (or amount financed)	65,000
Difference (trade-in received for old equipment)	$15,000

So, the real trade-in value is $15,000. Subtracting that from the book value at the end of the third year ($25,000) leaves a *loss on sale* of $10,000—the same as if the old equipment had been sold for cash.

The IRS has a different approach. Again, this book is concerned with accounting rules rather than tax rules; but, when the effect of using the IRS rule instead of the FASB rules does not result in material difference, many companies use the IRS rule. (Keep the bookkeeping simple.) The IRS would compute the cost of the new machine this way:

Book value of old machine when traded in (from depreciation record on p. 68	$25,000
Add amount for which a check is written or financed	65,000
Starting book value of new machine (before any depreciation)	$90,000

The result of using this IRS method is that there will be no immediate loss on sale of $10,000, but there will be more depreciation expense each year the new machine is used. Again, it is suitable for financial reporting *only* if the error introduced is immaterial. (See the discussion of materiality in Chap. 1.)

Repair or Refurbishment of Equipment

Angus, our old friend who runs a bagpipe and tartan store, took a different approach to new equipment. Whenever possible, he preferred to fix up the old. Specifically, he had a three-year-old copy machine that turned out gray copies with a vertical black line down the middle. Such copies gave a negative image to the newsletters and advertising that Angus mailed to bagpipe players all over the country. He considered replacing the copy machine, but when he priced a new one, he decided his only course was to keep his old one and have it repaired.

When Angus originally purchased the machine, the salesperson told him that it would easily last five years. It cost $3,000, and Gertrude (Angus' accountant) set it up on a depreciation schedule of five years at $600 depreciation per year. (She provided for no salvage value. Did you ever try to sell a five-year-old copier?)

Had Angus been lucky, the repair person would have turned a few adjusting screws, cleaned a part or two, and left the machine in good working order. The cost of such minor repairs would show up on his operating report as a *repair expense* and be subtracted from income. This repair expense would have no effect on the depreciation of the copy machine.

However, Angus was not so lucky. The machine needed replacement of several expensive parts. The total bill for parts and labor came to $1,600! When Angus came out of shock, he asked the repair person if the repairs would make the machine last longer.

"Yes," replied the repair person, "with just routine maintenance, it should last another four years." That meant the total useful life of the copy machine had been extended from five to seven years.

Would Gertrude put the $1,200 expenditure on the operating report as an expense? The accounting rules say she cannot. The rule is: *If a repair extends the life of equipment, it must be capitalized (added to the cost of the equipment) rather than treated as an expense.*

Before the repair was performed, Gertrude's depreciation record appeared as follows. (For simplicity, we'll assume that the machine was purchased on January 1.)

Cost of copy machine	$3,000
Subtract three years of depreciation at $600 per year	1,800
Book value	1,200
To this Gertrude added the cost of the life-lengthening repairs	1,600
New book value	$2,800

To compute the new depreciation, she computed a new remaining life of the copy machine. It is now the two years remaining of the original machine *plus* the two years by which the repairs lengthened the useful life—or four years. She divided the new book value of $2,800 by the new useful life of four years to compute a new depreciation rate of $700 per year.

Intangibles (Profit-Making Things That Aren't There)

Some things that a company acquires don't have any form or substance (although they may be represented by a piece of paper). However, the company spent money for them and they do add to the profitability of the company. Patents are one such item.

As I mentioned earlier, Rosie had a problem with spouses beating on the door of their Spouse House when the other spouse was inside. The result was damaged doors and unjustified warranty claims. She therefore developed an anticrush door, composed of spongy materials and spring-loaded panels, that would take tremendous beatings without harm. To make sure that the Spouse House Company would be the only vendor of backyard houses with that door, she applied for and was granted a patent for the Abuse-Proof Door. The patent fees, legal fees, and other expenditures totalled $17,000, and the patent would last for 17 years. Just like depreciation spreads the cost of a tangible machine or building over its useful life, *amortization* spreads the life of the patent over its useful life. So, each year, the annual income statement of the company reflects a patent amortization expense of $1,000 ($17,000 ÷ 17 years). As with depreciation, Jeff keeps a tally of the *accumulated amortization.*

Besides patents, items in this intangible category include copyrights, trademarks, and the costs of organizing a business—costs for lawyers, accountants, consultants, etc. that are incurred before the business opens and becomes operational.

Summary

Depreciation is a system by which the cost of equipment that will last more than one year is spread out, or allocated, to each of the years (or units of production) that it will be used. It can be computed in a variety of ways, some of which will load more depreciation into the early years of the equipment's useful life.

Book value of equipment is the original cost less the accumulated depreciation. It should not be confused with market value.

Income (gain) or *loss* on sale of equipment is computed by comparing the sale price (or true trade-in value) with the book value of the equipment.

IRS has its own rules for depreciation and computing gain or loss on sale of equipment. Companies often use these rules for financial statements when following them, instead of financial rules, does not create material errors.

Small items, even though they may last several years, are not put into a depreciation system. Instead, their cost is treated as an expense in the year in which they are acquired. The cost of these items needs to be small enough so that this treatment of their cost does not introduce *material* errors in the operating reports and financial statements.

Review Questions

1. The cost of equipment never becomes an expense or a subtraction from sales.   T   F

2. Salvage value is what the junk dealer has paid for a machine after it is worn out.   T   F

3. Useful life is how long a piece of equipment will be useful to a particular business.   T   F

4. Depreciation is the allocation of equipment costs to the years of its useful life.   T   F

5. When used by accountants with reference to equipment, the term *book value* refers to the market value of a piece of equipment.   T   F

6. *Accelerated depreciation* creates more depreciation in the early years of the life of a piece of equipment than in the later years of its life.   T   F

7. With most depreciation methods it is possible to determine what the depreciation of a new piece of equipment will be in each future year of its life. However, accurate determination of future depreciation expense is not possible when the *units-of-production* method is used.   T   F

8. Keeping two sets of books or records—one for financial reporting and another for income tax reporting—is always illegal.   T   F

9. You own a company doing $10 million in annual sales. You buy a $50 chair for your office. You should:
   a. Put it in your depreciation records and list a depreciation expense of $5 per year for the next 10 years
   b. Include the whole $50 in *office expense* this year

Case Study Question

George is in the golf-course building business. He bought an Automatic Sand Trap machine, on January 1, for $100,000. He estimated it will last him for five years, after which it will be worthless (no salvage value). However, after he had used it for two years, he wished he had bought the model that also installs water holes. In order to buy the fancier machine, he sells the first machine on December 31 of the second year for $45,000.

Your assignment: Using the following format, list the annual depreciation and remaining book value of the machine for each of the five years. Don't get fancy. Just use straight-line depreciation over the five-year life George originally expected to use the machine. Then determine his income or loss from the sale of the machine at the end of the second year.

Computation of annual depreciation expense:

Cost of machine ÷ expected useful life

= _____ ÷ _____ = _____

	Annual depreciation expense	Remaining cost of machine (book value) at end of year
Purchase price		_____
First year	_____	_____
Second year	_____	_____
Third year	_____	_____

Fourth year   _____   _____
Fifth year   _____   _____

   Book value at end of second year   _____
   Subtract $ received for old machine   _____
   Income (loss) on sale of equipment   _____

6

Buying, Leasing, or Doing Without

Justifying the Purchase of Equipment

In Chap. 5 we talked about the depreciation of the Automatic Window Machine that the Spouse House Company purchased, and I promised that in this chapter we would discuss the analysis that Rosie Rouse conducted before making the purchase.

During her first year of selling Spouse Houses, Rosie learned that customers wanted windows in the houses. (She had expected that the houses would be used for only one or two nights at a time, but apparently many were utilized for longer periods of discord.)

Initially, she met this need by having her supplier, Fred's Sheds, install the windows in the sheds that the Spouse House Company converted into Spouse Houses. For three windows, Fred charged $300. This made the wholesale cost of the sheds to Rosie $1,100. She would have to raise her retail price or find a cheaper way to install the windows. She hired Lem, a carpenter, to install the windows for her. He was efficient, but he could not keep up with Rosie's sales. She would have to hire another carpenter.

Onto the scene came Sam, the friendly equipment salesperson. For one week only, he had a special price on an Automatic Window Machine, which would automatically cut out the holes for the windows, cut the lumber and glass to make the windows, install them, paint the frames, and wash the windows.

Rosie made some quick calculations. They went like this:

Sam's machine would install windows in a Spouse House in *one hour.* It would require some lumber, glass, electricity, maintenance, and only one person to operate it.

Rosie estimated that for each house, the expenses of operating the machine would be $100, composed of:

Lem's salary for one hour	$ 12
Lem's social security, unemployment tax, medical and life insurance, vacations, etc. expenses for one hour	8
Lumber and glass	65
Maintenance	10
Electricity	5
Depreciation	15
Total cost per Spouse House	$115

It appears that the machine would provide a large saving: a window cost of $115 per Spouse House against the $300 that Fred's Sheds charges. However, there is more to consider. Rosie will have to plunk down $55,000 for the machine, either from her pocket or from a bank loan.

For that reason, justification of purchase of equipment is generally based on *cash flow,* which is jargon for the cash that can be generated by a company or by a project (such as the purchase of the Window Machine). To put it in terms of your personal financial life, if you insulate your house, and that results in your heating fuel bill falling from $2,000 a year to $800 per year, you have created an additional $1,200 per year that is available to you. That is a cash flow of $1,200 per year. Nice for you. Not so nice for your fuel oil person.

The computation of cash flow from the Automatic Window Machine was:

If Rosie used the services of the Fred's Sheds Company to install the windows, it would cost the Spouse House Company, per Spouse House	$ 300
If she used the Automatic Window Machine, the labor, etc. would cost, per Spouse House (as just computed, but without depreciation expense, which is not a cash expense)	100
Difference (which is the additional cash cost if Fred's Sheds is paid to install the windows, as opposed to doing it with the machine)	200
Multiply that times the 100 Spouse Houses that Rosie expected to sell during the year	× 100
Total extra money per year it would cost to have the shed supplier install the windows instead of using the machine (i.e., the cash that would be saved—cash flow generated—by using the machine)	$20,000

Payback Method

That's great, isn't it? An extra $20,000 per year by using the Automatic Window Machine! But, the Spouse House Company had to spend

$50,000* to buy the machine that would generate this saving. Let's assume the company borrowed the money, and for simplicity, we'll assume the bank charged no interest. (Yes, even finance books do contain some fiction.)

The first year the company can pay back the bank the $20,000 that it saved by using the machine, leaving a balance owing of $30,000. The second year the company can pay back another $20,000 that it saved, leaving a balance of $10,000; and it could pay back that last $10,000 halfway through the third year. So, the money invested in the machine is paid back in two and a half years. To put it in the lingo of accountants and financial people, "the machine will have a two-and-a-half-year *payback*." That's not a bad deal. The machine is paid for in two and a half years, so we have another two and a half years of its five-year life for free—almost.[†] So, a *payback period* is the time it takes to generate additional cash flow equal to the cost of the equipment.

This is a viable way to compare the feasibility of buying one machine as opposed to another. For instance, suppose Rosie can borrow no more than $55,000 from the bank, and she is also considering the purchase of a flatbed delivery truck, complete with a crane, for a cost of $50,000. By the same type of analysis she used for the Automatic Window Machine, Rosie finds that the truck's payback period is four years. Buying the window machine, with the quicker payback period, would be a better use of the money.

However, if she compares this to other uses of the money, there is a flaw in this payback computation: we had to assume the fiction that the bank would charge no interest. "But what," you ask, "if Rosie had an extra $55,000 kicking about in the Spouse House Company checking account? Then, she would not have to borrow the money from the bank and pay interest."

True. But there are alternative uses of the $55,000. She could put the $55,000 in an interest-bearing account. Assume the bank pays 10 percent interest to depositors. (More fiction, but it makes the computations easier.) If the company can earn $5,500 in interest, with virtually no risk, it would not make sense to invest in equipment unless it earns substantially more than 10 percent, or $5,500. I say *substantially*, for there is greater risk: the machine may not operate as promised, the demand for Spouse Houses may fall off, or the government may impose restrictions on putting windows in Spouse Houses!

Rosie could compute the payback by subtracting the $5,500 interest that she could earn at the bank from the $20,000 that the Automatic Window Machine would earn, and compute a payback from an annual cash flow— $20,000 − $5,500, or $14,500. (The payback would be $55,000 divided by

---

* This is the $55,000 cost to acquire the machine minus the $5,000 salvage value.

[†] What payback period justifies the purchase of equipment? That will vary with each company. Check with your financial department as to their payback criteria. Usually, if a manager requests a purchase of equipment with a payback period higher than the company's standard, it will automatically be rejected. So, it pays to find out what that number is.

$14,500, or 3.8 years.) However, even this refinement would not consider two more factors.

One, the interest, if left in the bank, would itself earn interest. In other words, the interest would compound, as follows:

Initial investment (present value)	$55,000
Interest, first year	5,500
Balance, end of first year	60,500
Interest, second year	6,050
Balance, end of second year	66,550
Interest, third year	6,655
Balance, end of third year	73,205
Interest, fourth year	7,320
Balance, end of fourth year	80,525
Interest, fifth year	8,052
Balance, end of fifth year (future value)	$88,577

The total interest earned is the balance at the end of five years minus the beginning balance, or $88,578 minus $55,000 ($33,578).

In effect, we now have two methods of including interest in this payback computation:

1. $5,500 per year (which would be withdrawn from the bank), for a total of $27,500
2. Leave the interest in the bank to earn interest on itself $33,578

As the cash stays tied up in the machine for five years, the second method of comparing an investment in a savings account makes more sense. However, this does become rather complicated, and there is a second shortcoming of the *payback* method of justifying equipment acquisitions: cash flows that occur in later years (interest on the bank account or cash generated by the machine) are not as valuable as cash-in-hand today. This brings up the next concept.

Time Value of Money

Don't let this phrase scare you. You have been using the concept since the third grade. If you were like me, you frequently either forgot your lunch money or spent it in the pinball machine or video game on the way to school. But you didn't starve. You could borrow a dollar from Pete, the guy with glasses and the class financial wizard. Then you had to pay him back $1.25 tomorrow. He understood the time value of money: A dollar today is worth a dollar and a quarter tomorrow. (Pete's rate was a little usurious, but the concept is valid.)

Put yourself in Pete's shoes. The *future value* (as of tomorrow) of the $1.00 he loaned you is $1.25. The *present value* (as of today) of the $1.25 he is to receive tomorrow is $1.00.

Suppose you borrowed the $1.00 from Pete on Monday, but you do not pay him back the $1.25 until Friday. Does the $1.25 he collects on Friday have the same value to him as it would have if you had paid him on Tuesday? It does not, for on Tuesday Susie asked to borrow a dollar from him and on Thursday Gene asked for a dollar loan. Pete had to turn them both down, because you still had his money. He lost both the 25 cents he could have earned from Susie and the 25 cents he could have earned from Gene. Because he did not have the $1.25 you owed him with which to take advantage of that opportunity to invest, he lost 50 cents. *On Tuesday, the present value of the $1.25 you will not pay him until Friday was only $1.25 − $0.50, or $0.75.*

We can put this in terms of the example on p. 86 of the Spouse House Company investing $55,000 in an interest-bearing bank account. The $55,000, invested today, is the *present value* of the $88,577 balance in five years. The $88,577 is the *future value* of the $55,000 invested today. In other words, a *present value* is the value today of a future payment. A *future value* is a value, in the future, of a payment today.

I have a deal for you. I will give you $88,577 five years from now, or I will give you $55,000 today. Which will you choose? (Assume you are not in dire straits.) Your answer should depend on how much interest you can earn on the $55,000. If you can earn more than 10 percent, then you could generate a higher future value in five years. If you can earn less than 10 percent interest, you would be better off to wait and collect the future value of $88,577 in five years, for that figure is generated by 10 percent interest. (Please understand that this is a hypothetical, illustrative example. I do not have $55,000 sitting on my desk, waiting for your phone call.)

Time Value of Money Computations

Is it necessary to go through the time-consuming calculations, as we did for $55,000, to find the present and/or future value of an investment? Fortunately, mathematicians have created tables which can be used to short-cut the computations. Excerpts from them are printed in Tables 6.1 and 6.2. (Please don't concern yourself, yet, with why I included a column for the odd number 25.365 percent interest rate. The reason will surface later.)

We can use Tables 6.1 and 6.2 to come up with the same answers as in our calculations about the $55,000.

Table 6.1 can shortcut our computation of what the $55,000 would be worth (future value) in five years if invested at the bank at 10 percent per year. Look under the column headed "10%," on the "year/number 5" row,

Table 6.1. Future Value of $1 Invested at Interest

End of year number	10%	15%	20%	25.365%
1	1.10000	1.15000	1.20000	1.25365
2	1.21000	1.32250	1.44000	1.57164
3	1.33100	1.52088	1.72800	1.97029
4	1.46410	1.74901	2.07360	2.47005
5	1.61051	2.01136	2.48832	3.09658
6	1.77156	2.31306	2.98598	3.88203
7	1.94872	2.66002	3.58318	4.86671
8	2.14359	3.05902	4.29982	6.10115
9	2.35795	3.51787	5.15978	7.64871
10	2.59375	4.04555	6.19174	9.58881

and you find "1.61051." Multiply that by the $55,000 original investment and you get $88,577—the same number we computed step by step.

You can use Table 6.2 to compute the present value of my insincere offer to give you $88,577 in five years. Look under the column headed "10%," across from "year number 5" to find the number "0.62093." Multiply that by the $88,577 and you get within a few pennies of $55,000.

What if I had offered you $100,000 in six years or the present value of that amount, at 15 percent, today? Would you wait for the $100,000 or take the present value today? Look in Table 6.2, under "15%" and across from "year number 6." The number is "0.43233." Multiply that by the $100,000 I insincerely offered, and you find a present value of $43,233. Can you make $43,233 grow to more than $100,000 in six years? Assume you found an

Table 6.2. Present Value of $1 Received in the Future*

End of year number	10%	15%	20%	25.365%
1	0.90909	0.86957	0.83333	0.79767
2	0.82645	0.75615	0.69444	0.63628
3	0.75132	0.65752	0.57870	0.50754
4	0.68302	0.57176	0.48225	0.40485
5	0.62093	0.49718	0.40188	0.32294
6	0.56448	0.43233	0.33490	0.25760
7	0.51316	0.37594	0.27908	0.20548
8	0.46651	0.32690	0.23257	0.16391
9	0.42410	0.28426	0.19381	0.13075

* Present value (today's value) of $1 received at the end of year for a given number of years.

investment that would pay 20 percent return (or interest) to you. Find the future value of the $43,233 by looking in Table 6.1, under the "20%" column and across the "year number 6" row. You will find the factor 2.98598. Multiply it times the $43,233 and you find your investment of the money I give you today will have grown to $129,092.87 at the end of six years (if you earn the 20 percent interest rate).

Present Value Method of Evaluating Investment in Equipment

To evaluate the wisdom of having the Spouse House Company buy the Automatic Window Machine, Rosie decided to compare the present value of that alternative with the present value of the interest-bearing bank account. That, we know, was $55,000, and the interest rate was 10 percent. To find the present value of the cash flow from the Automatic Window Machine, she listed the present values of the cash flow that would be received from the machine. Although the cash flow will occur throughout the year, she kept it simple (as do most finance people), by assuming the entire cash flow occurs on December 31.

By using the "10%" column in Table 6.2, she constructed the following list:

Year	Cash flow	Factor	Present value
1	$20,000	0.90909	$18,181
2	20,000	0.82645	16,529
3	20,000	0.75132	15,026
4	20,000	0.68302	13,660
5	25,000	0.62093	15,523
Total of present values			$78,920

Notice that year 5 includes the $5,000 that Rosie hopes she will receive for the used machine. As the total of the present values from the cash flow from the machine is $23,920.85 greater than the $55,000 present value of the bank investment, it would indicate that an investment in the machine would be justified. This concept is generally expressed by computing *net present value* as follows:

Total of present values (@ 10%)	$78,920
Subtract cost of machine	55,000
Net present value @ 10%	$23,920

That is, *net present value* can be defined as the *present value* of future cash flow from a piece of equipment minus the cost of the equipment. If the net present value is positive, purchase of the equipment would appear to be justified. If it is negative, the money is better left in the bank earning interest. Because of the higher risk of buying equipment as compared to banking the money, many companies use an interest rate substantially higher than the bank rate when making this computation.

Incidentally, if the cash flows had been the same every year, Rosie would not have had to list each year in order to make this computation. There are tables that will make the computation in one step—if the cash flow is the same every year. For instance, if she had not guessed that there would be additional cash flow of $5,000 from selling the used machine in year 5, the cash flow would have been $20,000 per year for every year. She then could use Table 6.3. Under the "10%" column, opposite "year number 5," is "3.79079." Multiplying that by $20,000 gives a total present value of $75,816. (Again, this is a different answer because it does not include the present value of the sale of the used machine in year 5.)

Internal Rate of Return

"I wonder," Rosie mused, "what *is* the interest rate the cash flow from the machine will generate, if it does save $20,000 per year and we receive $5,000 for the used machine." To compute this, Rosie has two choices: One, compute the present value as just shown for various interest rates until she finds one that generates a present value that equals the cost of the machine, so that net present value will be zero. (Such a computation by trial and error can be very time-consuming.) Second, use a computer or a financial calculator that has the necessary program built in. I used a computer spreadsheet program to determine that the answer was 25.365 percent. Using

Table 6.3. Present Value of $1 Paid at the End of Every Year (Annuity)*

End of year number	10%	15%	20%	25.365%
1	0.90909	0.86957	0.83333	0.79767
2	1.73554	1.62571	1.52778	1.43395
3	2.48685	2.28323	2.10648	1.94149
4	3.16987	2.85498	2.58873	2.34634
5	3.79079	3.35216	2.99061	2.66928
6	4.35526	3.78448	3.32551	2.92688
7	4.86842	4.16042	3.60459	3.13235
8	5.33493	4.48732	3.83716	3.29626
9	5.75902	4.77158	4.03097	3.42700
10	6.14457	5.01877	4.19247	3.53129

* Present value of $1 paid at the end of every year for a given number of years.

this rate in Table 6.2 computes a present value of the cash flow from the Automatic Window Machine to be:

Year	Cash flow	Factor	Present value
1	$20,000	0.79767	$15,953
2	20,000	0.63628	12,725
3	20,000	0.50754	10,150
4	20,000	0.40485	8,097
5	25,000	0.32294	8,073
Total of present values			55,000
Subtract cost of equipment			55,000
Net present value			$ 0

So, my computer computation of 25.365 percent was correct. The number is called the *internal rate of return* and is the interest rate the company is earning on the investment in the machine.* If you use a computer spreadsheet program to compute the internal rate of return (usually abbreviated IRR), you will probably find that you need to lay out the cash flow much as we did above, but the initial cash flow needs to be listed at the top as a negative number:

Year	Cash flow
0	−$55,000
1	20,000
2	20,000
3	20,000
4	20,000
5	25,000

The spreadsheet IRR formula will involve a range, and that will include the numbers from −$55,000 through $25,000, as shown.

It is not my intention to make this a book on using computers in finance. However, there is no easy way to compute IRR manually, so I resorted to discussing the computer method here. Of course, you can ask your finance department or CPA to compute the IRR for you, and then check their work using the manual present value tables, as we did above.† Or, you can purchase a financial calculator that will do most time-value-of-money calcula-

---

* There is one possible flaw in the assumptions for these present value and internal rate of return computations. Just as we assumed that the interest from the bank would be reinvested and itself earn interest (*interest-on-interest* or *compounding*), these concepts assume that the company will reinvest the interest (the internal rate of return) from the equipment cash flow at the same rate of interest. If it does not, the calculations will be somewhat in error.

† Your neighborhood library should have a supply of books full of time-value-of-money tables, computed at many interest rates.

tions, relieving you of the tedium of using tables. If you do have a computer and a sophisticated spreadsheet program, you will find the instruction manual will lead you through the computations.

Repair or Replace

It's time, again, to relax(?) with Angus' bagpipe music. In Chap. 5 we saw how his accountant handled the life-lengthening repair of Angus' copy machine. When I indicated that the repair bill was a shock to Angus, I engaged in a little literary license. Actually, Angus had asked for an estimate before the repairs started and had decided that repairing the old machine was the best course. Perhaps you thought that he made such decisions by flipping a coin or checking the consistency of his haggis.* That was not the case. Angus had several degrees in business, finance, law, and taxation. He just preferred playing the bagpipes.

Before he originally purchased his copy machine, he was paying a local printer 10 cents a copy for the 50,000 copies he made each year. (He mailed a lot of newsletters and fliers.) He projected his cash flow from purchasing the machine as:

Cash Flow from Purchase of Copy Machine

Existing cost (local printer)		$5,000
Subtract cash expenses		
if copy machine purchased:		
Paper	$ 500	
Maintenance	1,500	
Supplies	300	
Electricity	100	
Machine operator	1,000	
Total cash expense		3,400
Cash flow		$1,600
Cost of machine		$3,000

Payback period (machine cost ÷ cash flow) = 1.88 years

Angus used his financial calculator to determine that the internal rate of return (IRR) was 45 percent. The numbers looked good, so he bought the machine. Note that this IRR was computed on the expectation that the machine would last five years. Had he known that it would fall apart after three years, he would have computed it for only three years of the $1,600 cash flow. That would have been 28 percent, so he probably would have bought the machine anyway.

---

* Scottish "gourmet" dish best left to be eaten only by those who *must* prove their Scottish affinity.

When Angus was faced with the decision of whether to buy a new copy machine or repair the old one, he laid out the calculation in the manner just shown in two columns: one for the purchase of a new machine and one for refurbishing the old machine. Here are his computations:

Cash Flow Analysis—Repair or Replace

	New machine	Refurbish old
Alternative cost (printer)	$5,000	$5,000
Subtract cash expenses:		
Paper	500	500
Maintenance	2,000	1,750
Supplies	500	500
Electricity	100	100
Machine operator	500	1,000
Total cash expenses	3,600	3,850
Cash flow	$1,400	$1,150
Cost of machine	$5,000	$2,800
Payback, in years	3.57	2.43
Internal rate of return	12.4%	30.0%

The refurbishment won on both the payback period and the internal rate of return. That's why Angus decided to have the old copy machine repaired.

Some explanation of the numbers: The proposed new machine had more bells and whistles, so the maintenance expense would be a little higher. At the same time, there was more automation in the machine, so operator time was substantially reduced. The $2,800 cost of the refurbished machine was the number arrived at in Chap. 5. This was the book value of the old machine ($1,200) at the end of the third year of its use plus the cost of repair ($1,600).

The argument for repair would be even stronger if Angus followed this logic: without repair, the old machine was worthless. He would probably have to pay someone to take it away. Therefore, the remaining book value is a *sunk cost.* It is a cost that should have been allocated to prior years, and therefore should have no bearing on decisions as to future actions (i.e., with hindsight, Angus knows that the useful life used in computing depreciation expense should have been only three years). The remaining book value should be viewed as a *loss on disposition of equipment,* as covered in Chap. 5. Then the only cost of the refurbished machine would be the $1,600 repair. That makes the payback period only 1.4 years and the internal rate of return 66 percent!

Which is proper? Is book value a sunk cost or part of the cost of the refurbished machine? For financial reporting in accordance with the

GAAP rules, the latter is proper. For decision making, you can argue either way, all day. What is your company's policy? Ask. If you own the company, set a policy.

Leasing: Painless(?) Purchasing

What a boon leasing has been to American business! Not only has it provided some innovative financing, it has become a great marketing tool. Many sales have been made because the buyer became so absorbed in deciding between buying and leasing that he forgot to consider the question of whether to acquire at all. It's another completed sale for the salesperson: "Would you like a red one or a green one?" "Would you like to buy it or lease it?"

When Rosie Rouse bought her first Automatic Window Machine, she was offered four ways to acquire a machine:

1. She could write a check for $55,000, which would make the Spouse House Company the outright owner of the machine.

2. She could lease the machine (on a five-year lease for $1,270 per month) for 60 months. At the end of the lease, the Spouse House Company could buy the machine for one dollar, which it obviously would do. The company would be committed to the lease for the entire 60 months. There was no cancellation possibility.

3. She could lease the Automatic Window Machine for one year for $1,800 per month. At the end of the year she could return the machine to the leasing company and have no further obligation, or she could continue to rent it for $1,800 per month.

4. She could borrow the money from Herman, her friendly neighborhood banker, at the Easymoney National Bank.

Let's look at the details of each option.

1. *Pay cash.* Writing the check for $55,000 has one significant drawback—Rosie should have $55,000 in the company's bank account before she writes the check! Even if she has the money, she may have better uses for it (for business, not buying the yacht). For instance, if she bought 50 sheds (future Spouse Houses) at a time, the Fred's Sheds Company would give her a whopping additional discount of 12 percent. Rosie decided to look at other ways of acquiring an Automatic Window Machine.

2. *Five-year lease.* One of the suggested advantages of leasing equipment is that you are renting equipment that you do not own. You have not borrowed money to buy it, so there is no debt to put on the financial state-

ment that you give to your banker or to your stockholders. However, guess what works out to be the same amount as this five-year noncancellable lease? If Rosie went to the bank and borrowed $55,000 at 18 percent, payable over 60 months, the payments would be $1,870 per month—the same amount as the lease! So, is the Spouse House Company really renting the window machine, or is it actually buying it?

In the 1970s the FASB published a rule about this situation. The rule goes on for several pages, but it says, in essence, that substance rules over form. This lease has the substance of being an installment sale, for the payments are approximately what an installment loan payment would be, and the lessee (the Spouse House Company) would own the equipment at the end of the lease. The FASB calls this a *capital lease* and requires that it be treated as if the company borrowed the money and bought the machine. A *capital lease* can be defined as a lease that is substantially an installment sale rather than a rental arrangement.

3. *One-year lease.*   Is this arrangement like an installment sale? Hardly. Rosie would be obligated to only 12 payments at $1,800 each, for a total of $21,600. This comes nowhere near paying for the equipment and the interest that would be charged by the leasing company. This is no different than renting a chain saw from the local rental store for a week. It is a lease. There is no equipment acquired. There is just a monthly rental expense of $1,800 for one year only.

4. *Borrow from the bank.*   Herman may charge a lower interest rate, but he may also require a higher down payment than does the leasing company. Also, if the Spouse House Company borrows from the bank, that will use some of the credit limit that Herman, and the bank loan committee, has set up for the company.

Rosie mulled over the alternatives. Paying cash was out of the question, for that would have left her too little with which to meet the day-to-day cash needs of the business. Option 3, the short-term lease, would be too much monthly expense. Option 4, borrowing from the bank, was viable, but she did not want to use up part of her credit line there. She opted for option 2, the five-year lease.

However, leasing companies often sell their leases to banks. In providing the Spouse House Company with the Automatic Window Machine, the Softouch Leasing Company had to purchase it for $55,000. Then it signed a lease with the Spouse House Company for 60 monthly payments of $1,270 each, or a total of $76,200. Softouch then went to several banks, seeking to sell the lease to them, and found one in Chicago that would pay Softouch $63,000 for the contract. Softouch had made a profit of $8,000 (the $63,000 from the bank less the $55,000 the machine had cost). It also now had its $55,000 back, so it could buy other equipment to lease to other customers.

The bank would eventually collect $76,200 directly from the Spouse House Company as it made its lease payments.

As Rosie elected a long-term lease in order to keep her credit line at the bank open, she needed to guard against one possibility: the Softouch Leasing Company might sell the lease to the Easymoney National Bank. If that happened, the bank would look upon the lease as using up some of the Spouse House Company credit line. Rosie would not have accomplished her goal. What did she do? She insisted that the Softouch Leasing Company guarantee, in writing, that the lease for the window machine would *not* be sold to the Easymoney Bank.

A Word on Income Tax Lease Rules

There used to be some tax advantages in leasing, but generally the Internal Revenue Service now will treat a capital lease (discussed as option 2 above) as an installment purchase and make the company treat the transaction as a purchase. The equipment will have to be set up for depreciation, and the rental payments will not be deductible as rent (but the interest portion of the payments will be a deductible expense). However, there are some exceptions. If the size of the purchase is significant, get a good tax advisor to help you determine if leasing would be beneficial. The rental payments of an operating lease (option 3), sometimes called a "true" lease or "short-term" lease, generally are deductible.

A Budgeting Communication Problem

Has something like this happened to you?

Rosie Rouse's office manager, Doc, needed a new copy machine. After going through several demonstrations, he decided on a Goozus brand machine just before the end of the year. The Goozus salesperson talked about and quoted a lease, at $237 per month for 36 months. For the new budget year, Doc included in his budget a rental of $237 per month for the copy machine. His only other need was for three calculators at $35 each, so he requested an equipment purchase budget of only $105. The budgets were approved, the copy machine was delivered, and Doc sent the "lease" to the accounting department.

On the fifth of February, Doc received the January operating and budget report. It showed an equipment purchase of $6,500, which was over his $105 budget by $6,395! What was this figure and how was he going to explain such a horrendous budget overrun? Then he looked at the equipment rental category. His budget for the month was $237. His actual expenditure was zero. What happened? Jeff, the accountant, had examined the lease papers and decided the transaction was actually a purchase (a capitalized lease) and treated it that way, while Doc had submitted his budget on the assumption that the copy machine lease would be treated as a rental.

The moral? Communicate with your accounting department. Provide the finance people the facts and figures of your intended purchase and ask, using suitable buzzwords, "Will you treat this as a capital lease (equipment purchase) or as an operating lease (true lease)?" Then, submit your budget.

Summary

The acquisition of equipment should pass two tests. First, it should lower the cost of doing business and increase net income. Second, it should represent the best use of a business' cash and/or available credit. While analyzing the first test is a relatively simple procedure of comparing costs and expenses before and after the equipment is purchased, meeting the second test involves cash flow and the time-value of money. These can be measured by determining the payback period or the internal rate of return on the investment in the equipment. The numbers developed by these measuring tools can be compared to the numbers for other prospective equipment or numbers established by company policy. The decision to repair or replace old equipment can be helped by similar analysis of cash flow.

Leasing equipment can be a means of acquiring it without tying up cash or utilizing available lines of credit at banks and other institutions. However, leases often are disguised installment purchases and accountants may have to record and report them as installment purchases. Have your accountant review the lease terms before committing to an equipment lease.

Review Questions

1. While reduction of expenses may indicate that the purchase of a new piece of equipment is justified, the effect of the acquisition on _____ also needs to be considered.

2. Relative to equipment acquisition, *cash flow* is the additional cash that will be added to the company checking account because the equipment decreases costs and expenses or increases income.   T   F

3. In computing the *cash flow* from an item of equipment, the depreciation of that item reduces cash flow.   T   F

4. The *payback period,* in years, can be determined by dividing the cost of an item of equipment by the annual cash flow generated by the equipment.   T   F

5. The computation of a *payback period* includes consideration of the cost of money (interest).   T   F

6. *Present value* of a dollar is how much that dollar will be worth in some number of years down the road.   T   F

7. The *internal rate of return* (*IRR*) from an investment in a machine can be compared to the return from a same-size investment in certificates of deposit. Unless the IRR is higher, the purchase of the machine would not pass this test.   T   F

8. A *capitalized lease* is essentially an installment purchase.   T   F

Case Study Question

Sandra is in the drapery business. She is contemplating the purchase of an automatic drape-making machine. The machine costs $100,000 and Sandra estimates that it would save $40,000 per year in labor costs. That is, the cash flow from the machine would be $40,000 per year. She also assumed the machine would last five years, producing the $40,000 cash flow each of those years. Because of the risk involved, Sandra's policy is that any investment in equipment should earn at least 20 percent per year.

Your assignment: Help Sandra make her decision as to whether to buy the machine.

1. Compute the payback period for the machine.

2. Compute the present value of the cash flow over five years.

3. Compute the net present value of the investment.

4. Make a buy or don't-buy recommendation to Sandra.

This format should help you:

Purchase price of drapery machine   _____

Annual saving of labor cost (i.e., cash flow)   _____

Payback period = cost (purchase price) ÷ cash flow

= _____ ÷ _____ = _____ years

Present value of annual cash flow from Table 6.2:

Year	Cash flow	×	20% Factor	=	Present value
1	_____	×	_____	=	_____
2	_____	×	_____	=	_____
3	_____	×	_____	=	_____
4	_____	×	_____	=	_____
5	_____	×	_____	=	_____

Total present value _____

Subtract cost of machine _____

   Net present value _____

Recommendation (check one):

   Buy _____

   Do not buy _____

   Flip coin _____

7

The Balance Sheet

What's a Balance Sheet?
What Does It Mean?

So far, we have concerned ourselves mainly with generating income. After all, isn't that why a business exists? For it is the income that eventually translates into *cash,* and it is the cash that can buy the yachts, villas, and other good things for the owners and managers of an enterprise.

However, for most all businesses, success requires some tools. There was a time when many service businesses required only pencils, brooms, or shovels. That is no longer true. Bookkeepers need computers, janitors need vacuums and scrubbers, and ditch diggers need backhoes.

Assume you and I each own separate ditchdigging operations, and you have a good backhoe and I have only a shovel and a wheelbarrow. You obviously are going to be at a competitive advantage. When we (as managers of our businesses) or our bankers look at the relative merits of our businesses, we need to know not only how much profit we made last year, but what tools we have on hand with which to make those profits repeat this year.

An income statement or profit and loss report doesn't tell us much in this area. And there is another factor that is not revealed by an income statement—how much money did we borrow and do we still owe to buy that equipment?

Suppose the last year's income statement for my ditchdigging business looked like this:

Sales	$90,000
Cost of sales (labor)	50,000
Gross profit	40,000
Subtract general and administrative expense	
Bookkeeping/secretarial service	10,000
Operating income	30,000

Subtract interest expense		0
Net income		$ 30,000

And yours looked like this:

Sales		$125,000
Cost of sales (labor)		50,000
Gross profit		75,000
Subtract general and administrative (G&A) expense:		
Bookkeeping/secretarial service	$10,000	
Machinery repairs	5,000	
Depreciation	20,000	
Total G&A expense		35,000
Operating income		40,000
Subtract interest expense (loan to buy backhoe)		15,000
Net income		$ 25,000

Because you purchased equipment for $100,000, you were able to provide more service which generated more sales. But the additional repair, depreciation, and interest expense you had (which I did not have) made your net income lower. Nevertheless, you have a $100,000 backhoe, while I have only a shovel and wheelbarrow. You purchased the backhoe in July, so you are just getting cranked up in your efforts to keep it busy. Who has the greater potential? With my manual tools, I can never generate more than $90,000 in annual sales. You, with your backhoe, have a potential of $500,000 in annual sales and a commensurate net income.

Yet our income statements do not reveal this to the banker or whomever else we may wish to impress (such as in-laws, maybe?). Assume you want to borrow some money from the bank to pay your backhoe operator and secretary until you can collect for some work you are doing for a contractor. Of course, when you hand-deliver your income statement to the banker, you can verbally apprise him of your potential with the new machine.

A week later, when the banker must finally decide on your loan application, he has forgotten what you said. And what he has in writing before him provides no data about your equipment. The result: you hear a big "No" from him. To cover this need for information, accountants stick more pages into what they consider to be a complete set of financial statements.

Two of these additional pages would have provided the banker with reminders of what you told him:

1. *Balance Sheet.* This would include information as to what productive equipment you owned and how much you owed on it.

2. *Notes to the Financial Statements.* This is a narrative explanation of numbers in the income statement, balance sheet, and other elements of

financial statements. Numbers, by themselves, often do not tell a complete story. These notes are where you can describe the new backhoe and its capabilities.

Assets

There is a reason the first of these items is called a *balance sheet,* and we will cover the reason later. It has three main parts, the first being a list of things the business owns, the general term for which is *assets.*

At the end of the first year of operation, the Spouse House Company had several assets, which were listed on the balance sheet as follows:

Current assets:	
Cash	$ 30,000
Accounts receivable ($95,000 less $5,000 allowance for anticipated bad debts)	90,000
Inventory	100,000
Prepaid expenses	2,000
Total current assets	222,000
Property and equipment ($65,000 of equipment less $6,500 accumulated depreciation	58,500
Total assets	$280,500

What goes into each line?

Cash

Cash is just that, whether it's in the bank, the petty cash box, or stuffed in a mattress.

Accounts Receivable

This category covers what other people and companies owe the Spouse House Company. The most significant type of accounts receivable arises from credit sales to customers. It is also possible to have accounts receivable from employees, related companies, etc. However, what customers owe is usually the most significant, and what we will discuss here. It is commonly called *accounts receivable—trade,* to distinguish it from accounts receivable from other than customers. If there are amounts owing from employees, etc., they are listed separately in the asset section of the balance sheet.

Remember the conservatism principle? Accountants apply that to accounts receivable, based on this concept. If 100 people each owe the

Spouse House Company some money, one or two of them most likely will never pay the bill. They may be professional deadbeats, but checking out credit references and credit reports should have prevented the company from extending credit to them in the first place. More likely, they are individuals who recently felt the impact of a "reduction in force" (got fired), came home one night to find the spouse gone and a letter from a divorce attorney, or they have had some other misfortune. It's inevitable that some customers will have such a fate. Therefore, the accountants say that accounts receivable should reflect only what will eventually be collected and deduct an *allowance for bad debts* from the accounts receivable.

In Chap. 2 we saw how Rosie had decided that the Spouse House Company should anticipate that 4 percent of sales would never be paid for and would eventually become bad debts. Chapter 2 also explains the tally that Jeff (the accountant) kept of the anticipated bad debts less the bad debts the company actually experienced. (You may want to go back to Chap. 2 and review the disaster of shipping to an outfit called Adolf & Saddam.)

In Chap. 2, you may have gotten the impression that Jeff kept his tally on a note taped on the office wall. Actually, he kept it more formally, and just where he kept it is a detail with which only bookkeepers and accountants need to be concerned. However, the total of that tally is the amount of allowance for bad debts that is subtracted from accounts receivable on the balance sheet. It represents that portion of the accounts receivable that most likely will never be collected.

Inventory

We discussed inventory in Chap. 3, in connection with the cost of sales. Again, the tally of the *cost* of inventory from year to year is not kept on scratch paper, but in formal records, and the total appears here on the balance sheet. Actually, I should expand the term *cost* to *cost or market, whichever is lower.* (The conservatism principle again.) See Chap. 3 for a more detailed explanation.

Prepaid Expenses

We have not mentioned this category before. Again, the best explanation is an example. When Rosie rented her warehouse and started to stock extra Spouse Houses for immediate delivery, she should have immediately purchased fire insurance on that inventory. But, like many of us, she procrastinated and did not buy the insurance until July 1. The premium was $1,200 per year. She *prepaid* the $1,200 for 12 months, on July 1. Conveniently, if she divides the premium by the number of months covered, the result is a cost of $100 per month.

As Jeff makes up an income statement or report each month, he lists $100 as insurance expense. At July 31, he needs to reflect that the company has spent $1,200 for fire insurance, but has, at that point, only $100 in expense for the month of July. The other $1,100 is expense, for August through June of the next year, that has been *prepaid*. Jeff therefore lists it on the balance sheet as a *prepaid expense* of $1,100. By December 31, $600 has been listed as an expense ($100 each month, July through December) on the income statement and the remaining prepaid expense of $600 is listed as such as an asset on the balance sheet.

You can also envision it this way. If Rosie cancelled the insurance policy on December 31, half of the $1,200 of coverage has not been used. Theoretically, at least, the insurance company would owe her a refund of $600. If she has an account receivable of $600 due from the insurance company, that is an asset.

This is another area where materiality should be considered. The figures on small invoices are usually listed just as an expense, even though it may cover more than one month of service or product. For instance, most telephone companies bill for one month of advance service plus the long-distance calls the previous month. There is some prepaid expense involved in each bill, but I have never seen anyone think it is worth the time to try to separate the amounts and account for them as prepaid and/or current expense. I certainly would not do it.

Property and Equipment

In Chap. 5, we talked about the details of depreciation and the tally that accountants keep of the *cost of property and equipment*—and the *accumulated depreciation*. Again, the total of that tally appears here on the balance sheet. Most often it is listed on one line that says, "property, and equipment, net of accumulated depreciation," followed by a number in the figure column. In other words, all the cost of existing equipment is added up. All the accumulated depreciation is added up, the total accumulated depreciation is subtracted from the total of equipment, and the result, or *net* figure is put on the balance sheet. The details of equipment cost and accumulated depreciation, along with an explanation of how depreciation is computed, should then appear in the "Notes to the Financial Statements."

You may still find some balance sheets that title this classification with the old term of *fixed assets*. I suppose the concept was that buildings and machinery such as drill presses and refrigerators were "fixed" in place. But that doesn't apply to trucks, cars, boats, etc., so use of the term *fixed assets* is phasing out. (I wonder why these items were ever called "fixed." Before cars and trucks we had wagons, stagecoaches, and chariots, and they certainly were not "fixed" in place.)

Let me emphasize that buildings and equipment and depreciation are stated in *cost* figures, regardless of their market value. You might expect that conservative accountants would reduce the value of equipment to market value when the market value is less than the net of the equipment cost less accumulated depreciation. That does not happen. The cost of equipment is the only factor reflected in the balance sheet. Of course, being conservative, accountants would not increase the value of buildings and land to reflect increased values.

Intangible Assets

As does property and equipment, intangibles such as patents appear on the balance sheet. Rosie's patent for the Abuse-Proof Door (Chap. 5) will benefit the company over the patent's 17-year life, so it is considered an asset. The accumulated amortization (as described in Chap. 5) is deducted from the cost of the patent, leaving an item on the balance sheet of *cost of patent, net of accumulated amortization.* If there are several intangible assets, a breakdown of significant intangibles might then appear in the "Notes to the Financial Statements."

Goodwill is a special intangible asset. It sounds as if, at any time it chooses, management of a company could decide that its lists of loyal customers are worth some amount, and add that to the balance sheet. Such is not the case, for it arises only when going businesses are sold or reorganized. The details are in App. F, but I suggest you put off a perusal of it until after Chap. 8.

Other Assets

This is a catch-all category for assets that do not fit neatly into other categories. They might be loans that have been made to owners of the business, loans to related companies, and ownership of other companies.

The *Current* Concept

The grouping of certain assets under the heading of *current assets* is composed of those assets that are cash, or will be converted into cash within the next 12 months. For instance, the Spouse House Company has $90,000 in accounts receivable. Assuming that even the slowest customers will pay within 90 days, those accounts receivable will be collected (converted into cash) well within one year. So accounts receivable meets the test of being a current asset. Similarly, the inventory on hand at the end of any period should be sold in much less than a year, so it will be converted to cash.

The reason for this subclassification has to do with the business's IOUs. So, we will come back to looking at current assets after this next section on debt.

Liabilities

When we started our ditchdigging businesses, I needed $50 with which to buy a shovel and wheelbarrow. You needed $100,000 with which to buy that fancy backhoe. I had my own $50 to start my business, from my winnings in a football pool. For this example, we'll assume you did not have 100 thousand-dollar bills stashed in your mattress or that much sitting in a savings account, so you had to borrow it. In other words, there are two major classifications of the sources of funds to start or expand a business: investment by the owner, or investment by creditors. Obvious creditor sources of investment are banks, insurance companies, and others who loan money. But there are others: suppliers, employees, state tax departments, and even the Internal Revenue Service!

Borrowing from the Bank
(or Uncle Harry)

In December of the first year, Rosie was offered a deal by Fred's Sheds, the supplier of the sheds that become Spouse Houses. If she bought 100 of them at a time, Fred would give her an additional 5 percent discount. To take advantage of this savings, the company would need $90,000 with which to buy 100 sheds at $855 each and pay some related expenses.

Rosie did not have an extra $90,000 tucked away in her desk drawer or anywhere else. Therefore, she asked Herman, who managed the local Easymoney Bank, to loan the company the $90,000. Rosie had to fill out numerous forms. Herman performed many of the analysis procedures we will discuss in Chap. 12 and then agreed to the loan. As Rosie expects to sell the 100 sheds, converted to Spouse Houses, in less than six months, Herman expects her company to repay the loan in that time. Therefore, the terms of the loan call for repayment, in 180 days, of the $90,000 plus interest of $4,500.

Rosie was thankful she had decided to lease the window machine rather than borrow the money to buy it. Herman might not have approved the $90,000 loan had his bank already lent $55,000 to the Spouse House Company for the purchase of the window machine.

Notice that many business loans are not arranged as are mortgages and most loans to consumers—on an installment schedule. Loans like the $90,000 loan to the Spouse House Company are to be paid in full within a few months, often by a single payment. That $90,000 loan also could have been structured so that the Spouse House Company would pay it back to the bank as it sold the inventory, rather than in one lump sum in 180 days. For instance, Herman could have scheduled payments at $15,000 per month, plus the interest on the remaining balance.

That schedule is slightly different from what you and I see on our mortgage or car payment schedule, where the total payment is the same every month. The $15,000 per month plus interest results in the principal payment being the same every month while the interest will diminish as the loan balance diminishes. That results in the total payment decreasing each month.

Why are business loans often structured this way? Someone has suggested that it is because the commercial divisions of banks buy different calculators than do the consumer divisions, but the reason is more likely historical.

What if Rosie had started the Spouse House Company years ago and had applied for this loan in 1970, before the days of electronic calculators and desktop computers. Suppose some disaster had befallen the company, such as a fire, and there were no sales for two months. The company would not be able to make the principal payments on the loan. With the loan structured at equal $15,000 principal payments, it would have been easy for the bank officer to compute payments of only interest for two or three months. If the loan had been structured like your car payment, he or she would have had to do a lot of manual calculations to reschedule loan payments. In other words, there is more flexibility in structuring the loan with constant principal payments.

If you check a bank's computation of interest on a commercial loan, you often will find that the bank people computed it as if one year had 360 days. This, again, is a throwback to precomputer days. The 360-day year assumption simplified manual interest calculations.

The Spouse House Company needed a personal computer and some related equipment. Although it was only a $10,000 purchase, Rosie asked Herman if the bank would also loan the company the money with which to buy it. He agreed to advance those funds, repayable in 36 monthly payments of $278 plus interest. His logic in setting up different terms for this loan was this: The inventory purchased with the $90,000 would generate cash within a few months, as it was sold, so the loan would be due in a few months. The computer would generate cash more slowly, as it made some tasks more efficient and saved on clerical expense, so the loan for its purchase would be paid over many months.

Assume the Spouse House Company debt (for equipment acquisition) was all incurred on December 31, the last day of the first year of business. When this debt is listed on the liability section of the Spouse House Company balance sheet, it could be put this way:

Owed to bank for purchase of inventory (sheds)	$ 90,000
Owed to bank for purchase of computer	10,000
Owed to leasing company for purchase of window machine	55,000
Total owed	$155,000

Just as with assets, accountants usually break down liabilities into current liabilities and noncurrent, or long-term, liabilities. *Current liabilities* are those obligations that will become due within the next twelve months. *Long-term liabilities* are all the other IOUs. Unlike assets, the classifications of which seem to fit neatly in either *current assets* or *noncurrent assets,* many liabilities are partly current and partly noncurrent. For instance, consider the loan for the computer. The total liability is $10,000, but only 12 payments of $278 (principal) is due in the next 12 months. The other $6,667 is due later. The result is that this loan consists of two parts—current liability of $3,333 and long-term liability of $6,667.

Jeff made up a schedule of liabilities that are partially current and partially long-term. This is his schedule:

	Due within 12 months	Due after 12 months
Loan payable to bank for purchase of computer, $10,000 payable in 36 monthly payments of principal at $278 per month plus interest at 12% per year	$ 3,336	$ 6,664
Capital lease for acquisition of window machine, $55,000 payable in 60 monthly installments of $1,396.64 at interest computed to be 18% per year (as above, only the principal amount, without interest, is listed)	7,455	47,545
Total	$10,788	$54,212

The future interest payments do not show up in this schedule of loan payments to be made. Why not? The accountant and the economist will answer that interest expense is generated only as time passes, and the time (next year) has not yet passed, so there is no interest expense—and no liability to pay it—yet.

For example, Rosie borrows the money and buys the computer on December 31. Suppose that on January 1, she wins a rather large football pool of $10,000. As she had used company money to play the pool, she decides to pay off the $10,000 loan on January 2. She has used the bank's money for only two days, so the interest expense is only the immaterial amount of $7. The future interest expense on the amortization schedule adds up to $1,957. Had Jeff added that to the $10,000 principal and computed a total liability for this loan of $11,957, he would have overstated the liability by $1,950—the interest that would never be paid because the loan was paid off early.

Financing by Suppliers (Accounts Payable)

If, when Fred's Sheds ships $100,000 worth of sheds to the Spouse House Company, it collected cash on delivery, it would not be a supplier of cash to Rosie's Spouse House Company. However, Fred extends 30-day terms to Rosie's company, which then has the use of the $100,000 for 30 days. It could, for instance, use this money to hire more workers and install more Spouse Houses quicker, which should result in more income. Or, it could just put the money in the bank for 30 days and earn interest. Even at 5 percent, that would be an extra $415.

This money that is, effectively, loaned by suppliers is commonly called *accounts payable*. These normally arise when suppliers deliver merchandise, supplies, or services and expect payment in 30 days, the 10th of the next month, or at some agreed time.

Accrued Expenses

Can you borrow money from your employees? Certainly. Joe works for you for $400 per week, and you pay him monthly, on the first day of the following month. Assume it is February. By the end of the month, you have borrowed $1,600 from Joe. On your February 28 balance sheet you could list a liability of "borrowed from employee . . . $1,600." However, the usual terminology is *accrued wages*.

We ran into this *accrue* word before, in Chap. 1, where we defined *accrual accounting* as the process of recording transactions when they happen (which is not necessarily when they are paid for). That concept was applied to report version 2 for January, the first month of operations for the Spouse House Company. Although she had not paid for nor received a bill for it, Rosie had used the lights, calculator, and refrigerator during January. By asking other tenants in the office building, she could guess that her electric bill would be approximately $100. The expense was there, although the Spouse House Company would not have an account payable to the electric company until it received a bill in February. The estimated expense for the January electricity was put on the balance sheet for January 31 as an *accrued expense*. It also appeared on the operating report as an *expense*. (There is an interrelationship between income statements and balance sheets, which we will cover later in this chapter.)

This concept of accrued expenses pops up in several types of expenses. Among the more common are wages and salaries, unbilled utility service, insurance for which the bill has not yet been computed, and payroll taxes that are not yet due. Accountants make a fine distinction between accrued expenses and accounts payable for expenses, but they are both current liabilities and can be considered as the same thing.

Deferred Income

Here is another liability concept. Suppose Rosie is going to deliver a Spouse House to Frank, the yacht dealer. As his reputation is somewhat nefarious, she asks that he pay in advance. He pays her company on March 29 and she delivers the Spouse House on April 5. Jeff makes up a monthly balance sheet as of March 31. At that time, the company has Frank's $1,500, but it has not earned it, as it has not delivered the merchandise. Unless the terms of the sale specify otherwise, if he cancelled the order, the company would be obligated to return his $1,500 (i.e., the advance receipt of income is a liability until it is earned, and it gets listed as deferred income on the balance sheet). A short definition of *deferred income* would be: income that has been received but not yet earned.

An industry in which this deferred income concept is a major factor is magazine publishing, where subscribers pay for the subscription in advance. The magazine earns just a portion of that prepayment with each issue. If published monthly, it earns one-twelfth of the subscription price each month, so each month the deferred income is reduced by that one-twelfth amount and that one-twelfth moves to income. (Want to be a bookkeeper for a magazine?!)

You also may see deferred income called two other names: *customer deposits,* which is a reasonable name, and *deferred credits,* which is not a reasonable name. It was thought up and used by accountants who assume that everyone understands debits and credits, which is not a reasonable assumption. So don't worry about that last term. Just remember that it means *deferred income.*

Income Taxes Payable and Deferred

On some balance sheets, you may find two liabilities for income taxes: The first, *income taxes payable,* states the amount of the checks that the company soon will have to write to the IRS and state tax authorities. It's just a special type of account payable.

The source of the second category, *deferred income taxes,* is a little more complicated. Because GAAP and IRS have different accounting rules in certain areas (such as depreciation), the bottom line on the income statement (net income) may not equal the bottom line on the income tax return (taxable income). The income tax that is displayed on the income statement is based on what the tax would be if the IRS used the same rules as GAAP. Therefore, it may be a different amount than is shown as due on the tax return. If the difference between GAAP income tax and actual IRS income tax works out to be an additional liability, it appears as *deferred income tax*. If the difference shows up as a reduction in income tax liability, or as a tax refund due someday, it is ignored. (The conservatism principle has struck again!)

This is another area in which there is no point in spending a lot of time to decode the concept. Some accountants still argue over whether it should ever appear on a balance sheet, stating that it is some mythical number that may never have to be paid. When you see this liability, you are probably safe in ignoring it, unless it is an extremely large number (for the size of the company). In that event, there should be an explanation of it accompanying the balance sheet.

Now we can put together the liability section of the balance sheet for the Spouse House Company at the end of the first year.

Current liabilities:		
Payroll taxes	$10,000	
Loan payable to bank, principal and interest at		
10% due June 16	90,000	
Current portion of long-term loans payable	10,788	
Accounts payable	35,000	
Accrued expenses	8,000	
Deferred income	3,000	
Total current liabilities		$156,788
Long-term liabilities:		
Loan payable to bank, secured by computer,		
payable in 36 monthly installments of $332 of		
principal and interest at 12% per year	10,000	
Capitalized lease payable to lessor in 60 payments of $1,397 of principal and interest at 18%		
per year	55,000	
Subtotal	65,000	
Less current portion	10,788	
Total long-term debt		54,212
Total liabilities		$211,000

Notice that the *current portion* of long-term debt that is *subtracted* from long-term debt also jumps up the page to appear as an *addition* to current liabilities. The plus and the minus equal each other, so the liabilities total is correct.

Working Capital

Very shortly we'll talk about total assets, total liabilities, and their relationship. First, though, it's time to point out that we now have computed both *current assets* and *current liabilities*. For the Spouse House Company, at the end of the first year, the figures look like this:

Current assets	$207,000
Subtract current liabilities	156,788
Excess of current assets over current liabilities	$ 50,212

That last figure ($50,212), which is current assets minus current liabilities, is called *working capital*. The making of this calculation is why assets and liabilities are divided into current and noncurrent.

Why did we bother to compute these current items and working capital? Remember the definitions: *Current assets* are those assets that will turn into cash within the next 12 months. *Current liabilities* are those liabilities that should be paid within the next 12 months. If current assets are more than current liabilities, then the company should have, within 12 months, more cash than it has bills to pay. At least, that's the theory and the reason for computing working capital.

We will delve more into fortune-telling and prophesying the financial future in Chap. 12.

Notes to the Financial Statements

Up to this point, we have referred to what you owe as *loans,* which is quite proper. However, the term *note* is used almost interchangeably, although it is technically a written document that sets forth the terms of the loan.* (In this context, *note* is an abbreviation of *promissory note.*)

Unfortunately, note has another meaning in financial statements. This bit of confusion we can't blame on the accountants. The blame belongs squarely on Chaucer and all the other folks who developed the English language. The second meaning of *notes* is a narrative, akin to those notes to the sixth grade teacher that some of us used to forge—epistles that provided information such as how sick we were or how the house burned down.

Notes to financial statements are like the sixth grade notes—providers of information (but not forged). They will cover not only the details of the

* The distinction between loans and notes is unimportant until your cousin Corey refuses payback money that you have *loaned* him without having him sign a *note.* When in the courtroom, you will wish you had a written, signed *note.*

kind of notes owed to the bank, but some information about accounting principles followed (where GAAP allows some choices) and various other items. (If your factory really *did* burn, that should be included in the notes. It explains the low sales, the large insurance proceeds, and other unusual items.) There is a certain minimum of information that GAAP requires in the notes; other than that, the notes consist of explanations the management of the company wants to put in them. (An example of such notes will be found in Chap. 12.)

Notes payable are also called *bonds*. While a corporation may sign a note at the bank for a loan, if it signed hundreds of notes (usually for $1,000 each) and sold them to the public, they would be called *bonds*. Let's try to differentiate:

- A *loan* is a transfer of an asset (usually cash) to some person with the expectation it will be repaid.

- A *note* (*promissory note*) is the written document that describes a loan and its terms—interest, repayment, etc.

- A *bond* is one of a series of notes that are sold to investors.

Equity—The "Balance" Part

Why do they call this report a *balance sheet*? Because accountants always keep the same number of pencils in the left pocket as in the right? Not really. Historically, the term is based on attempts by goldsmiths in the middle ages to determine how rich they were, or what their *net worth* was. These were the forerunners of modern banks. They held gold in safekeeping for other people, they loaned gold to people they trusted, and at times might borrow gold themselves. If they added up the gold they had on hand (assets) and deducted what gold they owed to other people or were holding for them (liabilities), the difference was the gold that actually belonged to them (their net worth). That is, the gold that a goldsmith had on hand should equal, or *balance*, the gold he owed other people plus the gold that belonged to him.

For goldsmiths and others who dealt only in gold or other monetary media, this works well. However, when other merchants used the system and came up with a figure of net worth, it was not always a good indication of what they really were worth. If, in 1550, the Earl of East Overshoe had cornered and owned 80 percent of the oats in East Overshoe and West Sneaker, he might have computed his net worth as what he paid for the oats less what he had borrowed from the king to buy the oats. However, if he sold the oats all at once, he would flood the market, the price would go down, and he might not realize even enough to pay back the king, so his net worth would be a negative number. (And in those days, people literally lost their heads over predicaments such as that.)

In our times, this formula of assets-minus-liabilities-equals-real-net-worth is not valid for several reasons. One of the most significant reasons we have already discussed—property and equipment are included in the list of assets at *cost,* not present market value. Example: You bought your backhoe (at the beginning of this chapter) for $100,000, making a down payment of $20,000 and financing $80,000. The day after you bought it, you took it to a construction job site and dug a trench. It is now a *used* backhoe. It would bring, maybe, $55,000 at auction. But your list of assets still lists it at $100,000, and that is the number that is cranked into the assets-minus-liabilities-equals-net-worth formula, so your financial statement net worth has not changed. However, as the value of your backhoe has gone down $45,000, your *real* net worth is $45,000 less.

To try to avoid this confusion between financial statement net worth and market value (or real) net worth, accountants have phased out the *net worth* term and now use *equity* or, sometimes, *capital.* But the confusion has not ended. Look in today's newspaper. You will find some bank or mortgage company asking you to use the *equity* in your home for collateral with which to borrow money (so the bank or mortgage company can earn interest). The concept in this advertising is:

Your home, for which you paid $25,000 in 1974, now has a value of	$200,000
Subtract your mortgage balance which is now down to	10,000
Equity (available to be used as collateral)	$190,000

Yet, we have just learned that equity is computed by starting with property and equipment at cost. Confusing? Yes. Can we blame the accountants? Yes, along with the bankers and mortgage companies.

In the early 1980s, the accounting rule makers decided that while *business* financial statements would continue to list assets such as property and equipment at *cost, personal* financial statements would list them at market value! Equity is always something, but it's not always net worth!

This is probably a good place to point out that accounting is not an exact science. Because the experience of most nonaccountants is with checkbook balances and bank statements, they understandably may assume that all accounting is exact down to the penny. The truth is far from it. Accounting is full of estimates: What is the useful life of a piece of machinery? Which inventory is used first (or last)? What is the market value of old inventory? What will be the bad debt experience in the future? And so on.

As it is not an exact science, many accountants like to term it an art. It may not be even that. It may be only a futile attempt to quantify the unquantifiable. But, as Churchill said about democracy, no one has come up with anything better.

Why don't we list assets at their real value? We could, but at the expenditure of great time and money. Obtaining an appraisal on your home is relatively simple. Getting frequent appraisals on the value of a factory full of equipment would be expensive, time-consuming, disruptive, and the results would be arbitrary and open up countless disputes.

While we are discussing equity, I should mention another term, *net assets*. Earlier, we covered *net* as an accounting term meaning "what's left of one item after you subtract another item from it." *Net assets* is what is left of total assets after subtracting total liabilities from it—which is the same as saying *assets minus liabilities*, which is also the definition of *equity* (i.e., *net assets* and *equity* are synonymous).

So how is equity displayed on the balance sheet? The answer is in the next chapter, where I also will try to restore some of your confidence in accounting reports.

Summary

While an income statement can provide much information about the operations of a business, it leaves an incomplete picture. The balance sheet fills in some gaps, such as how much cash and other assets, including tools of the business, are on hand. It also reveals how much the business owes to suppliers, banks, taxing authorities, and others.

Assets and liabilities are classified into current and noncurrent categories. Current assets minus current liabilities generate a number known as *working capital*. The more working capital a business has, the better it is able to pay its bills and take advantage of buying opportunities.

Equity is the difference between total assets and total liabilities. While it is sometimes thought of as indicating the value, or worth of a business, such is not the case; for assets are not listed at market value, but at cost (usually).

Review Questions

1. A balance sheet provides information to a reader that is not available from an income statement or operating report.   T   F

2. Part of a balance sheet lists current assets, which are items that are cash or will turn into cash within 12 months.   T   F

3. The balance sheet of a company provides an estimate of what its real estate and equipment would sell for at an auction.   T   F

4. The interest that will be paid in the future on loans from banks is listed on the balance sheet as a liability.   T   F

5. A prepaid expense is an expense that will arise in the future and is therefore a liability.   T   F

6. Goodwill is the value of steady, satisfied customers. It can be included on the balance sheet whenever management of a company wants to list it there.   T   F

7. Accounts payable are actually loans made to a company by its suppliers. T   F

Case Study Question

1. Classify the following by making a check under the proper heading:

	Current asset	Noncurrent asset	Current liability	Long-term liability
Accounts payable	——	——	——	——
Inventory	——	——	——	——
Intangible assets	——	——	——	——
Deferred income	——	——	——	——
Loan due in 90 days	——	——	——	——
Cash	——	——	——	——
Accounts receivable	——	——	——	——
Property and equipment	——	——	——	——

2. When George, who built golf courses, bought his Automatic Sand-Trap Machine for $100,000, he paid $20,000 of his own money and borrowed $80,000 from the Easymoney Bank. He borrowed the money on January 1 of year 1 and was to repay it in annual payments of $16,000 principal plus interest (10 percent), due on December 31. He made all payments before the due date. Determine how this liability should be divided between current and long-term liability on George's balance sheet at the end of the second year.

Beginning balance of loan   _____

Subtract payments made   _____

   Balance   _____

Subtract current portion   _____

_____   _____

8
Ownership and Equity

Make a Killing in Equity?

Fortunes are made by many who build up *equity* in a business. They leave most of the net income in the business, so assets increase faster than liabilities, and that means the equity, and probably the market value of the equity, increases. Fortunes are also made by those who buy and sell the ownership (equity) interests in business.

Because ownership of a business ranks right up there with income in order of importance of financial figures, and because this equity is the conduit that ties income statements and balance sheets together, we'll look at it in more detail in this chapter.

The Spouse House Company balance sheet has grown to be somewhat complex, so to illustrate some basic concepts about equity, let's change the scene.

Building Equity

Suppose you have a young daughter named Lori, and the allowance you give her is by no means generous. To supplement your meager stipend, she starts a lemonade stand in front of your house. She borrows a pitcher and a card table from you, helps herself to your ice, paper cups, and sugar. You are out of lemons, so she buys a dozen at the local store for $1.20. She mixes up a pitcher of fresh lemonade, sits at the table on your front lawn, and sells 10 cups of lemonade to passers-by at 50 cents each. At the end of the day she returns the pitcher and unused cups to you, and drinks the remaining lemonade. She computes her profit as:

117

Sales (10 cups @ 50¢)	$5.00
Cost of sales (1 dozen lemons)	1.20
Profit	$3.80

She now has more than the $3.00 she needed to purchase a desired movie ticket, so she withdraws the entire $3.80 profit from the cigar box she had used for the business cash drawer. The business is closed and there is nothing of it left. There is no equity left.

Let's change the scenario of Lori's Luscious Lemonade. When she starts the business, she has only 20 cents, so she asks you to lend her the additional $1.00 she needs. You tell her that the paperwork involved does not justify loaning as little as $1.00 and insist that she borrow at least $3.00. She agrees. You draw up a formal promissory note, she signs it, and you advance the $3.00 to her.

The store is four blocks away, so she decides to avoid a possible second trip to the store by buying *two* dozen lemons. The other facts of her business are the same ($5.00 sales, free ice, sugar, and paper cups). However, she does not close the business at the end of the day, but takes out of the cigar box only the $3.00 she needs for the movie ticket. Because you, as her banker, insist, she computes her income by the *accrual* method, and she presents you with this accrual method income statement:

Sales (10 cups @ 50¢)		$5.00
Cost of sales:		
Beginning inventory	$0.00	
Add purchases (2 dozen lemons)	2.40	
Goods available for sale	2.40	
Subtract ending inventory (1 dozen lemons)	1.20	
Cost of goods sold		1.20
Profit		$3.80

When you see that, you ask that your $3.00 be repaid to you. (You're not quite greedy enough to charge your daughter interest—yet.) Lori looks in her cigar box and finds that she does not have $3.00. What happened?

The cash flow statement (not the income statement—review Chap. 1) looks like this:

Cash received:		
Lori's investment	$0.20	
Loan proceeds	3.00	
Sales	5.00	
Total cash received		$8.20
Subtract cash spent:		
Paid out for lemons	2.40	

Withdrawn by owner of business		
(for movie tickets)	3.00	
Total expenditures		5.40
Cash left		$2.80

You're concerned. How will you ever get your $3.00 back when the lemonade business has only $2.80? You could ask that she pay you out of the movie money, but if you have ever had a young daughter with her heart set on seeing a special movie, you know that you do not do that. However, you are relieved when she shows you this balance sheet:

Assets:	
Cash	$2.80
1 dozen lemons	1.20
Total assets	4.00
Subtract liabilities (the loan)	3.00
What the business owns less what it owes (equity)	$1.00

So, if Lori could return the lemons to the store for a refund of $1.20, she would have more than enough to pay back the $3.00 loan from you. If she continues in business, she does not, of course, return the extra lemons, but uses them tomorrow to make more lemonade (with thanks to Mom and/or Dad for the free sugar).

Now, we need to remember a little algebra. Does this portend that this book also will bring up simultaneous equations and algebraic factoring? No way. I don't recall what those things are, only their names. What I do recall, and ask you to recall, is:

$$\text{If } A - B = C, \text{ then } A = B + C$$

For finance, we can say:

If Assets − Liabilities = Equity, then
Assets = Liabilities + Equity

Applying this to financial concepts, Lori can prepare her balance sheet as follows:

Assets:	
Cash	$2.80
Inventory (1 dozen lemons)	1.20
Total assets	$4.00
Liability:	
Note payable to parent	$3.00
Equity in business	1.00
Total liability & equity	$4.00

Or, it may be presented in a classic format:

Assets		Liabilities and equity	
Cash	$2.80	Liabilities:	
Inventory	1.20	Note to parent	$3.00
		Equity	1.00
Total assets	$4.00	Total liabilities & equity	$4.00

Now we have arranged this report so that the left side (the assets) equals the right side (liabilities and equity). Because they are equal, accountants view this picture as if it were a balance scale. That is why it is called a *balance sheet*.

So far, we have computed equity by subtracting liabilities from assets. Lori could also have computed it by adding and subtracting those items that increase and/or decrease equity. What are they? We can follow it by making up a balance sheet after each of Lori's transactions.

First, she invested her 20 cents and borrowed $3.00 from you.

Assets		Liabilities and equity	
Cash	$3.20	Liability: loan from parent	$3.00
		Equity: investment by Lori	.20
Total assets	$3.20	Total liabilities and equity	$3.20

Then, she went to the store and exchanged $2.40 of one asset—cash (reducing it to 80 cents)—for another asset, the inventory of lemons. Note that this transaction does not change equity. The balance sheet would now look like this:

Assets		Liabilities and equity	
Cash	$ .80	Liability: loan	
Inventory (lemons)	2.40	owed to parent	$3.00
		Equity	.20
Total assets	$3.20	Total liabilities and equity	$3.20

Next, she sold 10 cups of lemonade for $5.00. This had the effect of increasing an asset (cash) by $5.00. What else changed? (Remember, the balance sheet has to stay in balance.) She used half of her lemon inventory (1 dozen) to make the lemonade that she sold, so inventory went down to $1.20. That leaves $3.80 ($5.00 minus $1.20) of the increase in cash without an offsetting item to keep this thing in balance. No other asset changed; the liability of the debt she owes you did not change; so, by elimination, equity must have changed. It did. It increased by the $3.80 profit to $4.00, as follows:

Assets		Liabilities and equity	
Cash	$5.80	Liability:	
Inventory	1.20	Owed to parent	$3.00
		Equity	4.00
Total assets	$7.00	Total liability and equity	$7.00

The last thing Lori did (much to your concern) was to take $3.00 out of the business.

Let's go back to an example of your home equity (as in Chap. 7, with new numbers):

Value of your home	$100,000
Mortgage balance	40,000
Equity (the difference)	$ 60,000

Suppose your next-door neighbor, who just won the lottery, does not have a garage in which to keep his Rolls Royce. You leave your old Splvit 4 in the driveway, never using your garage. So, you saw the garage off of the end of your house, put it on rollers, and roll it over to his property. He pays you $15,000 for it. This affects your equity in your home. By withdrawing the garage from your home, you have reduced the value of the house by the $15,000 value of the garage. Now the computation of your equity in the house is:

Value of your home	$85,000
Mortgage balance	40,000
Equity (the difference)*	$45,000

This is the same situation, and has the same effect, as Lori's withdrawing, or cutting out, $3.00 from her lemonade business. This, of course, reduces cash in the business by $3.00. It also reduces the equity of the business, so now the balance sheet is as we first saw it:

Assets		Liabilities and equity	
Cash	$2.80	Liabilities:	
Inventory	1.20	Note to parent	$3.00
		Equity	1.00
Total assets	$4.00	Total liabilities and equity	$4.00

This exercise in following revenue and expense transactions to the equity section of the balance sheet demonstrates the interrelationship between an *income statement* and its related *balance sheet*. It can be likened to watching

---

* We are discussing the equity in your *house* only. Of course, your total equity did not change, as your cash increased by the $15,000 that your neighbor paid to you.

the video of the soccer game Lori's team played last week. The running video records all the action as it happens, just as an income statement records a period of time in the life of a business. Put the video player on "pause" and freeze the picture, or take a snapshot of the game, and you have a record of what the situation was at that moment. Similarly, a balance sheet records the situation in which a business finds itself at a given time.

Note that we have been viewing Lori's business as if it were separate from herself. Even though she owns 100 percent of Lori's Luscious Lemonade, accountants consider it as a separate entity. When she took the $3.00 out of the cigar box and put it in her purse, that was a withdrawal from the business and a reduction in the equity of the business. This is another accounting concept, called the *entity* concept. An accounting *entity* is defined as consisting of people, assets, and activities devoted to a specific economic purpose.

Statement of Change in Owner's Equity

You could, but no one in their right mind would, keep track of every transaction for a large company by creating thousands of balance sheets—one after each transaction—as we did for the tiny lemonade business. Instead, accountants generate another report, or financial statement, that tells how and what changed equity from the first to the last day of a year, quarter, month, or for whatever period the report covers. For the first day of Lori's business, it would look like this:

Statement of Change in Equity for First Day

Beginning equity	$0.00
Owner's investment	.20
Net income, first day	3.80
Subtotal	4.00
Subtract *owner's draw*	3.00
Equity at end of day	$1.00

To summarize equity: income increases it; losses decrease it; investment by the owner increases it; withdrawals by the owner decrease it. (Occasionally, other items affect the equity section, but they are rare events such as the sale or purchase of a business or some catastrophe.)

Remember, various terms in this equity area are synonymous, for all practical purposes. *Owner's equity* is also referred to as *owner's capital* or *net worth*. *Owner's withdrawal* is often shortened to *owner's draw*. An *owner's investment* can be called a *capital contribution*.

Equity in a Partnership

Until now, our examples have dealt only with businesses that are owned by one individual as a proprietor.

May I change the scene again? When Lori comes to you for funds with which to start her business, you see "opportunity." She's eager, bright, ambitious, and can work hard. Lori's Luscious Lemonade may expand to thousands of locations that will someday sell billions of lemonades. You wouldn't want to miss out on a share of the wealth that she may generate.

So, instead of loaning $3.00 to Lori, you become her partner. You will invest $3.00; she will invest 20 cents, and you will share the profits 25/75. That is, you will receive 25 percent of the profits and she will receive 75 percent of the profits.* The Statement of Change in Equity for the first day now would look like this:

Statement of Change in Partners' Capital† for First Day

Mom or Dad:

Partner's capital contribution	$3.00
Net income, first day ($3.80 × 25%)	.95
Subtotal	3.95
Subtract *partner's draw*	.75
Partner's capital at end of day	$3.20

Lori:

Partner's capital contribution	$ .20
Net income, first day ($3.80 × 75%)	2.85
Subtotal	3.05
Subtract partner's draw	2.25
Partner's capital at end of day	$ .80

The format of this report could take many forms. If there were hundreds of partners, this report would display only the total of all partners' capital or equity. Each partner would receive a separate statement of the change in his or her capital.

Again, let's change one supposition about the partnership and assume it is a *limited* partnership. That is, Lori is the *general partner,* as she is active in

---

* Profits (and losses) of a partnership do not have to be shared in the same ratio as the investment in the business. In this situation, Lori provided the idea and will do the work, so her efforts make up for her smaller investment or capital contribution. Also, partners' withdrawals do not have to be equal to each other or in relation to the capital of each partner. How investments, profits, losses, and withdrawals are to be divided up is determined by the partnership agreement or by later agreement among the partners. (No wonder so many partnerships break up!)

† In reports on partnerships, the term *capital* is more likely to be used than *equity.* However, for practical purposes, they are interchangeable.

the business and manages it. You are a *limited partner* who is only an investor. How would the financial statement or report from the accountant change? It wouldn't. The word *limited,* when applied to a partner, refers to the liability of the partner for partnership debts. The reporting of partner's capital is not affected by the *limited* designation.*

Occasionally arising in the jargon of finance is the term *joint venture.* This is nothing but a partnership that is formed for one project, after which it will be dissolved. It is most commonly used when two construction companies form a joint venture to construct something that is beyond the financial capabilities of either contractor separately. Each *joint venturer* is basically a partner, and the reporting of capital in the joint venture is the same as for a partnership.

Corporate Equity

After seeing how you helped Lori become a successful businessperson, your son, Paul, asks for your help. He wants to go into the lawn business—not lawn care, but lawn replacement. For a respectable fee, he will replace a lawn and all the shrubbery with plastic replacements. That's right. A buyer's home will be surrounded by plastic grass and plastic shrubbery. The grass won't need mowing. The shrubbery won't need trimming. And there will be no expense for fertilizer, weed killers, and the like. The only maintenance would be rinsing off the dust during long dry spells.

Because there is a sizable population of people, like me, who just do not do lawns, you sense the large potential of this business. You agree to invest in Paul's business and insist that the business be set up as a corporation. You base your insistence on the advice of your attorney and expectations that you and Paul may want to sell some interest in the business to other investors later.

Let's dwell on that last point. It is the dream of many entrepreneurs that their business will grow to the size that, some day, they will be able to sell part of their business for millions of dollars. A businessperson cannot sell part of his or her sole proprietorship. By definition, a proprietorship has only one owner. Selling or buying part of a partnership creates some legal and accounting complications. It takes expensive lawyers and accountants to keep track of who owns what and who gets what part of the profits. As we shall see in the paragraphs that follow, the corporate form of business does permit relative ease in transferring portions of ownership.

---

* Income tax treatment of limited partners capital may be different from that of a general partner.

Why Have Corporations?

Weary of talking about financial statements? A change is as good as a rest, so let's change this to a history textbook for a few paragraphs. In the seventeenth century, investors in Europe had fabulous opportunities for gaining wealth by investing in the trade that was developing with the New World. For instance, my great-great-great . . . grandfather, Ezekiel, was a prosperous London merchant in 1682. He was offered an opportunity to invest, as a part owner, in what most likely would be an extremely profitable enterprise—the building of a ship that would sail to what is now Canada, load up with furs, and return to England.

However, Ezekiel had a family and had only £10 available to invest in this venture. There were many other investors, and of the five that Ezekiel knew, each wanted to invest a different amount, as £8, £27, £74 and £230. The other 495 investors each had different amounts they wanted to invest. Keeping track of this as a partnership, with each partner sharing a different amount of the profits, would have been an impossible task in those precomputer and precalculator days. Therefore, the promoters utilized a new concept of a *stock company*. The equity of the company, called the Fine Fur Trading Company, would be divided into five thousand shares of £1 each. Ezekiel bought 10 shares, his first friend bought 8, the next 27, and so on.

When he paid his £10 to the promoters, Ezekiel received a *stock certificate* stating that he owned 10 shares of the venture. When the ship returned and the furs were sold, Ezekiel received £2 as his share of the profits. Unfortunately, while the ship was on its second voyage, it was rammed by a deranged whale and sank. As the venture had borrowed some money from the king, he required that all holders of stock certificates (stockholders) in the venture pay their share of the loan. Not wishing to lose his head, Ezekiel paid his share, £15, to the king. As in a partnership, the stockholders were liable for the debts of the stock company. However, the Fine Fur Company continued in business and is in business today, although it has changed its name and now manufactures lawnmowers.

While £5,000 might launch a fur trading ship in the seventeenth century, the building of railroads and large factories in the nineteenth century required amassing millions of pounds or dollars. To encourage development, particularly of railroads, our state and federal governments, and most foreign governments, granted limited liability to the stockholders of these stock companies, or corporations. (This limited liability is established in a charter that the state grants to the corporation.) Had this limited liability been granted to the stockholders of the Fine Fur Company, Ezekiel would not have had to pay his share of the loan (£15) to the king. True, he would have lost his original £10 investment (minus his £2 profit), but no more.

As governments started granting the limited liability concept to corporations, they were no longer just vehicles for keeping track of hundreds or thousands of investors. They became attractive substitutes for proprietorships and partnerships, as the owners of these small businesses took advantage of the limited liability feature. That created the distinction between corporations whose stock is publicly traded and corporations whose stock is privately held. *Publicly traded stock* is stock issued and sold to the general public. It can be freely bought and sold, as through a stockbroker. The opposite animal, *privately held stock,* is owned by one or a few individuals and is not offered for sale to the general public. That is not to say that ownership of this stock is never changed, but it is infrequent and likely to be between family members.

The conclusions from the history lesson: A *corporation* is created by the state issuing a charter, and it becomes a legal person with unlimited life. *Stockholders* (also *shareholders*) are the owners of the corporation. *Stock certificates* are issued to each stockholder and state how many *shares* of stock he or she owns.

Most governments require that the name of a corporation contain a term that identifies it as a corporation. This is important to you if you extend credit to a corporation. You are warned that you cannot look to any of the owners of the corporation to pay the bill if the corporation becomes insolvent. Some of the terms used are Corporation, Incorporated, Inc., Limited, Ltd., P.C., P.L.C., and Company. Which ones are used vary with states and countries.

The Board of Directors

Another concept was developed for Ezekiel and his contemporaries: delegated management. Operations of large trading companies, with hundreds of owners, could not be managed by all those owners. So the stockholders elected a few people to be a board of directors, and that body actually hired the people to run the company—the people who today are the corporate officers: president, vice presidents, secretary, and treasurer of the corporation. If you want to take a meditation break, you can mull over whether this election of management was modeled after the emerging concept of a popularly elected legislature or vice versa.

Starting a Corporation and Issuing Shares of Stock

Back to Paul's business. Paul has saved $5,000 from his job with a landscape company, but believes he needs $10,000 to cover his start-up costs of advertising and paying for the materials needed to complete a contract. (He will be paid upon completion of a lawn replacement.)

You start the process to have the state grant a charter for your corporation, to be known as Paul's Permanent Lawns, Inc.* The state grants your corporation a *charter* and authorizes you and Paul, as the *incorporators,* to issue 100,000 *shares* of *stock,* at a *par* value of $10 for each share of stock.† So, you can bring 100,000 times $10, or $1 million into the corporate bank account by issuing and selling all of that stock. However, you and Paul will have to overcome a "small" detail. You will have to find people who are willing to buy the stock at $10 per share in your unproven company. It is, of course, unlikely you can do that. Also, when you sell stock to people who are not your family or close friends, you will have to comply with a jumble of regulations issued by the federal Securities and Exchange Commission and the equivalent agency of your state.

So, your corporation sells only 500 shares for a total of $5,000 each to you and Paul.

Why have the issuance of 100,000 shares authorized if you sell, or *issue,* only 1,000 shares? After Paul has sold his one billionth plastic shrub at generous profits, investors may be clamoring to buy stock in Paul's Permanent Lawns. The corporation has 99,000 shares to sell them, and it is not limited to selling them at $10 each. It can sell the shares for as much money as the buyers will pay. What a way to retire!

After you and Paul have purchased the 1,000 shares of stock, the corporation's balance sheet, before doing any business, will look like this:

Assets

Cash	$10,000
Total assets	$10,000

Liabilities and Stockholders' Equity

Liabilities	$ 0
Stockholders' equity:	
Common stock: 100,000 shares, $10 par value, authorized; 1,000 shares issued and outstanding	10,000
Total liabilities and stockholders' equity	$10,000

* The details of setting up a corporation vary from state to state, so what we outline here may not fit all the requirements of your state.

† *Par value* is a dollar amount specified in the corporate charter. Its only significance is that the original investors must pay at least that much for each share of stock. (They may pay more.) The par value has no relation to the real value of the stock.

The Equity Section of the Corporate
Balance Sheet

During the first year of business, Paul's Permanent Lawns, Inc. earns
$26,000. It also buys some assets, and at the end of the year it owes the plas-
tic grass and shrub manufacturer some money. The earnings, as in Lori's
Luscious Lemonade, increase equity. However, in financial statements for
corporations, the earnings are not simply added to *owner's equity,* but are
added to a subcategory called *retained earnings. Dividends,* which are the
same concept as *draw* for a proprietorship, are subtracted from retained
earnings.

That subcategory of *retained earnings* can be defined as the accumulation of additions of net income, or earnings, each year of the corporation's
existence, minus the dividends that have been paid over the years.

Dividends can be defined as the payments of part or all the earnings of
the corporation to stockholders. Generally, the dividend payments must be
made in proportion to the number of shares of stock owned by each stockholder. During this first year, the corporation paid dividends of $2,000
($1,000 each to you and Paul).

The equity section of the balance sheet at the end of the first year would be:

Common stock: 100,000 shares, $10 par value,
  authorized; 1,000 shares issued and outstanding $10,000
Retained earnings   24,000
   Total stockholders' equity $34,000

This would be accompanied by a *Statement of Changes in Retained
Earnings* as follows:

Beginning retained earnings $ 0
Add: net income, first year   26,000
  Subtotal   26,000
Subtract: dividends   2,000
   Retained earnings at end of year $24,000

The beginning balance of retained earnings would be zero only in the
first year. Thereafter, this statement would start with the ending balance of
retained earnings for the year (or whatever period) before. Dividends are
deducted from retained earnings on the day the dividends are declared by
the board of directors, regardless of when the checks are written to the
stockholders.*

* Appendix D lists several other dates that are pertinent to dividends on publicly held stock.

As corporations grow, equity sections of their balance sheets become more complex. Assume your wildest dreams come true. Paul builds his business into an international company with many millions of dollars in sales. Investors are clamoring to be let in, and you and Paul decide it's time to cash in, at least partially. You hold a stockholders' meeting (the two of you) and decide that the corporation will issue 1,000 additional shares of stock and sell it to the public. Your underwriter, which is the brokerage firm that will sell the new stock, recommends a price of $2,500 per share. It successfully sells the 1,000 shares at that price, for a total of $2.5 million.

That cash, of course, goes into the corporate bank account. But it also represents more equity in the corporation. How is it displayed in the financial statements?

Let's analyze what happened: 1,000 shares of stock were sold, and the par value of the stock is $10 per share. Yet the new stockholders paid $2,500 per share. If par value had any real financial significance (which it doesn't), the stockholders "overpaid" $2,490 for each share. The accountants, prodded somewhat by lawyers, treat it this way: they record the stock sold as 1,000 shares at $10 per share, for a total of $10,000. The balance of $2.49 million they call *additional paid-in capital, capital in excess of par value,* or they may still use the archaic term of *capital surplus.* The equity section of the balance sheet would now look like this:

Stockholders' equity:

Common stock: 100,000 shares, $10 par value, authorized; 2,000 shares issued and outstanding	$ 20,000
Paid-in capital, or capital in excess of par value	2,490,000
Retained earnings	490,000
Total stockholders' equity	$3,000,000

The $490,000 of retained earnings represents, of course, the accumulation of earnings, minus dividends, since the corporation started.

Now, how much of the business do you and Paul still own? The two of you, together, originally invested $10,000 and have invested $490,000 more by virtue of leaving that much of earnings in the corporation, for a total of $500,000. Your new stockholders have invested $2.5 million, so the total investment in the corporation is $3 million. One might think that, therefore, the new stockholders own 83 percent ($2.5 million/$3 million) and you and Paul own 17 percent (500,000/3 million) of the corporation, and that you and Paul no longer have control of Paul's Permanent Lawns, Inc. But such is not the case.

Ownership, and therefore control, of a corporation depends on the number of shares of stock owned by a stockholder, not the dollar amount invested by each stockholder. You and Paul still own 50 percent of the outstanding stock, so you have 50 percent ownership and virtual control.

This example is a little oversimplified, but it demonstrates the nature of paid-in capital. In real life, the underwriter would have suggested a stock split before the stock was sold, as perhaps 100 shares of new stock for every share already owned. In other words, you and Paul would each turn in, to the corporate treasurer, your certificate for 500 shares and receive a certificate for 50,000 shares. The par value for each share would now be ⅟₁₀₀th of $10, or 10 cents. Instead of issuing and selling 1,000 additional shares at $2,500 each, the corporation would sell 100,000 shares at $25 each. This is the reason for the stock split: $25 shares can be sold to any investor. $2,500 shares can be sold only to the wealthy.

Note that this stock split does not change the dollar amount of stockholders' equity. It changes only the number of shares that represent that equity. After the stock split, and before the stock sale, you and Paul each own 50 percent of the corporation, whether that 50 percent is represented by 500 out of a total of 1,000 shares issued, or 50,000 out of a total of 100,000 shares issued.

The most interesting result of all this, to you and Paul, is that by selling one-half of the corporation for $2.5 million, you have established a market price of $5 million for the corporation.

One essential ingredient of this scenario is that this stock becomes *publicly traded.* That is, anyone, through his or her stockbroker, can buy the stock in Paul's Permanent Lawns, Inc. By the action of the stock market, buyers and sellers agree on the price of the stock when they agree to buy or sell. That establishes a *market value* so that you can determine what your stock is worth. If the market value remains at the issue price of $2,500, then the stock you own is worth 500 times $2,500 or, $1.25 million. Theoretically, you could sell your one-quarter of the company for $1.25 million and retire! If the market value is more or less, then the value of your 500 shares is more or less. I say theoretically, as there are government regulations that may prevent you from immediately selling your stock. Also, if you tried to sell all of your stock at one time, you might create more supply of the stock than there is demand, so the price of the stock would go down.

Variations in Common Stock

Some corporations may have *no par value* stock and therefore no category for *additional paid-in* capital, but even in those situations, the finance people often create a *stated value,* treat it like par value, and wind up with *additional paid-in* capital.

I have been using the word "common" when referring to stock, and there is a reason. There is also an animal called *preferred stock.* In this instance, financial terms make sense, for *common stock* is far more commonly used than is preferred stock. Therefore, the latter is discussed in App. E, where you will also find a discussion of *classes* of common stock.

Valuation of Common Stock

Publicly Traded Stock

How much is the common stock of a corporation worth? That i answer if the stock is publicly traded. Just as in the example o.   . s Permanent Lawns, Inc., the stock is worth its market value multiplied by the number of shares outstanding; and the *market value* is whatever price a willing buyer and a willing seller will agree on. For Paul's Permanent Lawns, Inc., the market value of the stock is the 2,000 shares outstanding times the market price of the shares ($2,500 each), or $5 million.

Privately Held Stock

Can there be a market value for stock that is not traded, but just held in a safe deposit box by the owner(s) of the corporation? Yes, you will hear the *market value* term applied to these privately held companies, but it can mean a couple of different things:

1. The market value of the assets (minus the liabilities) is one way to compute the value of the equity of a business. (Review the discussion of the effect, on equity, of *market value* of assets versus *book value* of assets in Chap. 7.) Dividing that number by the number of shares outstanding would give us a so-called *market value per share,* but note that this does not guarantee that there is anyone out there who would pay that amount for the stock. A variation of this market value is *liquidation value.* Some people use the term synonymously with market value, although I think *liquidation* implies a lower value of assets, as one might receive at a public auction.

2. The *earnings value* of the company is another way to compute the value of the equity. This is, essentially, attempting to determine what the stock would be worth in the market place if it were publicly traded. For instance, Teresa owns a travel agency. Her assets consist of a desk, five chairs, a computer and various reference books and brochures—a total market value of $5,000. She has no liabilities, so the market value of her company, by method 1, is $5,000. However, after paying a reasonable owner's salary out of the business, it earns a net income of $50,000 per year. If you or I bought a business that earns $50,000 annually, after paying for a manager, we would certainly be willing to pay more than $5,000.

   How much more? We could arrive at a figure by the *capitalization of earnings,* which is a fancy name for a simple calculation. Assume we could earn 10 percent in a relatively safe investment. A travel agency is more of a risk, so we want to earn 20 percent. The question is: On what amount would $50,000 be a 20 percent return? The formula to compute the answer is:

Investment = earnings ÷ desired return = $50,000 ÷ .20 = $250,000

Would we really pay that much? There is more analysis we could do, much of which is covered in Chap. 12. The *capitalization of earnings* can be defined as the computation of that investment that will yield, at a desired rate of return, the net income of a company. As with publicly traded companies, this figure can be divided by the number of shares of common stock outstanding to determine a *market value per share*. Note that capitalization of earnings also can be computed for proprietorships and partnerships.

Book Value of Common Stock

Whether the stock is traded or not, and whether or not it is a corporation, the *book value* of equity is simply whatever number is on the balance sheet, for that is the number that the accountant extracts from the "books." It also can be divided by the number of shares of stock outstanding and stated as *book value per share*. Although you will hear this term from astute experts on "Wall Street Week" and other financial programs and in financial articles, it is often a meaningless term. It is, after all, based on *cost*, rather than on the *market value* of the assets.

Types of Corporations

What is the difference between "S" corporations and "C" corporations? For finance and accounting purposes, there isn't any, with one exception—that being the way in which income tax is collected on corporate profits.* "C" corporations have been around since the folks at the Treasury Department first collected corporate income taxes. Simply put, a "C" corporation pays taxes on its *taxable income*, which is a tax term that is akin to *net income*, except that it is computed by IRS rules, rather than GAAP rules. When stockholders receive dividends from a corporation, they have to pay income tax on the dividend they receive. In effect, a dollar of corporate net income is taxed twice: once as corporate income, and again as income of the stockholder.

An "S" corporation does not pay income tax. (There are some technical exceptions.) The *taxable income* is added to the individual incomes of the stockholders, and they pay taxes on it. Distinction: "C" corporation stock-

---

* This still is not a text on income tax. However, there is a widespread misconception that there are many other differences between "S" and "C" corporations, so I dip into the tax area here to dispel the rumors. Also, this tax status determines whether there will be an *income tax expense* line on the income statement.

holders pay tax only on the dividends they receive. "S" corporation stockholders pay tax on the total net income of the corporation, *whether or not they receive dividends.*

In the Statement of Retained Earnings on Paul's Permanent Lawns, Inc. on p. 128, the net income is listed as $26,000. Had the income statement also been printed, it would reveal that net income before income tax was $43,000 and the corporate income tax was $17,000, resulting in the net income of $26,000. In addition, each stockholder had to pay tax (at a hypothetical 30 percent) of $300 on the $1,000 dividend each received.

Had they elected "S" corporation status, each would have paid income tax on one-half of the $43,000 income, or $21,500. At the same 30 percent rate, that would be $6,450 each. To summarize:

Total tax as "C" corporation:
Corporation pays	$17,000
Stockholders pay on dividends	600
Total tax	$17,600

Total tax as "S" corporation:
Corporation pays	$ 0
Stockholders pay, on corporate net profit	12,900
Total tax	$12,900

For Paul and his corporation, as a whole package, it would be better to be an "S" corporation.* Want to switch from "C" to "S" status? It is possible for the same corporation to switch back and forth between "C" and "S" status, although IRS has some rules about how often you can do that.

You will not find large publicly held corporations with an "S" status. It is limited to corporations with no more than 35 stockholders.

Summary

Equity is not just a number arrived at by the equation:

$$Assets - liabilities = equity$$

It is also a running total of *owners' investment* plus *net income* minus *owners' withdrawals*—since day one of the business.† These rules of operation of the equity section of the financial statements apply to all types of

---

* These tax rates are hypothetical. If you have this "S" or "C" decision to make, have an accountant work out the numbers for you.

† There are a few rare and extraordinary items that directly affect equity rather than the income statement. When they occur, the accountant will list them in the Retained Earnings or Stockholders' Equity Statements.

business organizations, whether they are proprietorships, partnerships, or corporations.

Proprietorships, while simple to envision and operate, are suitable only for small businesses. *Partnerships* can become very complex if there are more than a few partners involved, so most businesses are organized as corporations. These animals are a creation of a government, and they can exist forever and have thousands of owners. Unlike proprietorships and partnerships, they provide *limited liability* to all the owners. The owners are known as *stockholders* or *shareholders* and each owner may own a different-sized piece of the corporation. The size of each one's piece is documented by a stock certificate that specifies how many shares, out of all the shares issued, he or she owns.

There may be several classes of shares of stock issued, and some of them may be promised certain dividends before the other shareholders are paid any dividends. The distinction is, respectively, *preferred* and *common* stockholders. The details as to classes of stock, and how much of each has been issued, will vary from corporation to corporation.

"S" corporation status is not a variation in the basic ownership of the corporation. It is a status that pertains to taxation of the profit of the corporation.

Review Questions

1. Fill in the blanks: The difference between an income statement and a balance sheet can be likened to a videotape. An income statement is like a video that is _____ and a balance sheet is like a videotape in a _____ status.

2. Unless there have been some extraordinary events, the equity section of the balance sheet of any business reflects an accumulation of owners' investments in the business plus net income of all years minus withdrawals or dividends paid to the owners, since the business started.   T   F

3. The *total stockholders' equity* section of a balance sheet provides an accurate estimate of the market value of the corporation.   T   F

4. Technically, the members of the board of directors of a corporation are appointed by the president of the corporation.   T   F

5. *Additional paid-in capital* is just a figure that accountants throw into the equity section of the balance sheet. It has no significance.   T   F

6. When a corporation splits its stock 2 for 1 (two new shares for each old share owned and turned in), the stockholders double their wealth.   T   F

Case Study Question _____

Gretchen's Gimmicks and Gadgets Stores, Incorporated, is a growing chain of specialty shops scattered around the country. The company specializes in such goods as left-handed letter openers and water-cooled ear muffs.

The corporation's balance sheet last December 31 can be summarized as follows:

Total assets		$10,000,000
Total liabilities		$ 4,000,000
Stockholders' equity:		
Common stock: 1,000,000 shares of $2.00 par value shares issued and outstanding	$2,000,000	
Retained earnings	4,000,000	
Total stockholders' equity		6,000,000
Total liabilities and stockholders' equity		$10,000,000

Net income last year was $1.5 million. The common stock is currently selling for $14.00 per share.

Your assignment: Compute the following: book value of the corporation and book value per share, value of the corporation if earnings are capitalized at 20 percent, and the capitalized value per share. Also, compute the market value of the entire corporation. Here's a format you can use:

Book value of the corporation   _____

Book value per share =

_____ ÷ _____ = _____

Value of the corporation by capitalizing earnings

_____ ÷ _____ = _____

Capitalized earnings value per share

_____ ÷ _____ = _____

Market value of the whole corporation at 20% capitalization

_____ × _____ = _____

9

Budgeting/Planning

What Is Budgeting?

Budgets—the word is scary. To many, it means a deadline, late nights, working weekends, explaining your numbers to your boss, revising numbers, failing to get the extra help or new equipment—another year of overwork and machines that don't work! And later in the year, explaining why you didn't meet your numbers. Why are sales lower? Why are expenses higher? Why so much overtime?

No wonder the very word causes paranoia. Budget procedures are followed mechanically, almost disregarded: "Budgets don't work, why try?" Many who break away from boss-imposed budgeting do so by going into business for themselves, and budgeting in their business is nonexistent. This state of affairs invites disaster.

So, you say, "Someone else needs to worry with this. I'm not good with numbers." Really?

Your friend, George, tells you that he is going to buy a $200,000 home, complete with mortgage payments of $1,900 per month. He says, "I can afford it. I make $3,000 per month."

You know he is married and his wife is a busy homemaker with five children. Do you agree that's a reasonable thing for him to do? Of course not.

How did you arrive at the conclusion that his decision is irrational? You probably made a quick calculation like this:

Income per month		$3,000
Subtract expenses:		
Federal and state income taxes	$ 600	
Social security	200	
Mortgage payment	1,900	
Groceries	500	
Clothing	200	

Automobile	400	
Miscellaneous	200	
Total subtractions (expenses)		4,000
George will go in hole, every month		($1,000)

What did you mentally do? Created a budget for George. Perhaps you abbreviated it. "Let's see. Five kids. Without the mortgage, living expenses must be at least $1,500 per month. Take out taxes. There's no way."

Even such rough estimating is better budgeting than no budgeting.

Keeping Score

In Chap. 1, I compared financial numbers with sports scores. There are many similarities, but up to now the scorekeeping was more like a game of solitaire. There was only one team playing at a time—Rosie Rouse's Spouse House Company, Angus' Bagpipe Shop, Lori's Lemonade, Paul's Permanent Lawns, and a few others. We could pick out two of those enterprises and pit them against each other, but it would be similar to a contest between the Toronto Maple Leafs and the Dallas Cowboys, played on a field that is one-half ice and one-half astroturf! And how do you make a playing piece that is a combination of a puck and a football? In other words, the Spouse House Company and Lori's Lemonade stand are not in the same league, so there is no point in comparing scores.

We could compare two companies of the same size, dealing in the same product or service, and we'll talk about that in Chap. 12. However, no two business entities are so similar that they can be matched on the same playing field. But two teams that can compete are:

Team One: Any company *last year, modified for new factors*

Team Two: The same company *this year*

Team One is the budget for this year, and when the year starts, Team One has already been at bat in this one-inning game (more like cricket, perhaps). It's up to all the players on Team Two (current owners and employees) to beat the budget (Team One).

The Starting Point

Where does budgeting start? Look at last year's numbers and add 10 percent? Lots of budgets are done that way, but do they really reflect what the process should be?

You can find several definitions of budgeting in dictionaries, accounting texts, and financial books. They all have one element in common—budgeting is directly related to *planning*. I like the definition that *budgeting* is the establishment of goals, making comparisons of actual results with those goals, and revising goals as results are known.

On one March day, I made up a plan, or budget, that I would break 90 at golf by July 15. On July 16, I compared results. My score the previous day of 102 meant that I, obviously, did not achieve budget. But I had performed the basic elements of budgeting. I made a plan. (I would improve my golf game.) I stated the plan in numbers. (I would score 90 or less.) I performed operations to implement the plan. (I played golf three times per week.) I kept track of results. (Scorecards.) I compared results with the plan. (Bust.) I changed operations based on budgeting results. (I gave away my golf clubs and bought a racing sailing dinghy—with which I have met my new budget plan and won a mantel full of trophies.)

My golf budget plan worked. It let me know when I was not reaching my goal, so that I could do something about it. (Change sports.) The purpose of business budgeting is no different. It provides a means of telling when the business is off track, so something can be done to get it back on track.

Business budgeting starts with planning. Planning at the department level? The always-optimistic sales department plans for a 20 percent increase in sales. The manufacturing department reads disheartening economic news and plans for a 25 percent decrease in production. Problems coming? You bet.

The planning will have to be coordinated, and no one is in a better position to coordinate than top management. It is they who are responsible for kicking off the budgeting process. Sure, there is important input from the sales manager: "How many Spouse Houses can we sell this year?" There also needs to be input from the production department. "In how many Spouse Houses can we install windows before we have to buy another window machine, or subcontract the work?"

The Spouse House
Company Plan

In December of her first year in business, Rosie Rouse had seen sales climb from 3 Spouse Houses in January to 40 of them in December. Can she sustain this growth? Would she have enough cash, employees, and equipment? These were questions to which she did not have answers. Answers about the future are not available to most of us, but *estimates* and "guessti-mates"* can be made, and if based on some logical planning, are extremely helpful.

Rosie took step number one in budgeting. She made up a plan. So far, her advertising had been limited to her local area. The demand for Spouse Houses had been great. She realized she must expand her market area, or competitors would appear and outrace her. Her first impulse was to sit down with Grace, her newly hired salesperson, and guess at what sales might be in the second year. A Ouija board might have been as good a method! Instead, she formulated a plan for the company, and it consisted of both a long-range and short-range plan, which follow. (Notice how similar these are to personal goal-setting.)

Long-Range Plan

The company is located in Great Sink, a city with a population of about 500,000. The only other cities of any size within commuting distance are East Basin and West Basin, each with about 250,000 people. The company plans to sell directly to customers within this area. Directly servicing cities farther away from the Great Sink locations would be unwieldy.

Yet, to discourage competition before it gets started, sales and warehouse locations should be set up over the whole country very quickly. To do this without a tremendous investment of cash, management has decided to seek distributors in all major cities. Also, there are other circumstances that favor setting up a network of distributors. For instance, some localities view the delivery and set-up of a Spouse House as no more than delivery of a retail item, such as a child's playhouse. Other localities view it as a building construction and require various permits and licenses. A local distributor is better able to cope with local regulations and bureaucrats.

Selling through distributors will require that the garden sheds the company converts to Spouse Houses be acquired for less than the current $900 cost price. While the company will negotiate price reduction with the current supplier, Fred's Sheds, management will proceed towards building its own facilities to manufacture Spouse Houses from raw materials, thus eliminating the dependence on suppliers of sheds.

---

* An *estimate* is a rough judgment formed from a rough calculation. A "guesstimate" is based on conjecture. "Guesstimates" should be used only when there is no information on which to base an estimate.

Short-Range Plan

To protect its competitive position, the company will immediately seek to register "Spouse House" as a trademark.

A feasibility study of the company owning its own production facility will be conducted. If the study indicates construction of production facilities would be advisable, and inasmuch as setting up manufacturing facilities will require additional capital, management will begin seeking financing and/or equity investors. Production facilities, if possible, will be operating by January 1 of year 3 (next year).

For year 2 (this year), advertising and sales will be expanded to the nearby cities of East Basin and West Basin. Compliance with local regulations in these nearby cities should be uncomplicated. This additional marketing should produce sales double those received from one city only. Demographics of these two additional market areas will be studied to confirm the sales increase expectation.

Resulting Sales Budget

Grace was an experienced salesperson in the construction and home improvement areas. Rosie conferred with her as to how best to translate the plan into real numbers. Also, she sought confirmation that the expectation of doubling the first year's sales rate was realistic.

"For there to be a market for Spouse Houses," Grace suggested, "there have to be some matrimonial difficulties—some flying pots and pans and that sort of activity. The divorce rate ought to be an indicator of how many marriages are nearly on the rocks and in need of separate quarters for one spouse. Let's check that out."

A call to the public libraries of the three cities generated the fact that the divorce rate was about the same in each city. Rosie and Grace then made up a sales budget. They began with the actual sales during the first year, which were:

Month	Number of Spouse Houses
January	3
February	3
March	4
April	8
May	10
June	10

July	12
August	15
September	12
October	15
November	20
December	40
Total	152

At $1,500 each, total sales of Spouse Houses in the first year was $228,000. Rosie and Grace looked at the first year's sales and decided that the record during the first four months was not meaningful, for the operations were just cranking up during that time. There is probably a lot of matrimonial harmony during February, with its highlight being Valentine's Day. So February sales naturally might be low. But January, coming just after office party season and New Year's Eve, should certainly be a high sales month for a product dependent on matrimonial dissension.

Therefore, as an estimate for the second year's sales, they doubled the first year's sales for May through December, but for January through April, they could only "guesstimate" what sales might be. This prediction then became the company's goal, expressed in numbers in this budget for the second year:

Month	Number of Spouse Houses to be sold	Budgeted sales in dollars*
January	18	$ 27,000
February	9	13,500
March	20	30,000
April	25	37,500
May	20	30,000
June	20	30,000
July	24	36,000
August	30	45,000
September	24	36,000
October	30	45,000
November	40	60,000
December	80	120,000
Total	340	$510,000

* While some Spouse Houses, with windows and other amenities, would sell for more than $1,500, Rosie anticipated selling some basic Spouse Houses, that were nothing more than garden sheds, for a little less. To make these calculations simpler, she considered that the average sales price would be $1,500.

They also needed to estimate sales of the service of daily or weekly cleaning of the Spouse Houses. The service appeared to be popular and easy to
sell to those who had purchased the houses, and Rosie had found that customers would accept a charge of $20 per hour for this service. The com-
pany had been using a contract cleaning service, but would now hire two
employees to perform this task. The productive time of each cleaning
employee was computed as:

	Hours	Hours
52 weeks @ 40 hours per week		2,080
Subtract:		
Vacation, 2 weeks @ 40 hours	80	
Maximum paid sick time (5 days)	40	
Administrative time (staff meetings)	50	
Training	16	
Total hours subtracted		186
Productive hours remaining		1,894

The total productive cleaning hours, therefore, are 1,894 hours (as
shown) times two people, or a total of 3,788 hours. Multiplying that times
the $20 billing rate equals a total service sales of $75,760. Dividing that
number by 12 months equals $6,313. That, rounded to $6,300, was the
monthly service budget.

Now, the sales budget for Spouse Houses and the service would be:

Month	Number of Spouse Houses to be sold	Budgeted Spouse House sales in dollars	Budgeted service sales	Total budgeted sales
January	18	$27,000	$6,300	$33,300
February	9	13,500	6,300	19,800
March	20	30,000	6,300	36,300
April	25	37,500	6,300	43,800
May	20	30,000	6,300	36,300
June	20	30,000	6,300	36,300
July	24	36,000	6,300	42,300
August	30	45,000	6,300	51,300
September	24	36,000	6,300	42,300
October	30	45,000	6,300	51,300
November	40	60,000	6,300	66,300
December	80	120,000	6,300	126,300
Totals	340	$510,000	$75,600	$585,600

Rosie has followed the recommended budgeting steps from the concept
of a long-range plan to a short-range (one-year) plan which has been trans-

lated into budget figures. Note the use of different methods of arriving at budget figures:

1. *Based on previous year's results.* (This was used for May through December.) The company was expanding its marketing efforts into two new cities that would double its market population. Therefore, the goal, or budget, would be double the previous year's sales.

2. *Based on available resources.* As there was ample demand for the cleaning service, the limitation of sales was the number of people available to do the work. Admittedly, additional cleaning people could be hired. However, Rosie and Grace felt that the existing demand would not keep three people busy. If they added another person, there would have to be a concerted sales campaign of cleaning service. As the long-range plan called for attracting distributors of Spouse Houses, it made more sense to concentrate sales efforts on the Spouse Houses (to impress potential distributors) rather than on the cleaning service.

3. *Based on "guesstimate."* (This was used for January through April.) This should be used only when no other means of estimating sales is available.

There are other sources of figures on which to base sales estimates, but they were not all relevant to creating a sales budget for the second year of Spouse House Company operations. Some such sources are:

1. *Experience of similar companies.* A comparable company in the same city, or market area, as the Spouse House Company would probably be reluctant to share monthly sales figures with Rosie. However, a similar company in a distant city may see no threat of competition and will be willing to share its figures. Rosie did not use this method, as she knew of no other companies producing living quarters solely for disgraced spouses.

2. *Trade associations.* Most associations compile statistics on operations submitted by their members. What they make available to members is a compilation of the experience of all members. For instance, if you owned a hardware store, you could join an association of hardware stores, or even a buying cooperative of hardware stores. From the statistics the association amasses, you could learn the obvious, such as the fact that lawnmowers sell better in the spring than in November. But you might learn other sales trends of which you were unaware. You could also find out what salaries are, for an average store, as a percentage of sales. If yours are higher, you have something to think about at 3:00 A.M.—why are they higher? (More on this in Chap. 12.)

3. *Government publications.* Government agencies, such as the Small Business Administration, publish information that may help a business set sales goals and establish other budget numbers.

4. *Commercial publishers.* Some publishers of business manuals print books of summaries of the averages of many companies' financial statements, industry by industry. If you use these, you need to take care that the statistics are for companies of the same size as yours.

5. *The company's own sales staff and/or distributors.* The people in the trenches often have insight that top management does not have. It is the people doing face-to-face selling that are the first to see sales trends developing and competitors' new tactics. Rosie used this as far as she could, in that she brought her only salesperson, Grace, into the planning process.

Cost of Goods Sold Budget

The most difficult part of the planning and budgeting process is the sales budget, for it is dependent not only on sales effort, but on many *external* factors, such as general economic conditions. Once that number is determined, numbers such as *cost of goods sold* can be ascertained. For the Spouse House Company, it looks like it will be very simple for this second year, when it is still buying unmodified sheds from Fred's Sheds for $900 each. If total sales are to be 340 Spouse Houses, it would seem the total cost of goods sold should be 340 times 900 or $306,000. Does this mean that the company will purchase 340 sheds for the $306,000? Not necessarily.

In Chap. 7, we learned that in December of the first year, the Spouse House Company had purchased 100 sheds from Fred's Sheds at a special price of $855 each. Additional purchases would again be at $900 each. On the December 31 balance sheet, the inventory was $100,000, and it was made up of:

100 sheds purchased @ $855 each	$ 85,500
16 sheds purchased @ $900 each	14,400
Extra doors	100
Total	$100,000

Rosie does not need to keep 116 sheds on hand. The inventory was stocked up only because of the special quantity price deal offered by Fred's

Sheds. When she determines that, by December 31 of the second year, she will need an inventory of only 75 sheds, she has established an *inventory budget*. Based on that inventory level assumption, she develops a *purchases* budget:

Sheds to be on hand on December 31, second year	75
Sheds to be sold during second year	340
Total sheds needed	415
Subtract sheds already in inventory	116
Need to purchase	299

So, the purchases budget will be 299 sheds at $900, or $269,100.

Now Rosie can construct a *cost of goods sold budget*. As the Spouse House Company uses the first in, first out inventory valuation method (refer to Chap. 3), this budget will look like this:

Beginning inventory of sheds	$ 99,900
Purchases budget (299 @ $900 each)	269,100
Sheds available for sale	369,000
Less ending inventory (75 sheds @ $900 each)	67,500
Cost of goods sold budget	$301,500

This cost of goods sold budget is less than the $306,000 we quickly computed earlier. The reason, of course, is that 100 of the sheds that will be sold as Spouse Houses will have a cost of $855 each, not $900.

Doesn't all this look familiar—like the "cost of sales" discussion in Chap. 3? It should. For an operating budget is nothing more than a *forecasted* income report. It's what we expect the income report to look like for each month of the next year and for the year in total. Note that although Rosie anticipates the cost of goods sold to be $301,500, the company needs to spend only $269,000 for the purchase of sheds. (This is not necessarily the total amount of the checks the company writes for sheds. See the section titled "Cash Budget" in Chap. 10.)

Expense Budget

This covers all the items that appear as expenses on an income statement, including sales expenses, salaries, rent, supplies, and so on. Making intelligent estimates of what these expenses will be is impossible for top management in any but the smallest companies. It falls to division and department managers to provide these budget numbers; and to many managers, the process is one of dreaming up some numbers (and enough numbers) to satisfy the boss. In companies where that is the attitude and the procedure, the company would probably benefit more if all the department managers went to the golf course for the day!

Once top management has determined the goals of the company, and once those goals have been translated into expected sales numbers for the coming year, department managers have a measure (sales volume) with which to determine their needs. If properly done, the process may appear tedious, but one hour on proper budget preparation can save many hours of sweating out explanations and justifications when results are far afield from budget expectations.

The Spouse House Company was not yet big enough to have formal department managers. Yet it did have people who might know more about details of their work area than did Rosie Rouse, the top management. Rosie decided to use good budget procedures and ask each of them for input into the budget.

Selling Expense Budget

Although Grace, the salesperson, was new to the Spouse House business, she was well experienced in similar sales and marketing. She submitted this sales department budget to Rosie:

Advertising	$36,000
Telephone, long-distance	1,020
Administrative assistant (50% of secretary's time)	9,000
Automobile use	15,300
Commissions (5% of sales)	29,280
Total selling expense budget	$90,600

Where did Grace get these numbers? For the commissions, it's obviously the commission rate of 5 percent of total sales, but from where did the other numbers come? She could have scratched them on a matchbook cover while waiting at a stoplight, but she was more conscientious than that. She made these underlying calculations, *and submitted them with the sales department budget.*

An addendum to the short-range plan provided a detailed advertising plan. It included mailing 2,000 direct-mail pieces each month and spending $1,000 each month on radio/television advertising and another $1,000 on newspaper advertising. The computation was:

Direct mail: 24,000 pieces @ 50¢	$12,000
Radio/TV @ $1,000 per month	12,000
Newspaper @ $1,000 per month	12,000
Total advertising budget	$36,000

The administrative assistant is one person. He or she will be answering the telephone, typing letters, maintaining files and other records for both Rosie (chief executive) and Grace (sales department), and changing from one to the other as priorities dictate. It would not be efficient for this person to try to keep track of how much time is devoted to which department. (The recordkeeping might take longer than the task!) When budget planners find this situation, there is nothing to do but make an arbitrary allocation. Therefore, one-half of the assistant's annual salary of $18,000 is listed under the sales department budget.

The forecasted long-distance telephone call computation was based on the assumption that one-half of the 340 annual sales would be made to the new markets in East Basin and West Basin. Each of these 170 sales would involve an average of three long-distance telephone calls, and the average cost per call would be $2. In other words:

$$170 \text{ sales} \times 3 \text{ calls} \times \$2.00 = \$1,020$$

There are two approaches to budgeting for automobile use by the sales department. The company could either own the car or it could reimburse Grace for using her own automobile. If the company owns the automobile, Rosie would have to estimate repairs, maintenance, gas, and depreciation. The simpler method, which is what Rosie did, is to reimburse Grace for using her own automobile. They agreed to a rate of 30 cents per mile.

Rosie's experience has been that one out of three sales calls results in a sale. Therefore, if 340 sales are to be closed, 3 times 340, or 1,020, sales calls will have to be made. Grace estimates that the average distance traveled for a sales call will be 50 miles. So the automobile budget expense is computed as:

$$1,020 \text{ calls} \times 50 \text{ miles} \times 30\cent = \$15,300$$

Warehouse Expense Budget

Rosie had the numbers for this budget, except for supplies. She asked Lem, the warehouse worker and carpenter, for an estimate, and he suggested that the supplies expense should run about $50 per month. He also gave Rosie a description of his typical day: receiving sheds, shipping out Spouse Houses, visiting the customer's location after shipment to install the amenities and check that doors and windows worked properly, plus operating the window machine that modified the sheds into Spouse Houses. He could handle the modification and delivery of about two houses per day, or at an annual rate of 500 houses (250 work days times 2).

Although the warehouse could hold no more than 10 Spouse Houses at a time, that limitation was not a problem. Fred was willing to hold extra sheds (as the 100 purchased in December) in his warehouse and deliver them five at a time.

At an annual volume of 340 sheds, it appeared that one person (Lem) and the present warehouse could handle the volume, so Rosie's warehouse expense budget was:

Rent @ $600 per month	$ 7,200
Supplies @ $50 per month	600
Salary (Lem)	24,000
Delivery (340 Spouse Houses with contract trucker at $100 each house)	34,000
Total warehouse expense budget	$65,800

General and Administrative Expense Budget

Let's look at the budget Rosie prepared and then discuss where she obtained the numbers. It looked like this:

Executive salary	$30,000
Administrative salary (½ here, ½ under sales expense)	9,000
Executive automobile	9,000
Workers' compensation insurance	3,040
Fire insurance	300
General liability insurance	600
Product liability insurance	2,930
Professional fees	12,000
Rent, office	4,800
Supplies, office	600
Telephone, basic service	1,800
Payroll taxes	10,130
Business license	2,930
Property taxes on machinery, etc.	600
Depreciation	12,000
Total general and administrative expense budget	$99,730

Rosie's executive salary budget is determined by Rosie. As is usual for small, growing companies, the owner's salary is based on her minimum need for living, rather than her worth.

Half the administrative salary of $18,000 is listed here and half under the sales expense budget. (See the discussion under "Selling Expense Budget" earlier in this chapter.)

There was no way to calculate miles for Rosie's car as there was for Grace's sales automobile budget. However, Rosie will be running around quite a bit, seeking capital and arranging for construction of facilities for manufacturing Spouse Houses. A guess of 2,500 miles per month at 30 cents per mile resulted in an annual budget of $9,000.

Budgeting insurance is a detailed task that often is not done. However, the numbers are available from the insurance company. For the Spouse House Company, it worked out as follows.

The premium for workers' compensation insurance is computed at 3 percent of total payroll,* and that is:

Sales commissions (Grace)	$ 29,280
Administrative assistant	18,000
Warehouse person (Lem)	24,000
Executive (Rosie)	30,000
Total salaries	101,280
Times rate	× 3%
Workers' compensation budget	$ 3,040

Fire insurance and general liability insurance are as quoted by the insurance company.

The product liability insurance covers injuries that may occur after a Spouse House has been delivered to a customer. There is a danger of a customer having a foot crushed in a half-closed door or being cut by flying glass from a broken window. Although such mishaps are usually caused by the aggrieved spouse, the courts could conceivably hold the Spouse House Company liable. As the risk increases with each house sold, the insurance company computes the premium based on .5 percent of sales. ($585,600 × .005 = $2,930.)

Professional fees (lawyers and accountants) will be high for this small company, since Rosie will need distributor and investor agreements, as well as audited financial statements with which to attract investors.

Rent of $400 per month can be accurately forecasted, as that is the amount stated in the lease.

Office supplies expense of $50 per month is, frankly, just a guess. The amount is small compared to other items and not worth spending a great deal of time over.

The telephone budget is for the lines into the office and the basic local service. As most long-distance calls are sales-related, that expense appears in the sales expense budget.

---

* The rates for this insurance, covering workers who are injured on the job, will vary with the type of work. Insurance rates for steel erectors who walk around on narrow beams 30 stories above hard pavement are much higher than for people sitting at a desk all day. To keep the example somewhat simple, I've used one rate for all employees. In actual practice, the rates would vary with the job description.

Taxes are inevitable and must be budgeted for. For the Spouse House Company, payroll taxes are estimated to be 10 percent of the total salaries and wages (same as computed for workers' compensation insurance). The city charges for a business license at a rate computed as .5 percent of total sales. Property tax is levied on the value of machinery and equipment, and the assessor's office has computed it to be $600 for the year.*

Budget Summary

Once Rosie and her crew decided on the numbers, she had her accountant, Jeff, put them together. One of the documents he created was this budget summary:

Sales budget	$585,600	
Cost of goods sold budget	301,500	
Gross profit budget		$284,100
Subtract expense budgets:		
Selling expense budget	90,600	
Warehouse expense budget	65,800	
General and admin. expense budget	99,730	
Total expense budgets		256,130
Budgeted operating income		$ 27,970

Rosie now has a budget for the second year of the Spouse House Company's operation. The figures are for the whole year. At the end of the year, she will be able to compare her actual income statement with the budget and exclaim, "Great! We did better than budget." Or, she will hang her head and mutter, "We didn't make budget."

Was making up the budget a worthwhile exercise? Not if the task stopped at the annual figures. After the year is over, who cares whether the company met its budget or not. What's done is done. Budgets are only useful as a management tool if they are broken down into at least monthly chunks. They work even better if divided into weekly or daily segments.

Rosie decided that, for her small business, breaking it down into monthly budgets was enough. To illustrate, the first four months of the budget are in Fig. 9.1.

---

* These rates are hypothetical. The actual rates will vary with the states and with the cities and counties within a state.

The Spouse House Company
Operating Budget
First Four Months of Second Year

Month	January	February	March	April
No. of Spouse Houses sold	18	9	20	25
Sales of Spouse Houses	$27,000	$13,500	$30,000	$37,500
Service sales	6,300	6,300	6,300	6,300
Total sales	33,300	19,800	36,300	43,800
Cost of goods sold	16,110	7,695	17,100	21,375
Gross profit	17,190	12,105	19,200	22,425
Expenses, by cost center:				
Sales expenses:				
Advertising	3,000	3,000	3,000	3,000
Telephone	54	27	60	75
Administrative assistant	750	750	750	750
Automobile	810	405	900	1,125
Sales commission	1,665	990	1,815	2,190
Total sales expenses	6,279	5,172	6,525	7,140
Warehouse expenses:				
Rent	600	600	600	600
Supplies	50	50	50	50
Salary	2,000	2,000	2,000	2,000
Delivery, per house	1,800	900	2,000	2,500
Total warehouse expenses	4,450	3,550	4,650	5,150
General and administrative expenses:				
Executive salary	2,500	2,500	2,500	2,500
Administrative salary	750	750	750	750
Executive auto	750	750	750	750
Workers' comp. insurance	230	210	234	246
Fire insurance	25	25	25	25
General liability insurance	50	50	50	50
Product liability insurance	167	99	182	219
Professional fees	1,000	1,000	1,000	1,000
Rent, office	400	400	400	400
Supplies, office	50	50	50	50
Telephone, basic	150	150	150	150
Payroll taxes	767	699	782	819
Business license	167	99	182	219
Property taxes	50	50	50	50
Depreciation	1,000	1,000	1,000	1,000
Total G&A expenses	8,056	7,832	8,105	8,228
Net income (loss) before tax	($ 1,595)	($ 4,449)	($ 80)	$ 1,907

Figure 9.1   Operating budget—Spouse House Company.

Note that some items vary from month to month, fluctuating with the changes in sales volume, while others stay at the same fixed amount every month. Sound familiar? We covered it as variable and fixed expenses in Chap. 4. Is it reasonable that what shows up as varying from month to month should vary? For instance, Grace's automobile expense was computed by determining how far she would have to drive in order to book 340 sales. That is, the expense would vary, year to year, with how many sales are budgeted.

However, when Rosie applied that formula to the monthly expenses, it appears that Grace will drive only half as far in February as she did in January. It is more likely that, when sales are slow, she will drive farther, making more calls. Perhaps, on a monthly budget, that expense should be budgeted as fixed, even though it will vary from year to year. The decision is a management judgment call.

Zero-Based Budgeting

This is another term that scares managers. It is the opposite of the "last year plus 10 percent" system I mentioned earlier. It should not scare you, though. Much of Rosie's budgeting that I described was zero-based—she had no previous years' experience to go on. Was it difficult, really, to compute the probable automobile expense for Grace, the new person in the newly created job?

Look what would have happened if Rosie had budgeted professional fees based on last year's expense, which was $2,500. If she had assumed "double sales, double the expense," the professional fees budget would have been $5,000. Actually, the fees the second year were $12,300—to cover the costs of raising capital and moving into the manufacturing business. Rosie did foresee this, for she budgeted $12,000 for the professional fee expense to cover the extra services she would need. She engaged in zero-based budgeting; she used common sense instead of some senseless formula. That is, *zero-based budgeting* is the process of creating a budget based on expectations for the coming year, without reference to previous years' budgets.

In the next chapter, we'll look at how to use these budget figures to avoid trouble.

Summary

Budgeting is essentially planning, with common sense liberally applied. It is not, or at least it should not be, a task undertaken only to satisfy the bureaucracy of some organization. It is a management tool that can provide a road map for your activities during the year. Different items in the budget can be determined in different ways: some by previous experience, some by developing new numbers. The more care and thought you devote to budget preparation before the year begins, the more useful the budget tool will be.

Review Questions

1. Final budgets for the following year should be prepared before any long-range planning is attempted. T F

2. Once prepared, budgets should never be altered. T F

3. Budgets should *always* be based primarily on the previous year's operating results. T F

4. Flexible budgeting is a system of changing budget figures as sales figures change. T F

5. Budgets should be (choose one):
   a. Easy to attain
   b. Virtually impossible to attain
   c. Attainable with strong effort and some luck
   d. Set in concrete after being computed by a set of formulas developed by some whiz kid

6. Rank the following in order of their reliability as sources of budget numbers:

   _____ Wild guesses

   _____ Last year's numbers

   _____ Estimates (educated guesses)

   _____ Industry averages

   _____ Probable actual expenses (zero-based concept)

   _____ Noncompeting similar companies

   _____ Company personnel "in the trenches"

Case Study Question _____

When Gretchen started the first Gimmicks and Gadgets Store, she instituted flexible budgeting within the first few months of operations (one reason she has been so successful). Her first monthly budget numbers were these:

Cost of goods sold	40% of sales
Advertising	10% of sales
Salaries	$5,000
Part-time help	5% of sales
Delivery expense	1% of sales

Fire insurance	$100
Rent	$2,000
Supplies	2% of sales
Telephone	$200

Your mission: Compute and list the budget figures for May, when sales were $30,000.

Item	Budget in dollars
_____	$ _____
_____	$ _____
_____	$ _____
_____	$ _____
_____	$ _____
_____	$ _____
_____	$ _____
_____	$ _____
_____	$ _____

10

Budget Reporting and More Budgets

Warning

There are many reports with many figures reproduced in this chapter. They could be injurious to your eyesight and your mental equilibrium, but don't sweat it. The reports are printed on these pages to demonstrate the *format* of the reports. Except for a few numbers I will point out, there is no need to study them line by line—unless you feel you just have to.

Budget Reports

As covered in Chap. 9, a budget is an expression of goals in terms of expected numbers. It's rather meaningless unless actual results are compared to these goals (budget numbers). That is, did results meet expectations? The best way to make this comparison is to lay out the actual and budget numbers, side by side. That is how Jeff prepared the report for January, second year, for the Spouse House Company. Figure 10.1 is the report.

The second column of the report is a copy of the January column in the monthly budget we looked at in Fig. 9.1. The first column is the report of what actually happened. The third column, called *variance*, is the difference between actual results (column 1) and the budget (column 2). The fourth column is the *percentage variance*, which is computed by dividing the variance in column 3 by the budget in column 2.

Some of the variances are positive and some are negative. Is positive good and negative bad, or vice versa? That depends on which item we are discussing. A positive variance in sales means sales have exceeded expectations, so that is good. A positive variance in an expense means that the company

The Spouse House Company
Budget Report
January of Second Year

Month	Actual January	Budget January	$ Variance	% Variance	
No. of Spouse Houses sold	21	18	3	17%	F
Sales of Spouse Houses	$31,500	$27,000	$4,500	17%	F
Service sales	5,500	6,300	(800)	−13%	U
Total sales	37,000	33,300	3,700	11%	F
Cost of goods sold	18,675	16,110	2,565	16%	F
Gross profit	18,325	17,190	1,135	7%	F
Expenses, by cost center:					
Sales expenses:					
Advertising	3,600	3,000	600	20%	U
Telephone	74	54	20	37%	U
Administrative assistant	750	750	0	0%	
Automobile	900	810	90	11%	U
Sales commission	1,850	1,665	185	11%	U
Total sales expenses	7,174	6,279	895	14%	U
Warehouse expenses:					
Rent	600	600	0	0%	
Supplies	40	50	(10)	−20%	F
Salary	2,000	2,000	0	0%	
Delivery	2,000	1,800	200	11%	U
Total warehouse expenses	4,640	4,450	190	4%	U
General and admin. expenses:					
Executive salary	2,500	2,500	0	0%	
Administrative salary	750	750	0	0%	
Executive auto	650	750	(100)	−13%	F
Workers' comp. insurance	236	230	6	3%	U
Fire insurance	25	25	0	0%	
General liability insurance	50	50	0	0%	
Product liability insurance	185	167	18	11%	U
Professional fees	300	1,000	(700)	−70%	F
Rent, office	400	400	0	0%	
Supplies, office	75	50	25	50%	U
Telephone, basic	150	150	0	0%	
Payroll taxes	785	767	18	2%	U
Business license	185	167	18	11%	U
Property taxes	50	50	0	0%	
Depreciation	1,000	1,000	0	0%	
Total G&A expenses	7,341	8,056	(715)	−9%	F
Net operating income (loss)	($ 830)	($ 1,595)	$ 765	−48%	F

Figure 10.1   January budget with variances—Spouse House Company.

spent more than was planned for this item. Generally, that is bad. Instead of saying "good" and "bad" to describe variances, financial people refer to them as *favorable* and *unfavorable*. Why? Possibly because accountants, fully aware of the inaccuracies in accounting and budgeting, like to use these weaker, or less dogmatic, terms. That provides more room for weaseling if the reports turn out to be wrong. (Accountants would say "possibly incorrect.") At any rate, so that Rosie does not have to ponder which is which, Jeff has indicated "F" or "U," for *favorable* and *unfavorable*, after each variance.

Let's look at the first item that is expressed in dollars, "Sales of Spouse Houses." In column 2 ("Budget") is the figure of $27,000. The column 1 ("Actual") figure of $31,500 reflects what really happened in sales. Jeff computed the variance by this computation:

Sales of Spouse Houses (actual)	$31,500
Subtract budgeted sales	27,000
Variance	$ 4,500

And he computed percentage variance as variance divided by budget, or:

$$\$4,500 \div \$27,000 = 17\%$$

So, sales of Spouse Houses are ahead of the goal that Rosie set by $4,500, which is 17 percent over her goal. Whatever she and Grace are doing to promote sales must be working.

On the next line, though, is the opposite situation. Sales of service are $800 under budget. This item needs some attention. Perhaps there should be more phone calls or mailings to old customers who should be using this cleaning service. However, the goals of the company included emphasizing Spouse House sales over service sales (to impress potential distributors). Perhaps this is a case where an unfavorable variance should just be accepted.

Why worry with computing and listing the percentages of variance? Again, let's look at advertising and sales telephone expenses. While advertising is $600 over budget, telephone is only $20 over. Yet, that $20 is a whopping 37 percent out of line, while the advertising variance is a more moderate 20 percent out of whack. That 37 percent figure will call Rosie's and Grace's attention to what may be a budding problem. Perhaps someone is using the business phone to call Aunt Nellie in Copenhagen. Or, Grace may know of several legitimate telephone calls that had to be made, in which case the $20 is really of no consequence.

Some items are next to impossible to budget. For instance, because of plans to expand the business and seek additional investors, Rosie anticipated needing help from lawyers and accountants to the tune of $12,000, so she budgeted $1,000 per month. At the end of January, she had bills from her accounting firm of only $300. Because the expansion plans were so flexible, the $12,000 was only a guess, and the way it was handled on this January report was the only reasonable way to do it. In other words, large variances are not always very good or very bad. They have to be read in light of circumstances.

Apropos of the warning at the beginning of this chapter, it should now be obvious that the important numbers to read in Fig. 10.1 are the percentage figures in the right-hand column. Only if one is a large figure do you need to look at the figures to the left on that line. Moral: Whenever possible, read two-digit numbers rather than five- or ten-digit numbers. It's easier.

Reports, Reports, and More Reports

Computers have made life easier, in some ways. Engineers and accountants no longer have to do tedious manual calculations. The electrons, elves, or whatever is inside the computers do it for them. We have automated grocery store shopping, although I still long for the time when we could visit with the clerk while he or she wrote the prices on the back of a paper bag and added them up. And computers have made it easier for the Internal Revenue Service to keep track of us, which, at best, is a dubious benefit.

For the business manager, accountants and programmers can produce volumes of operating and budget reports—hundreds of pages jam-packed with numbers—which could never have been generated with pencils and typewriters. Overkill? Of course. Solutions? Reform the accountants and programmers? Not likely. Managers, particularly those not number-oriented, have to learn to sort out the useful from the useless. For instance, Fig. 10.2 is the February operating report for the Spouse House Company. It looks formidable, and it is, but I'll try to simplify your visualization of it by breaking it down into components.

The point of printing it is that it is an example of a report with lots of information to sort out. Here are my suggestions for making it easier to read: The first four number columns (through "% Variance" under February) is the same report format as was the January report. Cover up the last four columns and you can read it simply as a report for February, like the January report.

Cover the first four number columns and look at the last four, and you are reading the same format for the total of January and February actual and budgeted amounts. Budgeted figures come from adding the first two columns of Fig. 9.1, and the variances and percentage variances are computed in the same manner as for one month. These year-to-date figures can be more meaningful because, as the year progresses, they iron out month-to-month fluctuations.

You can use this same technique with any busy reports you face. Cover up the parts that are not germane to what demands your immediate attention. It can cut down on eye fatigue and resulting frustration.

Flexible Budgets

Figure 10.3 is part of the operating report at the end of September. I omitted, or covered up, the columns for September only, as they are not germane to what is under discussion. What's here is what we want to look at—the nine-month, year-to-date, total.

Business is great! Sales are 47 percent over budget and net income before tax is 4,000 percent over budget. Now, look at the expenses. Most of them are over budget (bad or unfavorable variance). The Spouse House Company would make even more profit if it could boost sales like this and keep all the expenses within budget. Is that a reasonable goal? Hardly. Some expenses, such as sales commissions, will rise automatically with a rise in sales.

Some expenses will be equal to budget no matter what the volume of business is. For instance, property tax is assessed on the equipment on hand January 1. The bill arrives in January, so the amount is definite—Jeff can divide it by twelve and have a known monthly expense figure. It will always equal the budget figure.

Depreciation expense can be computed at the beginning of the year, for both equipment on hand and equipment for which purchase is planned during the year. It therefore should show no variance from the budgeted depreciation figure.

But look at advertising, sales commissions, warehouse supplies, product liability insurance, and the other items that are 40 percent or more over budget. When Rosie looked at this report, she said: "This budget's gone to the land of fire and brimstone." She told Jeff not to print the budget figures in the reports for the rest of the year.

Did she need to forsake the management tool of budgeting? Not if the budget had been constructed as a *flexible budget*. In such a budget, the budgeted variable expenses* are listed as varying with the sales volume. It is usually done in one of two ways.

First, Rosie can make up a schedule of budgets at different sales volumes, as in Fig. 10.4. When Jeff makes up the operating report at the end of a month, he would look across the "sales" line and find the number closest to actual sales for the month. Then he would use the numbers in that column for the "budget" column in the operating report.

The second way to construct a flexible budget is to state the variable and semivariable items as a *formula* based on *actual* sales volume. For the Spouse House Company, cost of goods sold budget would be 60 percent of actual sales, sales commissions budget would be 5 percent of sales, delivery expense budget would be $100 per unit sold, and so on.

* The distinction between and the definitions of *variable* and *fixed* expenses are covered in Chap. 4.

Figure 10.2 Month and year-to-date budget report—Spouse House Company.

The Spouse House Company
Month and Year-to-Date Budget Report
February of Second Year

	February				Year-to-Date			
	Actual	Budget	$ Variance	% Variance	Actual	Budget	$ Variance	% Variance
No. of Spouse Houses sold	11	9	2	22%	32	27	5	19%
Sales of Spouse Houses	$16,500	$13,500	$3,000	22%	$48,000	$40,500	$7,500	19%
Service sales	7,000	6,300	700	11%	12,500	12,600	(100)	-1%
Total sales	23,500	19,800	3,700	19%	60,500	53,100	7,400	14%
Cost of goods sold	9,405	7,695	1,710	22%	28,080	23,805	4,275	18%
Gross profit	14,095	12,105	1,990	16%	32,420	29,295	3,125	11%
Expenses, by cost center:								
Sales expenses:								
Advertising	2,700	3,000	(300)	-10%	6,300	6,000	300	5%
Telephone	45	27	18	67%	119	81	38	47%
Administrative assistant	750	750	0	0%	1,500	1,500	0	0%
Automobile	775	405	370	91%	1,675	1,215	460	38%
Sales commission	1,175	990	185	19%	3,025	2,655	370	14%
Total sales expenses	5,445	5,172	273	5%	12,619	11,451	1,168	10%

Warehouse expenses:								
Rent	600	600	0	0%	1,200	1,200	0	0%
Supplies	75	50	25	50%	115	100	15	15%
Salary	2,000	2,000	0	0%	4,000	4,000	0	0%
Delivery, per house	1,100	900	200	22%	3,100	2,700	400	15%
Total warehouse expenses	3,775	3,550	225	6%	8,415	8,000	415	5%
General and admin. expenses:								
Executive salary	2,500	2,500	0	0%	5,000	5,000	0	0%
Administrative salary	750	750	0	0%	1,500	1,500	0	0%
Executive auto	700	750	(50)	-7%	1,350	1,500	(150)	-10%
Workers' comp. insurance	215	210	5	2%	451	440	11	3%
Fire insurance	25	25	0	0%	50	50	0	0%
General liability insurance	50	50	0	0%	100	100	0	0%
Product liability insurance	118	99	19	19%	303	266	37	14%
Professional fees	500	1,000	(500)	-50%	800	2,000	(1,200)	-60%
Rent, office	400	400	0	0%	800	800	0	0%
Supplies, office	60	50	10	20%	135	100	35	35%
Telephone, basic	150	150	0	0%	300	300	0	0%
Payroll taxes	718	699	19	3%	1,503	1,466	37	3%
Business license	118	99	19	19%	303	266	37	14%
Property taxes	50	50	0	0%	100	100	0	0%
Depreciation	1,000	1,000	0	0%	2,000	2,000	0	0%
Total G&A expenses	7,354	7,832	(478)	-6%	14,695	15,888	(1,193)	-8%
Net operating income	($2,479)	($4,449)	$1,970	-44%	($ 3,309)	($ 6,044)	$2,735	-45%

The Spouse House Company
Budget Report—Fixed Budget Numbers
Nine Months of Second Year

Month	Actual 9 Months	Budget 9 Months	$ Variance	% Variance	
No. of Spouse Houses sold	280	190	90	47%	F
Sales of Spouse Houses	$420,000	$285,000	$135,000	47%	F
Service sales	80,000	56,700	23,300	41%	F
Total sales	500,000	341,700	158,300	46%	F
Cost of goods sold	247,500	166,500	81,000	49%	U
Gross profit	252,500	175,200	77,300	44%	F
Expenses, by cost center:					
Sales expenses:					
Advertising	40,000	27,000	13,000	48%	U
Telephone	900	570	330	58%	U
Administrative assistant	6,750	6,750	0	0%	
Automobile	12,000	8,550	3,450	40%	U
Sales commission	25,500	17,085	8,415	49%	U
Total sales expenses	85,150	59,955	25,195	42%	U
Warehouse expenses:					
Rent	5,400	5,400	0	0%	
Supplies	700	450	250	56%	U
Salary	22,000	18,000	4,000	22%	U
Delivery, per house	27,500	19,000	8,500	45%	U
Total warehouse expenses	55,600	42,850	12,750	30%	U
General expenses:					
Executive salary	22,500	22,500	0	0%	
Administrative salary	8,000	6,750	1,250	19%	U
Executive auto	6,200	6,750	(550)	–8%	F
Workers' comp. insurance	2,543	2,131	412	19%	U
Fire insurance	225	225	0	0%	
General liability insurance	450	450	0	0%	
Product liability insurance	2,500	1,712	788	46%	U
Professional fees	8,000	9,000	(1,000)	–11%	F
Rent, office	3,600	3,600	0	0%	
Supplies, office	600	450	150	33%	U
Telephone, basic	1,500	1,350	150	11%	U
Payroll taxes	8,475	7,112	1,363	19%	U
Business license	2,500	1,712	788	46%	U
Property taxes	450	450	0	0%	
Depreciation	9,000	9,000	0	0%	
Total general expenses	76,543	73,192	3,351	5%	U
Net operating income (loss)	$ 35,207	($ 797)	$ 36,004	4517%	F

Figure 10.3 Budget report with variances based on fixed budget—Spouse House Company.

The Spouse House Company Flexible Budget Figures for Various Levels of Sales					
No. of Spouse Houses sold during month	20	25	30	35	40
Sales of Spouse Houses	$30,000	$37,500	$45,000	$52,500	$60,000
Service sales	6,300	6,300	6,300	6,300	6,300
Total sales	36,300	43,800	51,300	58,800	66,300
Cost of goods sold	17,100	21,375	27,000	31,500	36,000
Gross profit	19,200	22,425	24,300	27,300	30,300
Expenses, by cost center:					
Sales expenses:					
Advertising	3,000	3,000	3,000	3,000	3,000
Telephone	60	75	90	105	120
Administrative assistant	750	750	750	750	750
Automobile	900	1,125	1,350	1,575	1,800
Sales commission	1,815	2,190	2,565	2,940	3,315
Total sales expenses	6,525	7,140	7,755	8,370	8,985
Warehouse expenses:					
Rent	600	600	600	600	600
Supplies	50	50	50	50	50
Salary	2,000	2,000	2,000	2,000	2,000
Delivery, per house	2,000	2,500	3,000	3,500	4,000
Total warehouse expenses	4,650	5,150	5,650	6,150	6,650
General expenses:					
Executive salary	2,500	2,500	2,500	2,500	2,500
Administrative salary	750	750	750	750	750
Executive auto	750	750	750	750	750
Workers' comp. insurance	234	246	257	268	279
Fire insurance	25	25	25	25	25
General liability insurance	50	50	50	50	50
Product liability insurance	182	219	257	294	332
Professional fees	1,000	1,000	1,000	1,000	1,000
Rent, office	400	400	400	400	400
Supplies, office	50	50	50	50	50
Telephone, basic	150	150	150	150	150
Payroll taxes	782	819	857	894	932
Business license	182	219	257	294	332
Property taxes	50	50	50	50	50
Depreciation	1,000	1,000	1,000	1,000	1,000
Total general expenses	8,105	8,228	8,353	8,475	8,600
Net operating income (loss)	($ 80)	$ 1,907	$ 2,542	$ 4,305	$ 6,065

Figure 10.4 Schedule of flexible budget figures—Spouse House Company.

At Jeff's urging, Rosie took the time to revise her figures into a flexible budget, using formulas, and now has a September 30 operating report with a budget and variances that she can use. If you like detail, the computation of the flexible budget figures may be found in App. A. If you would like to skip all the formulas, just take my word that they work out to be the numbers under the "Budget 9 months" column of Fig. 10.5.

Based on the fixed budget Rosie threw away (Fig. 10.3), sales telephone expense was unfavorable by 58 percent. When the flexible budget is utilized (Fig. 10.5), the sales telephone expense changed to 46 percent favorable. Doesn't it make sense to increase the budget for this telephone expense when sales increase well beyond expectations?

The variance between actual and budgeted sales is zero, as it should be, for the budget is computed on actual sales. The cost of goods sold is 2 percent under budget. This reflects the fact that the budget was computed at $900 per shed (60 percent of selling price), while 100 of the sheds were purchased on a special deal of $855 each.

Advertising is still way over budget—48 percent. This is probably tolerable, as sales are way over expectation. The advertising budget was computed as $3,000 per month, a fixed expense that would not change, regardless of sales volume. Perhaps it should be determined as a percentage of sales, making it a variable expense. This would work well as sales *increase.* However, there is this danger in making advertising a variable expense: If sales *decrease,* the budget would decrease and Grace would feel that she must spend less on advertising. Yet, when sales decrease may be the time to spend *more* on advertising. That is, making the advertising budget variable with sales may send the wrong message to the sales and marketing managers when sales bomb.

The solution to this advertising budget dilemma may be to set up that budget as variable when sales rise above the goal and fixed at a certain level if sales fall below the goal. Management can be as creative as it wants to be in setting up flexible budget formulas.

What goes on with the sales commissions in Fig. 10.5? If they are paid (and/or accrued) at 5 percent of sales, and the budget sales commission figure is computed at 5 percent of actual sales, they should be the same and there should be no variance. But there is a $500 unfavorable variance. Why?

Rosie and Grace had decided on a July-to-September sales referral promotion. Any existing customer who referred a friend who also became a customer during the period would receive a referral fee of $50. Ten customers had made successful referrals, resulting in additional sales commissions of $500, which caused the $500 variance.* When Rosie first looked at

---

* Because these referral fees are not subject to payroll taxes, and as this flexible budget computes the budgeted payroll taxes based on total salaries and commissions, this has also caused a small variance in payroll tax expense.

The Spouse House Company
Budget Report—Flexible Budget (by Formula)
Nine Months of Second Year

Month	Actual 9 Months	Budget 9 Months	$ Variance	% Variance	
No. of Spouse Houses sold	280	280	0	0%	
Sales of Spouse Houses	$420,000	$420,000	$ 0	0%	
Service sales	80,000	80,000	0	0%	
Total sales	500,000	500,000	0	0%	
Cost of goods sold	247,500	252,000	(4500)	−2%	F
Gross profit	252,500	248,000	4,500	2%	F
Expenses, by cost center:					
Sales expenses:					
Advertising	40,000	27,000	13,000	48%	U
Telephone	900	1,680	(780)	−46%	F
Administrative assistant	6,750	6,750	0	0%	
Automobile	12,000	12,600	(600)	−5%	F
Sales commission	25,500	25,000	500	2%	U
Total sales expenses	85,150	73,030	12,120	17%	U
Warehouse expenses:					
Rent	5,400	5,400	0	0%	
Supplies	700	450	250	56%	U
Salary	22,000	18,000	4,000	22%	U
Delivery, per house	27,500	28,000	(500)	−2%	F
Total warehouse expenses	55,600	51,850	3,750	7%	U
General expenses:					
Executive salary	22,500	22,500	0	0%	
Administrative salary	8,000	6,750	1,250	19%	U
Executive auto	6,200	6,750	(550)	−8%	F
Workers' comp. insurance	2,543	2,370	173	7%	U
Fire insurance	225	225	0	0%	
General liability insurance	450	450	0	0%	
Product liability insurance	2,500	2,500	0	0%	
Professional fees	8,000	9,000	(1,000)	−11%	F
Rent, office	3,600	3,600	0	0%	
Supplies, office	600	450	150	33%	U
Telephone, basic	1,500	1,350	150	11%	U
Payroll taxes	8,475	7,900	575	7%	U
Business license	2,500	2,500	0	0%	
Property taxes	450	450	0	0%	
Depreciation	9,000	9,000	0	0%	
Total general expenses	76,543	75,795	748	1%	U
Net operating income (loss)	$ 35,207	$ 47,325	($12,118)	26%	U

Figure 10.5 Flexible budget report, based on flexible budget by formula—Spouse House Company.

the September report, she had forgotten about this incentive program and questioned Grace about the $500 variance. Grace reminded her of the promotion, which explained the discrepancy.

There is nothing wrong with unfavorable variances, provided they can be justified by the responsible person (Grace, the sales manager) *to top management* (Rosie). Of course, "justifying" means that the result of an unfavorable variance should be a benefit to the company (such as increasing net income now or in the future). *Sloppy management is not a justification.*

If Rosie is bothered by the $500 variance, she has the option of revising the budget. *Budgets should not be carved in stone.* They can be changed at any time, by top management. Perhaps the "not carved in stone" statement does not always apply to the government, where top management consists of a committee (the United States Congress and the President). As we have often seen, getting over half of the committee of several hundred people to agree on a budget is akin to revising Roman inscriptions chiseled in a rock. But for many for-profit businesses, the chief operating officer, with an eraser and a pencil, can modify the budget.

You may have noticed, and questioned, the lack of interest expense on the operating budgets and reports we have discussed. It was intentionally omitted, as interest is not controllable in the day-to-day operations of the business, and it is not the responsibility of operating and administrative managers. Also, the amount of interest cannot be determined until borrowing needs are determined, and that involves cash planning, which is discussed in the next section. Payments of interest are included there.

Cash Budget

So far in this chapter, we have looked at what income and expenses Rosie expected, compared to what really took place. Remember that these income and expense items are listed as they *happen,* which is not necessarily when they are *paid for* (i.e., the reports are on the *accrual* basis, which was covered in Chap. 1).

When the company sells a Spouse House on account, the sale is made and appears on the operating report or income statement at that time. However, if the sale is made in May, but the customer does not pay until June, Rosie can't count that sale when she is trying to determine if she will have enough money to pay the bank loan that is due in May.

To help her answer that question, Jeff prepares a *cash budget* for the year. Note that this task is usually assigned to the accountant or accounting department. The decisions by top management and department managers now have been reflected in the accrual-basis operating budget. Converting that to cash is a mechanical function, but a rather complicated one that will drive most people into outer space. Factors involved in the conversion include: when customers will pay their bills (based on previous experience), how late the company can be in paying its suppliers (based on terms of purchases), due dates of loan payments, etc. It's best left to those people who love complicated number problems.

Most obligations become due monthly. That is, suppliers ask to be paid by the 10th of the month following a sale; and leases, installment loans, and many other items are payable once a month. So, cash budgets are normally made up on a monthly basis. Jeff started to make up a cash budget for the second year of the Spouse House Company, but when he got to May and June, he found that *cash* became a negative figure. As banks take a dim view of negative checking account balances, he stopped there. Figure 10.6 is the result of his efforts.

Under the January column, the beginning cash of $120,000 includes the proceeds of the $90,000 loan from the bank. The bank put the money in the Spouse House Company's checking account in December, although Fred's Sheds did not expect payment until January 10.

Based on last year's experience, Jeff estimates that 60 percent of sales will be collected in the month they are made (many are delivered COD), 36 percent will be collected later, and 4 percent will never be collected (bad

			The Spouse House Company Cash Budget Second Year			
Month	Jan.	Feb.	Mar.	Apr.	May	June
Cash, beginning of month	$120,000	$54,738	$63,085	$ 71,334	$ 84,157	($10,714)
Cash receipts for month:						
Collections, current sales	19,980	11,880	21,780	26,280	21,780	21,780
Collections, prior sales	19,800	13,590	7,938	12,078	15,318	13,518
Proceeds of bank loans	0	0	0	0	0	0
Total cash available	159,780	80,208	92,803	109,692	121,255	24,584
Cash disbursements for month:						
Payment, purchases of sheds	85,500	0	0	0	18,000	13,500
Sales expenses for month	6,279	5,172	6,525	7,140	6,525	6,525
Warehouse expenses for month	4,450	3,550	4,650	5,150	4,650	4,650
Total gen. expenses for month	7,084	6,672	8,565	11,516	6,565	6,565
Loan and lease payments	1,729	1,729	1,729	1,729	96,229	1,729
Total disbursements	105,042	17,123	21,469	25,535	131,969	32,969
Cash at end of month	$ 54,738	$63,085	$71,334	$ 84,157	($ 10,714)	($ 8,385)

Figure 10.6 Monthly cash budget, second year—Spouse House Company.

debts). As I said before, these can be rather complicated calculations, but the results are listed in the rows titled "Collections . . ."

Under January cash disbursements, we find payment for the 100 sheds ($85,500) for which the company borrowed the $90,000 from the bank. Under February, March, and April, there are no payments for sheds, as sales were delivered from the stockpile of 100 sheds bought on the special deal. Jeff has also computed what checks will have to be written for sales, warehouse, and general and administrative expenses, and listed the totals of these checks as disbursements on this cash budget.

Then he subtracted total disbursements from the "Total cash available" to compute the expected cash balance at the end of the month. That number then became the cash at the start of the next month, at the top of the next column. (The January 31 balance of $54,738 becomes the beginning balance in February.)

Revising the Cash Budget

When Jeff found the cash going into the minus sign realm, he conferred with Rosie. They cooked up this solution: Rosie called a competitor of Fred's Sheds, the Leaky Shed Company. To get her business, the Leaky sales

The Spouse House Company
Cash Budget, Revised
Second Year

Month	Jan.	Feb.	Mar.	Apr.	May
Cash, beginning of month	$120,000	$54,738	$63,085	$ 71,334	$ 84,157
Cash receipts for month:					
Collections, current sales	19,980	11,880	21,780	26,280	21,780
Collections, prior sales	19,800	13,590	7,938	12,078	15,318
Proceeds of bank loans	0	0	0	0	0
Total cash available	159,780	80,208	92,803	109,692	121,255
Cash disbursements for month:					
Payment, purchases of sheds	85,500	0	0	0	0
Sales expenses for month	6,279	5,172	6,525	7,140	6,525
Warehouse expenses for month	4,450	3,550	4,650	5,150	4,650
Total general expenses for month	7,084	6,672	8,565	11,516	6,565
Loan and lease payments	1,729	1,729	1,729	1,729	96,229
Income tax					
Total disbursements	105,042	17,123	21,469	25,535	113,969
Cash at end of month	$ 54,738	$63,085	$71,334	$ 84,157	$ 7,286

Figure 10.7 Cash budget revised for change in supplier terms and additional bank loan—Spouse House Company.

manager offered her 45-day terms. That is, invoices for sheds would not have to be paid until 45 days after Leaky invoiced for them. Rosie confronted Fred with this, to which he countered with even better terms. Invoices would not be due until the 10th day of the second month after the month of purchase. In other words, a shed purchased on April 1 need not be paid for until June 10. This actually represented an interest-free loan from Fred's Sheds.

Rosie also arranged with Herman, the banker, to borrow $10,000 in June. He agreed, provided the company had paid back the $90,000 in May, as promised.

Jeff revised the cash budget to reflect the extended terms from the supplier and the future $10,000 loan from the bank. As no negative cash balances showed up on his computer screen, he continued in this fashion for the entire year. His work product is shown in Fig. 10.7. The first six months are the same as in Fig. 10.6, with two exceptions:

1. The payments for prior months' purchases of sheds are scheduled 30 days later in Fig. 10.7 than in Fig. 10.6.

2. The $10,000 bank loan is an additional receipt in June and an additional disbursement in August, at which time the company will pay it back.

June	July	Aug.	Sept.	Oct.	Nov.	Dec.	Total
$ 7,286	$15,115	$19,741	$17,421	$22,407	$20,354	$ 22,328	$120,000
21,780	25,380	30,780	25,380	30,780	39,780	75,780	351,360
13,518	13,068	14,868	17,928	15,768	17,928	22,968	184,770
10,000	0	0	0	0	0	0	10,000
52,584	53,563	65,389	60,729	68,955	78,062	121,076	666,130
18,000	13,500	16,200	18,000	27,000	27,000	31,500	236,700
6,525	7,017	7,755	7,017	7,755	8,985	13,905	90,600
4,650	5,050	5,650	5,050	5,650	6,650	10,650	65,800
6,565	6,526	6,467	6,526	6,467	11,370	12,349	96,672
1,729	1,729	11,896	1,729	1,729	1,729	1,729	125,415
						5,000	5,000
37,469	33,822	47,968	38,322	48,601	55,734	75,133	620,187
$15,115	$19,741	$17,421	$22,407	$20,354	$22,328	$ 45,943	$ 45,943

Note that this cash budget contains items that do not appear in an income statement, such as bank loan proceeds and repayments. These are not income and expense items, only cash flow items.* (Only the interest part of loan payments shows up on an income statement as expense.)

Other Budgets

Just about anything that can be measured in numbers can be the subject of a budget. For instance, most companies have a *machinery purchase budget,* or they may call it something more esoteric, such as an *asset acquisition budget* or *capitalization budget.* They all mean essentially the same: what machines, automobiles, trucks, boats, buildings, land, etc. the company is going to purchase. Because some assets, such as buildings, have very long-range implications, these budgets are often made up for several years as part of the long-range company planning. Equipment purchase justification procedures (covered in Chap. 6) are essential in preparing these budgets.

As I mentioned in Chap. 6, when budgeting for equipment acquisitions that will be leased, be sure to determine whether the lease will be capitalized and show up on the balance sheet as an asset, complete with depreciation, or if the lease payments will show up on the income statement as an expense. Treating it one way on the budget and the other way on the reports of results can create some wild budget variances.

Some businesses prepare a budgeted balance sheet that will show what the balance sheet at the end of the year will look like if actual results are the same as the budget. Again, this is a rather complicated procedure, but it is mechanical, based on management decisions already determined in preparing the operating budget and equipment purchase budget.

Let the Accountants Worry with the Budget?

Perhaps you noticed that in describing the Spouse House Company budget preparation, Jeff, the accountant, did not show up until after Rosie, Grace, and Lem had made the management decisions. Why? Because the basic decisions as to what the numbers will be is best done by those who make the numbers happen—the operational managers. Jeff's expertise is not in the area of marketing, planning sales campaigns, or installing windows in Spouse Houses.

---

* If you want to get theoretical, you can consider that the repayment of bank loans to buy equipment shows up on the income statement as depreciation on the equipment financed by the bank loans. That's just some ethereal accounting theory. You can worry about it or not, as you see fit.

However, after the management decisions are made, it is the accountant who is best equipped—by aptitude and training—to put the details of the budgets together. He or she will compute flexible budgets, equipment purchase budgets, cash flow budgets, budgeted balance sheets, and any other budgets that are appropriate. Of course, it is the accountant's job to prepare the reports that compare actual results with budgets.

There is this interaction between the accountant and top management: As happened with the Spouse House Company, when the accountant puts together the cash budget, he or she may find that there is not enough cash to carry out management's goals. That may cause a revision of the plans and the resulting operating budget. This is one of the larger benefits of realistic budgeting. Cash crunches can be anticipated months ahead of time. Loan commitments can be secured early from the bank, or the company goals can be deferred or lowered until there will be cash enough to carry out plans.

Budget projections can also be used in price determination. For instance, if the price of Spouse Houses was raised from $1,500 to $2,000 each, the number of Spouse Houses sold* would probably decrease. However, the gross profit on each would rise by $500 and various expenses would have a different relationship to total sales. Construction of a new budget at the new price level would be a necessity if Rosie is to make an informed decision about raising prices.

Obligation
of Budgeted Amounts

Lem's budget for warehouse supplies for January was $50. On January 28, the rag salesman called on him, and Lem ordered $25 worth of rags, to be delivered on February 2. He had already spent $40 during January for some touch-up paint, caulking compound, and cleaners. On the tally that Lem kept, he added the $25 for the rags to the $40 already spent and determined that he would be $15 over the $50 budget. He would have an unfavorable variance of $15.

However, when he received the January 31 report for the warehouse department, it showed actual expenses of only the $40, so the variance was a favorable one of $10. What happened to the $25 he "spent" on rags? The operating report is an accrual-basis report. As discussed in Chap. 1, purchases occur when title to the goods transfers. In this case, that is when the rags are delivered to the Spouse House Company warehouse, and that is in the next month. As of January 31, the rags had not been purchased, but only ordered. Therefore, there was no expense for rags in January.

---

* Exactly how many sales there would be at an increased price would be determined by market surveys, test sales, and other marketing tools.

Lem was confused. He went to Jeff for an explanation. Jeff pointed out that Lem was keeping a record of *obligated* funds. In other words, once he made a commitment to spend the money, he considered it spent. But Jeff was preparing reports based on GAAP. There was no expense until the rag man delivered the rags. (In actual practice, Jeff would probably not record the expense until the rag man's invoice arrived.)

How can Lem, or any department manager, resolve this discrepancy between obligated budget amounts and recorded expenses? Lem could take his tally of obligated amounts to Jeff at the end of each month and compare what has been ordered with what has been recorded as an expense. This would be time-consuming and irksome to both Lem and Jeff.

A more efficient method would be strict adherence to a purchase order system. When Lem orders the $25 worth of rags, he fills out a purchase order and sends a copy to Jeff. When the supplier's invoice comes in, Jeff records it as an expense ("done deal") and marks his copy of the purchase order as "completed." In our example, as of January 31, the rag purchase order has not been completed, so Jeff would list it on the operating and budget report, in another column, as "obligated but unfilled purchase orders." Lem could immediately reconcile his tally with the actual expense Jeff recorded.

Transaction Steps

You can think of a transaction, such as the purchase of these rags, as occurring in steps:

1. Lem orders the rags. The Spouse House Company is now obligated to pay $25 to the rag vendor.
2. The rags are delivered to the Spouse House Company warehouse.
3. The Spouse House Company receives the invoice from the rag vendor.
4. The Spouse House Company sends a check for $25 to the rag vendor.

Step 1 is the creation of the *obligation*. The accounting department should record the expenses at step 2, but probably will not record it until step 3. Step 4 has no effect on the reports of actual results versus budget for the warehouse department. It is of concern to the company treasurer (or whoever handles the checkbook).

Summary

Budget preparation is only worthwhile if the budgets are used, and they have to bear some reasonable relationship to actual results if they are to be useful. Some form of flexible budgeting is necessary to ensure this, unless the business entity is stagnant.

Budgets, which should be compared frequently to results, provide a track on which to run the business. Those that are made up and chucked into a desk drawer are a waste of time. Those that are viewed and used as a management tool are well worth the time spent on their preparation and monitoring.

Review Questions

1. Variance in dollars is usually computed as (circle one):
   a. Actual result minus budget number
   b. This year's budget number minus last year's budget number

2. Variance in percentage is usually computed by (circle one):
   a. Dividing variance (in dollars) by actual results
   b. Dividing actual results by variance (in dollars)
   c. Dividing variance (in dollars) by budget
   d. Dividing budget by variance (in dollars)

3. Budgets don't work unless sales are steady and there are no unforeseen problems.   T   F

4. If a cash budget predicts a negative cash balance at some time in the next year, file for bankruptcy immediately.   T   F

5. The best way to coexist with budgets and accountants is to recognize that budgeting is for accountants and let them deal with it.   T   F

6. Once a manager obligates a company to spend some money, that decision will immediately show up as an actual expense on his budget report.   T   F

7. Some items will show up on a cash budget and not on an operating budget, and some will be vice versa. Other items will show up on both. Complete the following table by checking which items will show up where.

	Operating budget only	Cash budget only	Both budgets
Advertising	___	___	___
Interest expense	___	___	___
Payment, loan principal	___	___	___
Receipt of loan from bank	___	___	___
Depreciation expense	___	___	___

Case Study Question

The operating results for the first Gretchen's Gimmicks and Gadgets Store were as listed in the following partially completed report. The budget figures are those that were developed in the problem in Chap.

9. Your mission is to compute the variances (in dollars and percentages) for the third and fourth columns. In the last column indicate "F" or "U" for favorable or unfavorable nature of the variance.

	May actual	May budget	Dollar variance	Percent variance	F/U
Sales	$30,000	$30,000			
Cost of goods sold	17,000	18,000			
Gross profit	13,000	12,000			
Expenses:					
Advertising	3,300	3,000			
Salaries	3,000	3,000			
Part-time help	1,000	1,500			
Delivery expense	330	300			
Fire insurance	130	100			
Rent	2,000	2,000			
Supplies	500	600			
Telephone	250	200			
Total expenses	10,510	10,700			
Net operating income	$ 2,490	$ 1,300			

11

Manufacturing and Construction

Up to this point, computing gross profit earned by a business has been fairly simple. When Angus sold a set of bagpipes from his shop for $600, having purchased them for $400, his gross profit was the difference of $200. When the Spouse House Company bought a shed and windows for $900 and sold the unit for $1,500, its gross profit was $600. But now, when Rosie Rouse determines that the Spouse House Company will cut out the intermediary shed supplier and manufacture Spouse Houses from raw lumber, it has become a manufacturer, and gross profit becomes harder to compute.

Consider what the Spouse House Company was buying when it bought a shed from Fred's Sheds and then resold the shed as a Spouse House. It was buying the lumber, nails, shingles, hardware, and other items that went into manufacturing the shed. In addition, it was buying the labor that put the shed together. When Rosie bought the sheds from Fred, she did not need to worry about how much of the $900 cost was for lumber and how much was for labor. All she needed to know was that Fred charged her $900 for the shed, and that she sold it for $1,500.

Rosie, the marketing genius, knows very little about manufacturing. But she has a brother, Reggie, who was a production supervisor with Amalgamated Consolidated Manufacturing Company. By offering him stock options and other generous benefits, she enticed him to head up her manufacturing operation. Part of the deal was that a separate company, the S.H. Manufacturing Company, would be set up, and Reggie would be its president. It was to manufacture Spouse Houses and sell them to distributors and the Spouse House Company at the same price that Fred's Sheds was selling them.

During January, February, and March, Reggie organized the S.H. Manufacturing Company for the start of operations on April 1. He met his timetable: April was a full month of production. On May 1, Rosie and Reggie were anxious to see how the costs of manufacturing Spouse Houses compared to buying them from Fred's Sheds. As does any self-respecting accountant, Jeff celebrated the end of tax season by becoming unavailable. He went white-water canoeing. Reggie and Rosie thought they could easily figure out an income report by themselves, as Rosie had seen Jeff do it several times during the company's first two years.

Cost of a Manufactured Spouse House

On April 1, Rosie and Reggie made a list of the various materials on hand. The cost price of the list of lumber, hardware, prefabricated windows and doors, roofing, siding, wiring, light fixtures, carpet, and other materials added up to $10,000. At the end of the month, the list of the same items added up to $5,000, and purchases of those items during April totalled $50,000. They made this computation:

Beginning inventory April 1	$10,000
Add: purchases of materials	50,000
Total materials available	60,000
Subtract: Ending inventory April 30	5,000
Materials used to produce Spouse Houses	$55,000

Then they divided the $55,000 by the 70 Spouse Houses that had been sold to distributors and the Spouse House Sales Company that month:

$$\$55,000 \div 70 = \$882$$

They were horrified. It took a factory worker eight hours to put together a Spouse House, and he or she was paid $12 per hour, for a total of $96 per Spouse House. Add that to the $882 above, and it looks like it costs more to manufacture the Spouse Houses than it did to buy them already made from Fred's Sheds!

Rosie and Reggie wanted to send out a helicopter to yank Jeff out of his canoe and have him tell them (they hoped) that their calculations were wrong; but they survived, albeit impatiently, a few sleepless nights until he returned.

On the next Monday, Jeff spoke diplomatically, lest he lose a client. "You made a good start, but let's consider a few more factors. How many unsold Spouse Houses did you have at the end of April?"

"Thirty-nine," Reggie replied. "They were distributor orders that were not shipped until May 2—the trucking company fouled up."

"And as of the first of April you had not begun manufacturing, correct?"

"Right."

"And one other factor," Jeff continued. "How many partially built Spouse Houses did you have on the factory floor at the end of the month?"

Reggie consulted his production records. "Looks like we had four under way at quitting time on April 30."

"Okay. Let's review your calculations and add to them," Jeff said as he picked up a pencil and cleared a space on Rosie's desk. "Here's what you had computed, and it was fine as far as it went." He repeated Rosie's calculation:

Beginning inventory April 1	$10,000
Add: purchases of materials during April	50,000
Total materials available during April	60,000
Subtract: Ending inventory April 30	5,000
Materials used in April to produce Spouse Houses	$55,000

"That $55,000 looks like a good number, but those materials went into more than the 70 Spouse Houses you sold in April. You had an inventory of 39 unsold houses. You also manufactured those out of the $55,000 of materials you used."

"Uh-huh. We should have divided the $55,000 by the 70 sold plus the 39 increase in inventory, or 109. Let's see." Rosie punched her calculator keys. "Dividing $55,000 by 109 . . . that brings the cost down to $505 for each house."

"Almost, but we're not quite through. We need to consider what is called a *work in process inventory*. That's the half-completed products that are still being fabricated on the factory floor."

"I see. There are lumber, hardware, windows, and so on that went into those half-done Spouse Houses, too. But, Jeff, they weren't all halfway finished. Some might have been just with the floor frames in, and others might have been all done except for the roof," Reggie said.

"True," responded Jeff. "We'll try to refine that determination in the future, but for now we'll be close enough if we just assume that *on average*, they were all 50 percent manufactured. In other words, the four houses in process were equal to two completed houses."

"You're saying, then," Reggie continued, "that we built the equivalent of 111 houses with $55,000 of materials."

"Exactly," Jeff agreed. "So the material cost of each house was $55,000 divided by 111, or $495 each."

Rosie and Reggie both said they felt much better, as they looked at the figures Jeff had written down as he talked. They looked like this:

Spouse Houses manufactured in April:	
Sold during the month	70
In inventory at the end of the month	39
Four in process at end of month, equivalent to	2
Total houses manufactured during month	111

Jeff continued his explanation, for there were more costs involved in this manufacturing operation. Obviously, even with prefabricated components, power saws, nailers, and other devices, there was some labor involved in putting the Spouse Houses together. During April, the labor *and* the benefits cost $12,520. Note that this is the cost of *direct labor,* which is the cost of the people who actually do the work of putting the product together. It does not include salaries for supervisors such as Reggie, for janitors, stock clerks, or others who do not labor directly on the product.

The word *direct* is also used to describe materials. The materials that Rosie and Reggie included in their calculation at the beginning of the chapter were *direct materials.* They were the materials that end up being part of the finished product. The term does not include such items as rags, paint brushes and other items that do not become part of the product.* Direct materials, before they are processed or "cooked" into finished products, are also called *raw materials.*

There are more costs of manufacturing the Spouse Houses. If Reggie could put the houses together in Rosie's backyard, he could save a lot of rent. But for efficiency and continuous operation in all weather, the production needs to be in a building. Like your home, factories need electricity, water, heat, insurance and other services. The local tax collector looks to taxes on large commercial buildings to pay his or her salary. These things, along with the labor and material that is not *direct* labor and *direct* material, are usually called *indirect costs* or *factory overhead costs.* I like the latter term. It's these costs that put a roof over the heads of the workers in the production area. Like to have a definition? How about: *Factory overhead* is all the costs of operating a factory that are not direct materials and direct labor.

You will hear the terms of *indirect labor* and *indirect material* associated with overhead. Essentially, these terms cover the labor and materials that do not fit the definitions of *direct labor* and *direct material* and are, therefore, included in overhead. Examples are the wages of the janitors and supervisors, and such materials as rags, sandpaper, and other supplies.

For April, for the S.H. Manufacturing Company, factory overhead was as follows:

---

* The term *direct materials* is often defined as materials that are *traceable* to the product. Does that include the paint brush? Ask your finance people; the concept will vary with each company.

Factory overhead, month of April:

Rent (landlord pays the property taxes)	$1,500
Utilities	200
Supplies	200
Insurance	100
Depreciation	1,000
Supervisor's (Reggie's) salary	2,500
Total overhead, April	$5,500

Now Jeff could compute the total cost of manufacturing the 111 Spouse Houses during April:

Total cost of manufacturing, month of April:

Materials	$55,000
Direct labor	12,520
Factory overhead	5,500
Total manufacturing costs, April	$73,020

Note that sales, marketing, and general and administrative expenses—the expenses of selling the product and running the office—do not get cranked into manufacturing expenses. They are costs of doing business and are listed, on the income statement or report, as expenses during the *period* in which they occur.

When these computations are put together, we have a "Schedule of Cost of Goods Manufactured and Cost of Goods Sold," which is Fig. 11.1.

Costs/Expenses— Which Went Where?

In Chap. 1, I touched on the distinction between costs and expenses. The distinction, along with the need for it, becomes more obvious in the manufacturing area.

Let's look at the S.H. Manufacturing Company figures for April (Fig. 11.1). Where did the costs of materials, labor, and overhead end up? Here's the cost flow:

The *cost of raw materials purchased* went partly to the cost of *raw materials inventory* and partly to the *cost of raw material used in production*. That material used in production, along with the *cost of direct labor* and the *cost of overhead* went partly to *cost of work in process* and partly to *cost of finished goods*. And that cost of finished goods was split into *cost of goods sold* and *cost of ending inventory of finished goods*. The costs that end up in *inventory* show up on the balance sheet as *assets,* while the costs that end up in the *cost of goods sold* appear, of course, on the income statement.

The S.H. Manufacturing Company
Schedule of Cost of Goods Manufactured and Cost of Goods Sold
Month of April, First Year of Manufacturing

Direct materials:		
Beginning inventory	$10,000	
Purchases	50,000	
Raw materials available for use	60,000	
Ending inventory	5,000	
Cost of materials used		$55,000
Direct labor:		12,500
Factory overhead:		
Building rent	1,500	
Utilities	200	
Supplies	200	
Insurance	100	
Depreciation, equipment	1,000	
Supervisor salary	2,500	
Total overhead cost		5,500
Total manufacturing cost		73,020
Add: Beginning work-in-process inventory		0
Subtotal		73,020
Subtract: Ending work-in-process inventory		
(4 units in process = 2 completed units)		1,316
Cost of goods manufactured		
(109 finished, ready for sale)		71,704
Add: Beginning inventory of finished goods		0
Subtotal		71,704
Subtract: Ending finished goods inventory		
(39 units)		25,662
Cost of goods sold (70 units)		$46,042

Figure 11.1 Schedule of cost of goods manufactured and sold, April—S.H. Manufacturing Company.

Confused? Perhaps the diagram shown in Fig. 11.2 will help. It describes where the raw materials, direct labor, and overhead have gone by the end of the month. Of course, what ends up in inventory at the end of the month doesn't stay there. In the following months, that inventory goes, respectively, to work in process, finished goods, and cost of goods sold.

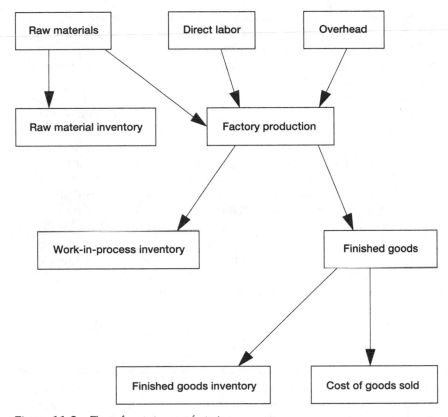

Figure 11.2 Flow of costs in manufacturing.

As discussed in Chap. 1, the costs that end up in *cost of goods sold* are also expenses. That is, they are subtractions from revenue during the period reported on—April, in our example. However, they are usually called "costs," as in "cost of goods sold."

Inventories and Fluctuating Costs

In May there were more considerations in determining the cost of the Spouse Houses manufactured and sold.

First, at the end of April, there was an inventory of $5,000 of material for putting together Spouse Houses. This will, of course, become the beginning inventory in May.

Second, the work in process inventory was, at the end of April, the equivalent of two finished Spouse Houses. So, in May, there is a beginning inventory of the equivalent of two finished Spouse Houses.

Third, the ending inventory, in April, of finished goods becomes the beginning inventory of finished goods in May.

Labor, as far as inventory is concerned, is a little easier to handle—there is no inventory involved. As yet, no one has figured out how to extract advance hours of labor from people and stockpile those hours in the corner of the warehouse, as one would stockpile raw materials. (Remember, though, that past labor does become part of the inventories of work in process and finished goods.)

Figure 11.3, the manufacturing cost for May, is essentially the same format as the April report, but I included it here for two reasons.

One, you can follow the inventories from the end of April to the first of May. Unlike the Spouse House Company or the other retail companies we have used as examples, the S.H. Manufacturing Company has three categories of inventories to carry from the end of one period to the beginning of the next: raw materials, work-in-process, and finished goods.

Unit Costs

The second reason to include the April report is to help in a discussion of *unit costs,* which are defined as the total cost of production divided by the number of units (Spouse Houses, in our case) manufactured. For instance, in April (Fig. 11.1) total cost of goods manufactured was $71,704. Total of Spouse Houses (units) produced was 109 plus the four in process that are equivalent to two finished Spouse Houses, for a total of 111. Dividing the cost of $71,704 by the production of 111 computes to a unit cost of $658. Similarly, the unit cost of the Spouse Houses sold would be the cost of goods sold ($71,704) divided by the number sold (70), or the same figure of $658.

Now, look at the May report (Fig. 11.3). When you divide the cost of goods manufactured ($66,881) by the number produced (95 plus the equivalent increase in work-in-process of 1, for a total of 96), we find the unit cost is $705—a considerable increase over the $658 in April. If you compute the unit cost for ending inventory of finished goods, it is the same $705. That seems reasonable, as the ending inventory was produced in May. However, when we compute the unit cost of the cost of goods sold ($82,673 divided by 120) the unit cost is $689. This is partway between the unit cost of goods manufactured in April and the same cost in May. On reflection, that makes sense also. Some of the Spouse Houses sold in May were produced in April at the lower cost, and the rest were produced in May at the higher cost.

The S.H. Manufacturing Company
Schedule of Cost of Goods Manufactured and Cost of Goods Sold
Month of May, First Year of Manufacturing

Direct materials:		
Beginning inventory	$ 5,000	
Purchases	58,000	
Raw materials available for use	63,000	
Ending inventory	13,500	
Cost of materials used		$49,500
Direct labor		12,480
Factory overhead:		
Building rent	1,500	
Utilities	250	
Supplies	200	
Insurance	250	
Depreciation, equipment	1,000	
Supervisor salary	2,500	
Total overhead costs		5,700
Total manufacturing costs		67,680
Add: Beginning work-in-process inventory		
(4 units in process = 2 completed units)		1,316
Subtotal		68,996
Subtract: Ending work-in-process inventory		
(6 units in process = 3 completed units)		2,115
Cost of goods manufactured		
(95 finished, ready for sale)		66,881
Add: Beginning inventory of finished goods		
(39 units)		25,662
Subtotal		92,543
Subtract: Ending finished goods inventory		
(14 units)		9,870
Cost of goods sold (120 units)		$82,673

Figure 11.3 Schedule of cost of goods manufactured and sold, May—S.H. Manufacturing Company.

In other words, the cost per Spouse House, both in inventory and in cost of goods sold, will vary each month with the costs that the S.H. Manufacturing Company incurs that month. Good economic sense would dictate that when it costs more to build a product, the manufacturer will have to charge more to its customers. That could mean that the company should charge a different amount each month for the Spouse Houses it sells, depending on what the costs of manufacturing were that month. Reasonable? Of course not. The marketplace takes a dim view of manufacturers who are constantly revising prices, particularly if the revisions are up!

How can these fluctuations in monthly costs be leveled out? Let's start with the direct labor per unit, which was:

	April	May
Direct labor and benefits during month	$12,520	$12,480
Divide by number of units manufactured	111	96
Direct labor cost per unit	$ 113	$ 130

That's a big jump, from one month to the next, but there is an explanation. The number of hours put in by the five factory workers was 720 in April and 760 in May. Reggie had watched the workers going about the assembly of Spouse Houses in several inefficient ways. He therefore shut down the production for two days of training. Yet, the report made no allowance for this nonproductive time, which is usually called *idle time*. Despite its name, it does not imply lazy workers. *Idle time* consists of all time not actually spent producing products. It includes training, machine set-up, waiting for materials, etc.

Many manufacturing companies break that time out of the *direct labor* cost and include it in the *indirect labor* in factory overhead. That will result in a *unit labor cost* that is based only upon time that was available for production, so the unit labor cost should be nearly the same each month.

You may be ahead of me. Moving the idle time may help the direct labor numbers, but it really just moved the fluctuation to the "overhead" classification. Now it will vary more, and the total unit costs will still vary month to month.

Standard Costs

To try to meet this problem and make the unit cost of manufacturing a consistent figure from month to month, accountants have devised concepts of *standard costs*. One way to envision these animals is: *Standard costs* are budgets based on unit costs rather than on monthly or annual figures.

After looking at the April and May reports (Figs. 11.1 and 11.3), Reggie felt that he did not have a good grasp of what the cost of manufacturing a Spouse House really was. He asked Jeff to help.

They made a lot of detailed computations as to costs of items in a Spouse House, from plywood to door knobs. We don't need to get involved in that, but only in the results, which were that a standard Spouse House should contain materials costing $500 and labor (including benefits) costing $115.

That left the question of overhead cost. Jeff stated the question as: "How much overhead should be *absorbed* by each Spouse House?" He saw Reggie's perplexed expression and added, "Think of overhead as a pool, like a swimming pool, full of costs—electricity, rent, supplies, indirect labor, etc. The cost-accounting sheet for each Spouse House is written on a sponge. We throw the sponges (one sponge for each Spouse House) into the pool so they each will soak up some of the cost, and we hope that we throw in enough sponges to soak up all the overhead costs in the pool. In other words, *absorbed costs* are overhead costs that have gone into the cost of products that have been manufactured."

"What if we don't manufacture enough Spouse Houses? Or, as you put it, what if we don't throw enough sponges in the pool?" Reggie asked.

"Then we have *unabsorbed costs*. That's not a good situation. It means we have some costs that did not get included in the cost of manufactured Spouse Houses, so they were not cranked into pricing decisions."

Of course, Reggie wanted to avoid that situation, and asked Jeff to come up with a solution. Unfortunately, there is no accounting solution. The solution is a marketing challenge, for the Spouse House organization has to sell enough houses such that the overhead cost will be spread over (soaked up by) many houses.

To arrive at some kind of standard overhead costs, Rosie provided an estimate that the company would sell 1,200 Spouse Houses during the year. Jeff divided the $66,000 of overhead expense by the 1,200 Spouse House projected production, and that resulted in a standard overhead cost of $55 per Spouse House. That figure, times the number produced, will be included in the costs of production on the monthly reports.

For example, during July only 90 Spouse Houses were manufactured, so the overhead costs that were *absorbed* by those houses was 90 times $55, or $4,950. Yet the total actual overhead costs were $5,750. The *unabsorbed* costs were the difference of $800. That number does not go away. It will appear on the operating statement as just what it is (an expense):

Unabsorbed costs $800

If, in August, the production run is 110 Spouse Houses, the overhead that will be included in the cost of the manufactured Spouse Houses will be

110 times $55, or $5,500. As actual overhead expenses totaled only $4,700, there is an *overabsorption* of costs of $800 in August. July and August under- and overabsorptions will cancel each other out.

Variations in Standard Costs and Budgets

As is often the case, particularly in internal reports, there are no hard and fast accounting rules for internal reports. Financial managers can develop systems that best suit their company and their industry. Some variations (but not an all-inclusive list) follow:

Segregation of Variable and Fixed Factory Overhead Costs

By separating overhead costs into variable and fixed costs,* the problem of allocating overhead costs can be isolated to only the fixed overhead costs. For instance, supplies may vary with the pace of production, while rent just exists as a fixed cost whatever the production rate. This segregation isolates the problem of how much to consider as a cost of each house, but it does not make the problem go away.

Allocation of Overhead by Labor Hours

This would be unnecessary for the S.H. Manufacturing Company, as long as it manufactured only one model of Spouse House. However, what if Rosie and Grace, her sales manager, found a market for Deluxe Spouse Houses? They would be larger, with jacuzzi, plumbing, air conditioning, heat, and other amenities, and would take three times as long to manufacture. As these fancy houses take up more time, factory floor space, and management attention, it is only right that they should bear more of the overhead costs. It might be relatively easy to decide that they should bear three times the overhead burden of the regular Spouse Houses, or $165 (3 times $55). But, if customers could order with or without the jacuzzi and other options, there could be virtually unlimited variations in Spouse House models. As the company received each order for a Spouse House, Jeff and Reggie could confer and decide how much overhead that order should bear. For

* The concept of variable and fixed costs or expenses was covered in Chap. 4.

example, they might decide that a special order for a Deluxe Spouse House, without the jacuzzi, but with air conditioning, was the equivalent of $2\frac{3}{16}$ of a regular Spouse House. So it would be hit with overhead costs at $2\frac{3}{16}$ times $55, which is $120.31. It becomes pretty unwieldy.

A simpler method is to determine an overhead rate per productive-worker hour, or direct-labor hour. Rosie projected that 1,200 regular Spouse Houses would be manufactured during the year. If each Spouse House takes eight hours of direct labor, the total direct labor for the year would be 9,600 hours. Dividing the total projected year's overhead costs of $66,000 by the 9,600 hours results in a labor overhead rate of $6.88 per hour. (Notice, we include the pennies here. When things are multiplied out, they do become material.)

For a regular Spouse House which takes eight hours of direct labor, the overhead hit would be eight times $6.88, which is the same $55 we used previously. However, when a custom model takes $17\frac{1}{2}$ hours, the overhead is found by multiplying 17.5 times $6.88 to get $120. That was easier than guessing it was equivalent to $2\frac{3}{16}$ regular Spouse Houses.

In fact, because most manufacturers produce a variety of products and models, the allocation of overhead expense by labor hour is the most common way of doing it.

Controllable and Uncontrollable Costs

This cost system can assign only those costs that the production manager can control to the cost of the product. Uncontrollable costs, such as rent and some utilities, show up elsewhere on the operating report, as general overhead. This is great for nailing a manager if he or she runs over the standard costs (over budget), for the report lists only the budget items he or she can control. However, it obviously does not assign all of the cost of production to the product, so it is dangerous if pricing decisions are made solely on these cost records. Also, assigning only controllable costs to the cost of production is not acceptable for GAAP, so another set of cost records has to be kept for preparing financial statements for use by outsiders.

Other Methods and Systems

The variations in cost determination and budgeting are limited only by the imaginations of production managers and cost accountants. Managers who ask their finance/accounting people how they do things in this area are not showing ignorance. They are demonstrating knowledge that questions need to be asked.

Process Costs/Job Costs

These are some more manufacturing terms you will hear. Their distinction is as follows:

Process Costs

The *process costs* concept applies to the manufacturing of a continuous stream of an identical product. Think, if you will, about your favorite chemical company. The chemical company will produce a stream of a product, such as garden fertilizer. All the fertilizer that is produced in a production run, be it for a day or a month, will be assigned the same cost per pound. What size container it is sold in does not change its production costs, although the packaging and marketing costs may vary with package size. If the process is highly automated (little or no direct labor), the overhead may be assigned by machine-hour, pound of product, or some other yardstick.

Job Costs

At the other end of the spectrum of cost systems is the *job cost* concept. This is applicable when every product that is produced is different from every other product. A good example is the custom home builder. Each house is different, so a well-managed builder will keep track of all direct materials and labor that are used in a particular job. Although there is no factory (just the great outdoors), there are overhead costs such as supervision costs and equipment costs that need to be allocated to each job. Many builders allocate equipment costs by the number of hours the equipment is used on the job (as if the equipment were being rented by the company to the job). Supervision costs can be allocated by the number of direct-labor hours, total job cost, or whatever management thinks is equitable.

Where does the S.H. Manufacturing Company fit in these categories? When it started manufacturing one standard Spouse House with no variations, its reporting needs were closer to *process cost* procedures. When it became involved with several models and custom variations, its system became that of *job cost.*

Work-in-Process Inventory

So far, about all I have said about the work-in-process inventory is that it's there and has some value. For the Spouse House Company, Jeff assigned it a value by assuming that, *on the average,* the unfinished Spouse Houses were 50 percent completed. In other words, two Spouse Houses in process were equal to one finished Spouse House. For an assembly line that is putting together the same or similar products, one after the other, this assumption sounds reasonable.

The same concept is true of most process-cost operations, such as a fertilizer factory. In such bulk operations, though, it is often necessary to estimate how much partially cooked product is in the pipes, vats, settling tanks, etc.

For some operations, a reasonable estimate of the cost of the work-in-process inventory can be made only by estimating the cost incurred, as of the end of the period, for each job. Consider the custom home builder again. What if, on December 31, the builder had two houses in process? One house had nothing but the foundation laid and the other house had the foundation and only the exterior first-floor walls framed in. In other words, one is 10 percent completed and the other is 20 percent completed. It would not be reasonable to estimate that, on average, they are one-half completed. The only way to compute this work-in-process inventory is to look at each project and, from cost estimates and actual invoices, determine the cost to that date.

The Contracting Business

As the Spouse House business grew, Rosie received more and more orders for fancier Spouse Houses. Wealthy customers wanted plumbing, built-in television and stereo, a kitchen, deluxe furniture, and a security system. Some of the orders were for houses so large that they could not be built in the factory and delivered on a truck, but had to be built on location. That put the Spouse House Company into the construction business. Rosie set up another company to engage in this and called it the S.H. Construction Company.

Guess who she hired to manage this construction business? Fred, who used to sell her sheds. He had become somewhat bored with sailing around and around the world and found his cash depleted. From their earlier association, Rosie knew he was a diligent manager, so she picked him to run this segment of her growing empire.

Completed-Contract Method
of Computing Income

Compared to the average residence being built these days, even these custom Spouse Houses were small. They could be completed in 60 days from the start of construction. Until the building was complete, the S.H. Construction Company owned the building. When it turned the keys over to the buyer, the buyer became the owner, so the sale took place at that time. Until then, even though the buyer owned the land, the building was part of the work-in-process inventory of the S.H. Construction Company.

There is little difference between this concept of inventory and that of the standard Spouse Houses being assembled on the factory floor.

Percentage-of-Completion Method of Computing Income

After the construction company had been operating for a year, a multimillionaire named Jack found that he was frequently banished from home and needed a Spouse House. However, even the custom-built deluxe models did not fit his needs. His conception was that such a place should be at least a 20-room residence on a tropical island, complete with boat dock, swimming pool, tennis courts, a landing strip for his jet, and various other amenities.

Jack found an appropriate island, bought it, and negotiated a construction contract with Fred. The contract price was $10 million and the schedule indicated it would take 30 months to build, starting in March. This was Fred's first endeavor with a contract that would take more than a year to complete, and it caused him a lot of concern. Not only was he worried about the scheduling, selection of subcontractors, purchase of materials, and so on, but there would be an unintended effect on the whole of Rosie's Spouse House operation. He discussed it with her.

"It'll be three years before we can deliver this project to Jack. In the meantime, there is no profit or income from the job."

"Guess we'll have to be patient," Rosie commented.

"But," Fred continued, "because of this job, I will have to hire two more office workers, buy another computer and other office equipment, and have some other general expenses. As I understand it, those are not part of the job cost. That added expense will just push down the net income from the rest of the company's operations."

"That could hurt our whole operation when we need to borrow money. We need advice from our accountant," added Rosie, picking up the telephone to call Jeff.

As Jeff explained, every rule has its exception. Through 10½ chapters of this book, the rule has been that a sale occurs, and income is recorded, only when merchandise is delivered or service is performed. Now that changes. For a long-term contract, the contractor may record a proportionate share of the expected income each year that the contract is in progress. This supposes, of course, that engineering studies and financial forecasts are detailed enough to provide a sound basis for estimating the profit that will be earned from the contract. Where these estimates are available, GAAP requires that this percentage-of-completion method be used.

The engineering estimates developed a total cost estimate of $7.5 million for the contract. Subtracting that from the contract price of $10 million indicated a total gross profit of $2.5 million. (In the context of long-term contracts, the gross profit is often called *earnings* from the contract.)

At the end of the first year, the numbers on this contract stood as follows:

Total costs to end of first year	$1,500,000
Total billed to Jack, throughout year	$1,800,000

In order to determine how much of the expected profit on the job is to be reported as gross income in this first year, Jeff had to determine how much of the contract had been completed. He computed that by dividing the total cost to date ($1.5 million) by the total expected cost of the contract ($7.5 million), which works out to 20 percent. He then multiplied that percentage by the total revenues to be earned on the entire contract. So, the revenue earned this first year is 20 percent times $10 million, or $2 million. He can then make up this abbreviated income report on the contract:

Jack's Spouse House Island Contract
Summary Report—First Year of Contract

Revenue earned, first year	$2,000,000
Subtract cost of contract, first year	1,500,000
Gross profit on contract, first year	$ 500,000

At this point, let's digress to discuss just what is in the cost of the contract that Jeff used in the above computation. Just as do manufacturers, contractors have different types of inventory. Their raw material inventory is the lumber, cement blocks, door knobs, and everything else that has been delivered to the job but has not yet been installed, or become part of the building. The work-in-process inventory is the partially complete building, dock, airstrip, bridge, or whatever is being built. In a contract such as the S.H. Contracting Company has with Jack, there will be the equivalent of a finished goods inventory only momentarily, for the building and accoutrements will be delivered to the customer as soon as completed. That is not true for all construction firms. For home builders who build houses on speculation (speculating that they will be able to sell them), there is a finished goods, or finished houses, inventory.

Jeff needs to be certain that, in computing what percentage of the contract is completed, he uses as cost only the costs of materials and labor that have gone into construction. Raw materials do not count.*

Using the cost figures in order to compute the percentage of completion is not the only method of determining that figure. Jeff could have used labor hours in the first year divided by total labor hours for the entire job. He could have used estimates from the engineering firm, or any other method that would reflect how much of the work has been

---

* Obviously, it would be a great finagling tool if contractors could count the raw materials on the job site. They could have thousands of dollars' worth delivered on December 30 and boost the percentage of completion and the resulting profit for the year.

done. There are no rules as to which method to use. It's a judgment call to be made by people experienced in the type of construction covered by the contract.

Notice also that the *revenue earned* is not necessarily equal to the *revenue billed* during the year. For the S.H. Contracting Company, the billing was less than what was earned. This may be due to sloppy billing procedures, but it is more likely due to the terms of the contract. For instance, the contract may state that 18 percent of the revenue may be billed when the foundation of the house is complete, so that is what has been billed. Yet the cost computation would indicate that 20 percent of the project is complete. Perhaps a little more care should have been used in drawing up the contract, or maybe Jack is a super negotiator.

This difference, between the revenue earned and the revenue billed is called *overbilling* and *underbilling*. For their formal reports, accountants generally use more complicated terms that mean the same thing. To understand their words, we need to consider the above summary report again. It states that the revenue less the cost of the contract equals the gross profit. Applying algebra again (sorry), it is also true that the cost plus the gross profit, or earnings, equals the revenue. Based on this, accountants can then make this substitution of complicated phrases for simple words: "Overbilling" becomes *billings in excess of costs and estimated earnings*. "Underbilling" becomes *costs and estimated earnings in excess of billings*. We'll use the shorter, simpler terms of *overbilling* and *underbilling* in the examples that follow.

To reflect this difference between revenue and billings, the summary report on p. 191 now grows by adding another line which says:

Underbilling $200,000

By the end of the second year, total cost of the *work in process* related to this contract was $5.625 million. Again, Jeff computed the percentage of completion by dividing that number by the total cost of the contract ($5.625 million ÷ $7.5 million), which generates a completion percentage of 75 percent. At the same time, the total of billings to Jack from the start of the contract to the end of the second year was $8.3 million. Now Jeff prepared this report:

Jack's Spouse House Island Contract
Summary Report—First and Second Year of Contract

Revenue earned, first and second year	$7,500,000
Subtract cost of contract, first and second year	5,625,000
Gross profit on contract, first and second year	$1,875,000

When Jeff puts together an income statement for the construction company for the second year, he will have some problem using these numbers, for they are for *two* years. To generate the figures for year 2 only, he has to deduct the first year's revenue and cost figures from the total for both years, as in this report:

Jack's Spouse House Island Contract
Summary Report—Second Year of Contract

Revenue earned, first and second year	$7,500,000	
Subtract revenue earned, first year	2,000,000	
Revenue earned, second year		5,500,000
Cost of contract, first and second year	5,625,000	
Subtract cost of contract, first year	1,500,000	
Cost of contract, second year		4,125,000
Gross profit on contract, second year		$1,375,000
Total billings, through end of second year		$8,300,000
Revenue earned, first and second year		7,500,000
Overbilling		$ 800,000

Is there an inconsistency here? Did Jeff goof? For revenue, cost, and gross profit, he deducted the first year's figures. For the over-/underbilling computation, he used the total figures for both years!

Sorry, Jeff wins. The revenue, cost, and gross profit figures are those that end up in the *income statement*. They report the operations of only one year, as would a video of just the one year. The over-/underbilling is a figure that reports a status (a snapshot)—of what the situation is now, as a result of all the years of operations (two, in this example). Therefore, there is no subtraction of the first year when reporting the balance sheet item of under-/overbilling. (Don't worry too much about this. It's one of those concepts that will be murky for weeks, then at 3:00 A.M. one day, it will suddenly make sense.)

For the third and final year of the contract, Jeff would not use estimated costs for total cost of the contract. By then, he will know what actual total costs are, and, of course, the percentage of completion will be 100 percent. The report will show the total revenues and costs, including those for any changes that were made in the contract. Then he will deduct the revenue and costs for the first two years to arrive at the revenue, costs, and gross profit for the third year.

This report that Jeff made up works well if the company has only one contract in progress. If there are many contracts under way, this format would require a page for each contract plus a total page, and that is unwieldy. The usual procedure is to turn what Jeff did 90° to a columnar format. An example is shown in Fig. 11.4.

The S.H. Construction Company
Contract in Process Schedule
(Numbers are in $1,000s—the last 000 is omitted)

Contract name	Total contract price	Total est'd costs	Est'd total gross profit	Actual costs to date	Est'd percent complete	Revenue earned to date	Gross profit earned to date	Billings to date
Jack's S.H.	$10,000	$ 7,500	$2,500	$ 5,625	75%	$ 7,500	$1,875	$ 8,300
Karen's S.H.	8,000	6,000	2,000	4,800	80%	6,400	1,600	6,000
Just started	2,000	1,600	400	400	25%	500	100	650
Completed	3,515	2,850	665	2,850	100%	3,515	665	3,515
	$23,515	$17,950	$5,565	$13,675		$17,915	$4,240	$18,465

Figure 11.4 Schedule of longer-term contracts in progress—S.H. Construction Company.

Government Contracts

Because of laws that attempt to limit the earnings of government contractors to a *reasonable** amount, reports on government contracts are different. In computing the cost that a contractor can claim, as a subtraction from contract revenue, the contractor is allowed to deduct various *overhead* and *administrative* expenses. That is, part of the cost of paper clips, paper towels, computer paper, and so on, will end up in the cost of the government contract. For nongovernment contracts, of course, these expenses are listed on an income statement as *general and administrative expense.*

Summary

The complications in reports of factory production and its cost arise from the nature of the inventories involved: raw materials, work-in-process, and finished goods. It is also complicated by the fact that the cost of a finished item is not, as in a mercantile business, the price billed by a supplier, but it is a total of several items that include materials, labor, and overhead.

Reports on construction contracting involve the same considerations as manufacturing but, in addition, the fabrication of a "product" may take years. This is, therefore, one area in which GAAP permits, or may require,

* What is reasonable? I don't know. Government regulations attempt to define it, but it is elusive. For that reason, there is no definition in the text and you will not find one in the glossary.

Costs and Earnings in excess of billings	Billings in excess of costs and earnings	Cost recognized previous periods	Costs this period	Estimated revenue in previous periods	Estimated revenue in this period	Estimated gross profit or (loss) previous periods	Estimated gross profit or (loss) this period
$ 0	$800	$1,500	$4,125	$2,000	$5,500	$ 500	$1,375
400	0	4,000	800	4,200	2,200	800	1,400
0	150	0	400	0	500	0	100
0	0	2,500	350	3,000	515	0	165
$400	$950	$8,000	$5,675	$9,200	$8,715	$1,300	$3,040

that part of the expected total contract gross profit be reported as partial gross profit each year the contract is under way.

The details of the reporting process will vary somewhat from company to company, as it will be dependent on the professional philosophy of the accountants and managers involved.

Government contracts are often a different animal, in that the concept of *overhead cost* often includes *general and administrative expense.*

Review Questions

1. A manufacturing operation is concerned with three categories of inventory. They are _____ , _____ , and _____ .

2. Labor is part of the cost of at least two classes of inventory in manufacturing. T   F

3. In an operation that produces only one product, all of the items in inventory will have the same cost. T   F

4. Normally, a factory floor sweeper would be classified as indirect labor. T   F

5. In the long-term-contract method of reporting income, some of the profit is assumed to be earned during each time period the contract is in progress. T   F

6. If it appears that a contractor is going to have a loss on a long-term contract, that loss should be spread out and reported as some loss in each period the contract is in progress. T   F

7. *Underbilling* and *overbilling* have to do with whether all the work performed on a contract has been billed to the customer. It does not affect the profit that is reported. T   F

Case Study Question _____

The Flying Paper Company manufactures the Executive Paper Airplane. These are sophisticated versions of the third-grade models, folded by a patented process, and manufactured from special mylar-reinforced paper, which is heat-fused for durability in the boardroom.

The only copy of the October manufacturing-cost report was inadvertently left on the fusing machine. The motivated operator, not wishing to waste material, folded it into the patented shape and sent it through the fusing machine. When the plant manager realized what had happened and retrieved it, she was able to unfold and flatten most of the report, but some of the numbers were erased by the fusing process. Your mission: Insert the numbers at the dotted lines.

Raw material (special paper):
Inventory October 1: 100,000 sheets @ 20¢	$ 20,000
Purchased during October, 300,000 sheets @ 20¢	60,000
Total paper available	80,000
Inventory October 31: 50,000 sheets @ 20¢	10,000
Used in production _____ sheets @ 20¢	. . . .

Direct labor:
8,750 hours @ $10 per hour	87,500
Factory overhead	17,500
Total manufacturing cost	. . . .

Work-in-process (valued at cost of 25¢ each):
Inventory October 1: 1,000 units	250
Total manufacturing cost	175,000
Subtotal	. . . .
Inventory October 31: 1,500 units	. . . .
Cost of goods manufactured (finished goods)	. . . .

Finished goods:
Inventory October 1: 100,000 paper airplanes @ 50¢	50,000
Goods available for sale	. . . .
Inventory October 31: 40,000 airplanes @ 50¢	20,000
Cost of goods sold	$. . . . . . .

12

Analysis of an Enterprise

Through 11 chapters, we have looked at income statements, balance sheets, budget preparation, and budget reports, as well as the ingredients of these reports such as sales, cost of goods sold, expenses, assets, liabilities, and equity. We have looked a little more deeply into components such as depreciation, manufacturing cost, and long-term contract cost. We've talked about how to use the information in the reports, prepare budgets, and justify equipment purchases.

Time now to discuss one of the most important reasons for all the records and reports: Answering the question, "How is the enterprise doing?" ("Will it survive and will it prosper?") Obviously, a business that is going to survive will have to make a profit (net income), but how much profit does it need to make? If it extends credit to its customers, how much can it afford to lose in bad debts? How much inventory should it have on hand? What guidelines as to the amount of profit, bad debts, inventory, and other elements of finance should there be?

If you are a small business owner, the answers to these questions are critical to your survival. If you are a part-owner (stockholder) of a large business, the information is critical to the success of your investment program. If you are, or hope to become, a manager of a division of a large company, you will be judged on the operation of your division as if it were a separate business.

Again, let's explain by example. I wish we could continue with Rosie Rouse, our friend in the Spouse House business. However, her operation has become quite complex—involved in retail sales, wholesale sales, manufacturing, and construction contracting. Consequently, her financial reports are far more complicated than we need for our purposes.

Let's, therefore, move down the street to her uncle Harry and Harry's Hardware Store, Inc. Harry purchased this store about five years ago, borrowing most of the money he needed to purchase the business and add to the inventory of tools, nails, buckets, and all the items that hardware stores are supposed to have. Of course, he also carried the candy bars, toothpaste, and (occasionally) the free hot dogs that progressive hardware stores carry these days. How well is he doing? Have the 80-hour weeks and glad-handing of customers paid off? Let's look at his financial statements as of the end of last year. The complete package consists of:

- Income Statement
- Balance Sheet
- Retained Earnings Statement
- Cash Flow Statement
- Notes to the Financial Statements

Harry has Alice, his accountant, prepare this complete set of financial statements. Let's look at each one separately, starting with the income statement in Fig. 12.1.

The Income Statement

When you look at Fig. 12.1, you may have questions. Probably one of them is, "so what?", and that would be a logical question. Yes, the company did make a profit, but did it make as much profit as it should have? How do you determine what profit the company should have made?

Do all the numbers on this statement indicate a good operation? Or are all the numbers bad? Or are some good and some bad? From looking at only this statement, I don't know. Unless you are in the retail hardware business, you probably don't know, either.

The answers are in that last statement—"unless you are in the retail hardware business." Harry, who obviously is in the retail hardware business, does have a feeling for which numbers reflect good management. He mentally compares the numbers with what they should be, and he probably bases "what they should be" on what they were last year for his company.

However, Harry has been known to leave his glasses in the house paint section and spend an hour looking for them among curtain rods and cabinet hinges. Could he really remember last year's numbers? He could have dug out the income statement for the year prior to last year and compared it to last year's income statement, but there is an easier way. He asked Alice

Harry's Hardware Store, Inc.
Income Statement
Year Ended Last December 31

Revenue:			
Sales			$1,300,000
Subtract: Sales returns and allowances		$ 40,000	
Sales discounts (cash discounts)		13,000	53,000
Net sales			1,247,000
Cost of goods sold			680,000
Gross profit			567,000
Selling expenses:			
Sales salaries	$150,000		
Advertising	50,000		
Delivery expense	25,000		
Bad debt expense	8,000		
Credit card fees	5,000		
Total selling expense		238,000	
Administrative expenses:			
Administrative salaries	100,000		
Rent	50,000		
Employee benefits	30,000		
Payroll taxes	25,000		
Insurance	15,000		
Utilities	5,000		
Office supplies	4,000		
Depreciation	20,000		
Total administrative expense		249,000	
Total selling and administrative expense			487,000
Net operating income			80,000
Other income: Interest income			10,000
Income before interest and income taxes			90,000
Other expense: Interest expense			19,000
Net income before income tax			71,000
Subtract: Income tax			18,000
Net income			$ 53,000

Figure 12.1   Income statement for one year—Harry's Hardware Store, Inc.

to make up his financial statements in *comparative* format. That format consists of two (or more) years of financial statement figures presented side by side, so they can be *compared*. The comparative income statement Alice put together is shown in Fig. 12.2. Now it is fairly easy to make this computation:

Harry's Hardware Store, Inc. Comparative Income Statements		
Year ended December 31,	Last year	Prior year
Net sales	$1,247,000	$1,125,000
Cost of goods sold	680,000	615,000
Gross profit	567,000	510,000
Selling expenses:		
Sales salaries	150,000	140,000
Advertising	50,000	45,000
Delivery expense	25,000	25,000
Bad debt expense	8,000	7,000
Credit card fees	5,000	0
Total selling expense	238,000	217,000
Administrative expenses:		
Administrative salaries	100,000	95,000
Rent	50,000	48,000
Employee benefits	30,000	23,500
Payroll taxes	25,000	23,000
Insurance	15,000	13,300
Utilities	5,000	4,200
Office supplies	4,000	4,000
Depreciation	20,000	18,000
Total administrative expense	249,000	229,000
Total selling and administrative expense	487,000	446,000
Net operating income	80,000	64,000
Other income: Interest income	10,000	8,000
Income before interest and income taxes	90,000	72,000
Other expense: Interest expense	19,000	22,000
Net income before income tax	71,000	50,000
Subtract: Income tax	18,000	13,000
Net income	$ 53,000	$ 37,000

Figure 12.2 Comparative income statements—Harry's Hardware Store, Inc.

Sales last year	$1,247,000
Sales prior year	1,125,000
Increase in sales	$ 122,000

Dividing that increase by the prior year's sales will give us a percentage of increase over the prior year:

$$\$122,000 \div \$1,125,000 = 11\% \text{ increase in sales}$$

So, sales are increasing by a healthy amount. Let's see how the more important figure—net income—is doing:

Net income last year	$53,000
Net income prior year	37,000
Increase in net income	$16,000

As above, dividing the increase by the prior year's net income will provide a percentage increase over the prior year:

$$\$16,000 \div \$37,000 = 43\% \text{ increase in net income}$$

Harry must be doing some things right. With only an 11 percent increase in sales, he increased net profit by 43 percent. Some of those right things can be discerned from the numbers shown in the income statement in Fig. 12.2:

- There was no increase in delivery expense, though sales increased.
- Sales salaries increased only $10,000.
- There was no increase in office supplies expense.

By examining each line item, you can determine how Harry managed to increase his net income so dramatically.

There is an additional set of numbers that can help analyze the changes in an income statement. If every item on the statement is expressed as a percentage of net sales, rather than in dollars, it makes it easier to compare the year-to-year figures. Figure 12.3 is the same as Fig. 12.2, but all the numbers are expressed as a percentage of net sales.* Now, in Fig. 12.3, we can see that delivery expense has *decreased* from 2.2 percent to 2 percent of net sales. Although administrative salaries *increased*, in actual dollars, from $95,000 to $100,000, as a percentage of net sales, this item *decreased* from 8.4 percent to 8.0 percent of net sales.

---

* Each percentage is computed by dividing the number for that item by net sales. For instance, sales salaries last year (Fig. 12.2) were $150,000. Dividing that by net sales of $1.247 million gives us 0.120 or the 12.0 percent listed for sales salaries in Fig. 12.3. For the prior year, the computation is $140,000 ÷ $1.125 million, or 12.4 percent.

Harry's Hardware Store, Inc.
Comparative Income Statements
Common Size

Year ended December 31,	Last year	Prior year
Net sales	100.0%	100.0%
Cost of goods sold	54.5%	54.7%
Gross profit	45.5%	45.3%
Selling expenses:		
Sales salaries	12.0%	12.4%
Advertising	4.0%	4.0%
Delivery expense	2.0%	2.2%
Bad debt expense	0.6%	0.6%
Credit card fees	0.4%	0.0%
Total selling expense	19.0%	19.2%
Administrative expenses:		
Administrative salaries	8.0%	8.4%
Rent	4.0%	4.3%
Employee benefits	2.4%	2.1%
Payroll taxes	2.0%	2.0%
Insurance	1.2%	1.2%
Utilities	0.4%	0.4%
Office supplies	0.3%	0.4%
Depreciation	1.6%	1.6%
Total administrative expense	19.9%	20.4%
Total selling and administrative expense	38.9%	39.6%
Net operating income	6.6%	5.7%
Other income: Interest income	0.8%	0.7%
Income before interest and income taxes	7.4%	6.4%
Other expense: Interest expense	1.5%	2.0%
Net income before income tax	5.9%	4.4%
Subtract: Income tax	1.4%	1.2%
Net income	4.5%	3.2%

Figure 12.3 Comparative common size income statements—Harry's Hardware Store, Inc.

This sort of analysis may put you in mind of *flexible budgeting* that was discussed in Chap. 9. It is based on the same concept of variable expenses being analyzed and controlled in relation to the level of sales, rather than in absolute dollar amounts.

A financial statement, expressed in percentages only, is called a *common size* financial statement. It allows similar businesses of differing size to be compared. For instance, by looking at common size statements of Harry's Hardware ($1.25 million in sales) and the Amalgamated Putty, Paint & Nail chain of stores ($500 million in sales), we can compare each item on Harry's Hardware income statement with that for the large company. This comparison of the percentage figures can be meaningful. Comparison of actual dollar figures would be meaningless, because of the difference in size.

What can Harry learn by comparing his percentage figures with those of a large chain? For example, his rent runs about 4 percent of sales. If the large operation's rent is 2 percent of sales, Harry could conclude that he must do substantially more business in his present store before he considers expanding it. Of course, this comparison is not the absolute determinant of whether or not he should expand his space; it is just a decision-making tool.

Better than a comparison with only one other hardware store company would be comparing Harry's operation with average percentage figures of many hardware stores. Such *industry average* figures are available from publishers who compile these numbers for many lines of business. (See App. B.) Also, many trade associations compile average numbers from their members. For instance, Harry could obtain statistics on retail hardware stores from the National Retail Hardware Association.

The Balance Sheet

Figure 12.4 shows Harry's Hardware Store, Inc. Balance Sheets for last year and the prior year. There is no concept here that was not covered in Chaps. 8 and 9, except for the idea of putting two years' balance sheets side by side so that comparisons can be made. Example comparison: although sales increased, accounts receivable decreased. This could indicate:

1. Harry is pursuing more aggressive collection policies.

2. He is being more selective in deciding to whom he will extend credit. (This may be good or bad. See the discussion of bad debts in Chap. 2.)

3. He is using third-party credit cards (Visa, MasterCard, etc.) instead of adding to his accounts receivable. (Most credit cards result in either immediate cash to the business, or cash within a few days.) This is apparently the case, for there is an expense item of *credit card fees* on last year's income statement, but no such expense for the prior year. (The *credit card fees* are what the banks or credit card companies charge the retailer for assuming the work of collecting accounts and bearing the burden of bad debts.)

You probably can think of other situations that could cause the decrease in accounts receivable.

Harry's Hardware Store, Inc.
Comparative Balance Sheets

December 31,	Last year	Prior year
Assets		
Current assets:		
Cash	$ 95,000	$ 85,000
Accounts receivable (net of bad debt allowance)	190,000	200,000
Inventory	350,000	325,000
Prepaid insurance	10,000	12,000
Total current assets	645,000	622,000
Equipment:		
Furniture and fixtures	75,000	75,000
Office equipment	30,000	25,000
Vehicles	65,000	55,000
Total equipment	170,000	155,000
Subtract: Accumulated depreciation	100,000	80,000
Net equipment	70,000	75,000
Total assets	$715,000	$697,000
Liabilities		
Current liabilities:		
Notes payable to bank, due within 1 year	$ 82,000	$ 92,000
Accounts payable	57,000	45,000
Accrued expenses	20,000	22,000
Income taxes payable	5,000	6,000
Total current liabilities	164,000	165,000
Long-term liabilities:		
Notes payable to bank, due after 1 year	96,000	120,000
Total liabilities	260,000	285,00
Stockholders' equity:		
Common Stock: par value $10 per share; 100,000 shares authorized; 5,000 shares issued and outstanding	50,000	50,000
Retained earnings	405,000	362,000
Total stockholders' equity	455,000	412,000
Total liabilities and stockholders' equity	$715,000	$697,000

Figure 12.4   Comparative balance sheets—Harry's Hardware Store, Inc.

As with the income statement, the balance sheet can be expressed in percentages, as a *common size* balance sheet. One for Harry's Hardware is shown in Fig. 12.5. As is usually done, all the balance sheet items are expressed as a percentage of total assets. Again, these can be compared to prior year and to industry average figures.*

Retained Earnings Statement

Figure 12.6 is the Retained Earnings Statement of Harry's Hardware in comparative form for two years. It also could be presented as common size (in percentages), but it would not provide any information that is not already expressed in the percentage figures from the income statement and the balance sheet.

In the financial statement package of corporations that have, during the years covered, issued more stock or accepted additional contributions of capital from stockholders, you will find the Retained Earnings Statement replaced by a Stockholders' Equity Statement. The latter statement includes the information about changes in retained earnings, as well as the changes in issued stock or paid-in capital.

Ratios

Here's another scary term from somewhere in the eighth or ninth grade. It is also from yesterday if it's baseball season and you are a baseball fan. If not, please pretend that it is and you are. A batting average is a ratio—a comparison of hits to number of times at bat. It is usually expressed as the number of hits per thousand times at bat, such as 333 in 1,000. In finance, the same concept would be expressed as 0.333 to 1 (often written as 0.333:1) or as a percentage (33.3 percent).

In deciding on loan requests, bankers and other credit types are extremely fond of determining their "yeas" and "nays" by computing these ratios. That is why it behooves any business owner, before taking his or her financial statement to the bank, to compute certain ratios (or have the accountant compute them). If a ratio doesn't come up to par, the business owner needs to have a whale of a good story to present as an explanation.

What is par for the ratio game? Just as the percentages in the common size statements, ratios can be compared to the company's ratios for the prior year or to industry averages. Some of the more common ratios follow:

* For instance, in Fig. 12.4, inventory at the end of last year was $350,000. Dividing that by total assets of $715,000 gives us 0.490 or 49.0 percent. Dividing the prior year's inventory by the prior year's total assets ($325,000 divided by $697,000) equals 0.466, or 46.6 percent.

Harry's Hardware Store, Inc.
Comparative Balance Sheets

December 31,	Last year	Prior year
Assets		
Current assets:		
Cash	13.3%	12.2%
Accounts receivable (net of bad debt allowance)	26.6%	28.7%
Inventory	49.0%	46.6%
Prepaid insurance	1.4%	1.7%
Total current assets	90.3%	89.2%
Equipment:		
Furniture and fixtures	10.4%	10.8%
Office equipment	4.2%	3.6%
Vehicles	9.1%	7.9%
Total equipment	23.7%	22.3%
Subtract: Accumulated depreciation	14.0%	11.5%
Net equipment	9.7%	10.8%
Total assets	100.0%	100.0%
Liabilities		
Current liabilities:		
Notes payable to bank, due within 1 year	11.5%	13.2%
Accounts payable	8.0%	6.5%
Accrued expenses	2.8%	3.2%
Income taxes payable	0.7%	0.9%
Total current liabilities	23.0%	23.8%
Long-term liabilities:		
Notes payable to bank, due after 1 year	13.4%	17.2%
Total liabilities	36.4%	41.0%
Stockholders' equity:		
Common Stock: par value $10 per share;		
100,000 shares authorized; 5,000 shares issued		
and outstanding	7.0%	7.2%
Retained earnings	56.6%	51.8%
Total stockholders' equity	63.6%	59.0%
Total liabilities and stockholders' equity	100.0%	100.0%

Figure 12.5 Comparative common size balance sheets—Harry's Hardware Store, Inc.

Harry's Hardware Store, Inc. Retained Earnings Statements		
For the years ended December 31,	Last year	Prior year
Beginning balance	$362,000	$330,000
Add: Net income for year	53,000	37,000
Subtotal	415,000	367,000
Subtract: Dividends paid	10,000	5,000
Balance at end of year	$405,000	$362,000

Figure 12.6 Comparative retained earnings statements—Harry's Hardware Store, Inc.

Current Ratio

This is one the credit manager or banker always computes. It is supposed to measure how well a company will be able to pay its bills from its assets on hand. The computation of the *current ratio* is total current assets divided by total current liabilities. For Harry's Hardware, for December 31 last year (Fig. 12.4), it is $645,000 divided by $164,000, or 3.9 to 1. In other words, current assets are 3.9 times as much as current liabilities. As current assets represent cash or assets that should turn into cash within a year, it would appear that Harry should have no trouble in paying the debts that are represented by current liabilities. Note that *the higher the ratio, the better.*

What should a current ratio be? The rule of thumb is 2:1, but it varies with each industry. One industry average source indicates the average current ratio for those retail hardware stores that are about the same size as Harry's to be 2.4:1. So, compared to that average, Harry's Hardware is in better shape. We can also compare the current ratio to that for the prior year, when it was $622,000 divided by $165,000, or 3.8:1. The ratio of 3.9:1 for the later year is an increase. There are more current assets per dollar of current liabilities at the end of last year than there were at the end of the prior year, so the trend is improving.

Quick Ratio

This is similar to the current ratio, except that cash and accounts receivable are the only assets considered. It takes into consideration that inventory does not always turn into cash, due to spoilage, obsolescence and nature of the items. (Harry still has a pair of ox yokes, purchased by the previous store owner in 1934.) The computation of the *quick ratio* is cash and accounts receivable divided by total current liabilities. Harry's Hardware has remained the same for both years at 1.7:1. A source of industry averages lists this ratio as 0.4:1, so again, he is ahead of the averages.

As with most financial analysis tools, there is a caveat. The quick ratio was computed at December 31 of both years. For a hardware store that carries a lot of holiday decorations and gift items, there should be a large amount of cash and accounts receivable on hand from the big sales season just completed. In April, when the company has to pay for an abundance of garden supplies that are still in inventory, there may be a pinch on cash and accounts receivable, so the quick ratio will be much smaller.

Inventory Turnover

When I refer to "turnovers," I am not referring to pastries, nor to failure to carry the ball over the line of scrimmage on fourth down. The finance concept of turnover is more akin to automobile racing. How many times, after it spins out, can the car turn over between the track and the hay bales along the fence?

One hot July day, Harry drops by Lori's Luscious Lemonade stand. "How's business?" he asks as she pours some lemonade and ice into a glass for him.

"Great! I am now going through 10 dozen lemons a week," Lori replies.

"Fantastic. How many lemons do you keep in inventory?"

"Ten dozen—a week's supply."

"And you're open for how long—what's your season?"

"All year," Lori answers. "We serve it hot in the winter. It's great for flu and colds. I buy 10 dozen lemons every week, all year."

"That's wonderful! You sell the equivalent of your inventory each week. I wish I could do that," said Harry.

"Right," Lori commented. "My inventory *turns over* every week, or 52 times per year."

Harry was amazed to hear this term from one so young, but Lori is smart. (Obviously—she's *your* daughter, remember? See Chap. 8.) "I wish my inventory turnover was even a tenth of yours," he said as he finished his drink.

So, *inventory turnover* can be defined as how many times an inventory can be turned into sales, measured in equivalent units, within a time period (usually a year). Note the *equivalent units* requirement. Because inventory is measured in *cost* dollars, for this ratio sales need also to be measured in cost dollars, and that is the same as the *cost of goods sold*.

The higher this ratio number, the less inventory the company keeps in order to generate a certain sales volume. Less inventory ties up less money, so, generally, *the higher the inventory turnover, the better it is.*

Assume the unlikely circumstance that the price that Lori pays for lemons is $1.00 per dozen all year. As she sells lemonade made from 10 dozen lemons per week, her cost of goods sold* can be computed as follows:

$$\text{Cost of goods sold} = 52 \times 10 \times \$1 = \$520$$

Applying the definition of turnover gives us:

$$\text{Inventory turnover} = \text{cost of goods sold} \div \text{inventory} = \$520 \div \$10 = 52$$

We can do a similar computation for Harry's Hardware, taking the figures from the income statements and balance sheets in Fig. 12.1 and 12.4 for last year.

$$\text{Inventory turnover} = \text{cost of goods sold} \div \text{inventory}$$

$$= \$680,000 \div 350,000 = 1.9$$

The inventory turnover figure for Harry's Hardware is certainly far afield from that of Lori's Lemonade, but, given the nature of the two businesses, the difference makes sense. If Lori had Harry's inventory turnover of only about two times per year, she would be stocking a six months' supply of lemons. Spoilage, of course, makes that impracticable. It would also be foolish of her to tie her money up in so many lemons, when they can be purchased each week, as needed. For the hardware store, however, there is a need to keep a large selection of items, even though some hardly ever sell. While the inventory of ¼-inch electric drills may turn over 10 times a year, it may take three years to go through a box of 1½-inch, #6 flat-head stainless steel wood screws. Yet Harry needs to stock that item so that the customer who needs that size of screw will find it at Harry's and won't go to a competitor, where he may also buy a ¼-inch electric drill. Such is the nature of the retail hardware business.

One national average for retail hardware stores' inventory turnover is 2.7. Harry, at 1.9, takes longer to turn over his inventory—he has more money tied up in inventory for his volume of sales than do most hardware stores. Keep this in mind and look back at his *common size* income statement in Fig. 12.3. Harry's gross profit is 45.5 percent of net sales, while the average for hardware stores is 34 percent of net sales. Perhaps, because Harry keeps a bigger selection of items, he can charge a little more for them and earn a larger profit. Maybe his lower inventory turnover works to his advantage. Again, analysis only by the numbers is seldom justified. It has to be accompanied by some knowledgeable judgment.

---

* For simplicity, I have ignored the cost of sugar, ice cubes, etc. Perhaps we can assume Lori sold only sour lemonade.

Many scholarly finance texts suggest that a turnover ratio, such as inventory, should be based on *average* inventory. That could be computed by averaging the opening and ending inventory, or we could average the ending inventory at the end of each month. This may be a more accurate computation, but if you use such methods, be careful when comparing the results to industrywide figures. Chances are that the compiler of the industry figures was not that detailed.

Accounts Receivable Turnover

If customers owe Harry's Hardware money, that is money he cannot spend for other things, such as a raise in his own salary. Is too much owed to him? He can compute *accounts receivable turnover* ratio by dividing net sales by accounts receivable.

$$\text{Accounts receivable turnover} = \text{net sales} \div \text{accounts receivable}$$

$$= \$1,247,000 \div \$190,000 = 6.6$$

Just as with inventory turnover, *the smaller the accounts receivable turnover, the better.* Note that in this case, we are dealing with *sales* dollars, as compared to the inventory turnover that dealt with *cost* dollars. That is because accounts receivable are expressed in sales dollars.

Days of Receivables

The accounts receivable turnover is often phrased in the more meaningful term of *number of days of receivables*. This can be computed by dividing 365 days by the accounts receivable turnover. For Harry's Hardware, it is:

$$365 \text{ days} \div \text{accounts receivable turnover} = 365 \div 6.6 = 55 \text{ days}$$

This means that, on the average, it takes Harry's customers 55 days after the sale to get around to sending him a check. That appears to be miserable when compared to the industry average of 19 days. *The fewer days it takes to collect an account receivable, the better*—it puts more money in the bank to earn interest. There may be a reason for Harry's high number here. We have already discussed that he has just started using bank credit cards instead of carrying all of the receivables himself. Probably, most of the hardware stores in the industry average figures have been using bank credit cards for some time, so their receivables should be much lower, compared to sales, than are Harry's. For the retailers who use bank charge cards, the only receivables they carry themselves might be contractors and other business accounts.

A more comparable accounts receivable turnover figure can be developed by using only *credit sales* in the computation. This would be more meaningful for Harry, for it would eliminate cash sales and sales on bank credit cards from his year-to-year comparisons of the results of his credit policies. However, in comparing industrywide figures, a ratio based only on credit sales may not be available.

Interest Coverage

I am planning a trip to Atlantic City and need to borrow $100,000 from you, on which I will pay 10 percent interest until I pay you back—some day. Please send me the check for $100,000.

Before you mail the $100,000, you should ask some questions, such as: Do I earn enough to pay you the interest every year? Well, I do; I earn $10,000 a year at my job. So, I earn enough to be able to pay you. Obviously, you will turn down my loan request. After I pay for food, housing, and other necessities, I would *not* be able to pay interest to you. However, if I can prove to you that I earn $120,000 per year and owe money to no one else, you would be more willing to loan the money to me. (This assumes you have an extra $100,000 kicking around and that I could provide collateral, etc.)

If I earn only $10,000, my earnings are only one times my interest cost of $10,000. If I earn $120,000, my earnings are 12 times my interest expense. Obviously, *the higher this number, the better the business looks to a banker, supplier, or investor.*

In computing this coverage for a business entity, it is common to use, for earnings, the net income before interest expense and income taxes. The definition, then, of *interest coverage* is the number of times interest expense will go into earnings before subtraction of interest expense and income taxes. For Harry's Hardware, for last year, it is (from Fig. 12.1):

Interest coverage = income before interest and income taxes ÷ interest

$$= \$90,000 \div \$19,000 = 4.7$$

Industry averages for this coverage are about 2, so Harry is in good shape on this ratio.

Debt-to-Equity Ratio

Just as the name implies, the *debt-to-equity ratio* is the total liabilities of a company compared to the total equity. For Harry's Hardware, we can compute it from the numbers in the balance sheets in Fig. 12.4. For last year it is:

Debt to equity = total liabilities ÷ total stockholders' equity

$$= \$260,000 \div \$455,000 = 0.6$$

which is often expressed as 0.6 to 1

For the prior year, by the same formula, the debt-to-equity ratio is 0.7 to 1. Is this ratio for last year better than it was for the prior year? Let's take the extreme. Alphonse owns the hardware store in the suburb of East Basin. Herman, the banker, is making a comparison between Harry's balance sheet and Alphonse's. Money is tight, and Herman must decide to which company he will make a loan. Alphonse's balance sheet, for his hardware store, lists total liabilities of $400,000 and equity of $100,000. His debt-to-equity ratio is $400,000 divided by $100,000 or 4 to 1. Alphonse has $4.00 of other people's money invested in his business for each $1.00 he has invested himself. Harry has only $0.60 of other people's money invested for each $1.00 he has invested himself.

Herman, remembering that equity represents the *excess* of assets over liabilities, could draw this conclusion: If times became tough, Harry could sell some of his assets (such as excess inventory) to raise cash with which to pay his bank loans and still remain in business. Alphonse would have to sell so many of his assets to pay his liabilities that he probably could not stay in business. Indeed, if he had to sell his assets for less than their book value, he may go bankrupt. *In other words, the smaller the number of the debt-to-equity ratio, the better shape the business is in.*

As with any concept that involves assets, this one is subject to the caveat that it is based on the cost, or book value, of assets.

Look at how this affected my nautical friend, Noah. He bought some riverfront land 30 years ago, on which he has built a thriving boat-yard business. The land originally cost him $50,000. It is now worth $2 million. His summary balance sheet looks like this:

Noah's Boat Yard
Balance Sheet as of Today

Assets:	
Current assets	$150,000
Buildings and equipment, net of depreciation	200,000
Land	50,000
Total assets	$400,000
Liabilities:	
Current liabilities	$100,000
Long-term liabilities	250,000
Total liabilities	350,000
Owner's equity	50,000
Total liabilities and equity	$400,000

The debt-to-equity ratio of the boat yard would be:

$$\text{Total liabilities} \div \text{equity} = \$350,000 \div \$50,000 = 7$$

On the surface, this would appear way too high to anyone analyzing this company's financial statements. However, if we made the same computation based on market value, it would appear like this:

Noah's Boat Yard
Balance Sheet as of Today
(With land stated at market value)

Assets:	
Current assets	$ 150,000
Buildings and equipment, net of depreciation	200,000
Land	2,000,000
Total assets	$2,350,000
Liabilities:	
Current liabilities	$ 100,000
Long-term liabilities	250,000
Total liabilities	350,000
Owner's equity	2,000,000
Total liabilities and equity	$2,350,000

Now, the debt-to-equity ratio of the boat yard would be:

$$\text{Total liabilities} \div \text{equity} = \$350,000 \div \$2,000,000 = 0.18$$

Now, of course, this very low number would make it appear the company is in excellent shape, debtwise. So, in computing this ratio, the computation should be adjusted for market value.

Do bankers and other financial analysts blindly ignore market values of assets and make their ratio calculations and decisions entirely on the financial statements as prepared by the conservative accountants? No. They take the accountant's balance sheet and modify it, changing asset numbers to market value by adjusting them up or down, as appropriate. They also usually eliminate some assets created by the accountant, such as *prepaid expenses*. (See Chap. 7 for a discussion of why accountants create balance sheets using cost figures.)

Return on Assets

Pretend you had $715,000 sitting idle in the bank. (Nice feeling, isn't it?) You could put it in a 5 percent savings account and earn $35,750 ($715,000 times 5 percent) per year. What if, instead, you invested it in a hardware store? Look at Harry's Hardware balance sheet for last year (Fig. 12.4).

Theoretically, you could buy the same $715,000 worth of assets that he has and earn, according to his income statement, $93,000. This is the operating income *before* interest expense and income taxes. If you put $715,000 into the business, you would not need to borrow any additional cash, so there would be no interest expense. The $35,750 you could earn in a 5 percent bank savings account would be *before* income tax. So, to be comparable, the return on both the hardware store and the savings account are computed *before* income taxes.

Also, to make comparison easy, the earnings from the hardware store are reduced to a ratio, or percentage, that can be compared to the 5 percent at the bank. (Think of the 5 percent as a ratio of 5 to 100.) The ratio, *return on assets,* is income before interest and taxes divided by total assets. The return on assets of Harry's Hardware is therefore:

Income before interest and tax ÷ total assets = $90,000 ÷ $715,000 = 13%

A return of 13 percent is greater than one of 5 percent, so you would be better off to invest the $715,000 in a hardware store—or would you? Risk is another consideration, of course. But, Harry's Hardware balance sheet lists assets at original cost (less depreciation on equipment), not at what it would cost you to buy them today. You would have to compute this return on assets at today's replacement cost in order to come up with a meaningful return you can compare with other investments (i.e., this concept has the same *market value* problem as we had with the *debt-to-equity* ratio).

Return on Equity

This ratio, expressed as a percentage, is similar to the return on assets percentage. The difference is that in this case, the return is computed on equity. As I trust you remember from Chap. 8, *equity* can be computed by subtracting total liabilities from total assets. Take the figures from Harry's Hardware balance sheet and again make the assumption that you want to invest in a hardware store. It should be evident that you do not need all of the $715,000 in cash in order to get started selling hammers and nails. Just as Harry did, you could borrow for some of your needs. If you duplicated Harry's operation and invested the same amount as he has in equity in his hardware store, your return on your investment, or *return on equity,* would now be defined as income before income taxes divided by total equity. For Harry's Hardware (and for you, if you duplicate his numbers), it is:

Return on equity = income before taxes ÷ equity = $71,000 ÷ $455,000

= 16%

That's better. You would be earning more than three times the 5 percent rate the bank would pay you! This scenario, incidentally, demonstrates the effect of *leveraging*, which is the borrowing of some of your investment needs at an interest rate below that which you will earn on the assets in which you invest. Using the numbers we have up to now, you would borrow from the bank at 10 percent and earn 13 percent on the investment in the hardware store assets you buy. You put the 8 percent difference in your pocket, or rather, it goes to push the return on *your own* money up to the 16 percent computed as shown. That's leveraging. Caveat: It also works the other way—if you borrow at 10 percent and earn only 5 percent on the assets you buy with the loan proceeds, you are in real trouble.

Notice that this computation of return on equity uses *income before income taxes* rather than the *income before interest and income taxes* that was used for return on assets. That is because you are now borrowing for some of your cash needs and will have interest expense.

Again, this computation has the built-in error derived from using cost figures, rather than market value figures, for assets. The same comments as for *debt-to-equity ratio* and *return on assets* apply.

Profit Margin

For the purpose of evaluating operating management, the *profit margin* is income before interest and taxes divided by net sales. It produces a percentage that measures how much of net sales is left after all expenses have been subtracted. Actually, Alice has already computed this percentage when she prepared the *common size* financial statements in Fig. 12.3. For Harry's Hardware, this percentage was 4.5 percent. As with the other ratios we have looked at, it can be compared to prior years' figures and to industry averages.

Anyone can dream up all sorts of ratios from financial statements—what the relationship of any item is to another item. However, those I have listed are the most common for evaluating management performance. There are other ratios that relate more to investments in the stock market (or more precisely, investments in publicly traded stocks). Some examples follow.

Earnings per Share

We could compute this number for Harry's Hardware, Inc., but it would be rather meaningless for a small corporation whose stock is owned entirely by one individual. Therefore, let's look at the International Deflated Balloon Corporation. The corporation has 1 million shares of common stock outstanding, of which you own 100 shares. It earned a net income of $12 million last year. Do you care how much profit the corporation made, in total?

Not really. What you are interested in is how much your little piece of the corporation earned. You could make this computation:

> You own 100 shares out of 1 million, which is 100/1 million or 1/10,000 of the corporation. So, your share of the earnings would be 1/10,000 of $12 million or $1,200.*

There is an alternative way to figure this:

> Divide the earnings of the International Deflated Balloon Corporation by the number of shares outstanding. That would be $12 million divided by 1 million shares, or $12 per share. That is the *earnings per share,* which can be defined as the net income of the corporation divided by the number of shares of common stock issued and outstanding.† Now, you can multiply your 100 shares by the $12 earnings per share to arrive at the same $1,200 as your share of the earnings of the corporation.

Price-to-Earnings Ratio

This ratio, often abbreviated *P.E. ratio,* would be impossible to compute for Harry's Hardware Store, Inc. or any corporation whose stock is not actively traded. So, let's look again at the International Deflated Balloon Corporation. This morning, you looked in the financial pages of the newspaper and found that the stock in this corporation was trading at a price of $120 per share. The *price-to-earnings ratio* is then the market price of the stock divided by the earnings per share. For the International Deflated Balloon Corporation, it is $120 (the price of a share of stock) divided by $12 (the earnings per share), which equals 10.

What does this "10" mean? By itself, it means little. However, it is meaningful if it is compared to price-to-earnings ratio of the stock of other corporations. Suppose you check out the Collapsed Tent Corporation and find that the price-to-earnings ratio of its stock is 8. We can compare that to the stock you own this way:

Balloons: to get a dollar of earnings you will have to invest $10.

Tents: to get a dollar of earnings you will have to invest only $8.

---

* Remember, this does not mean you will find a check for $1,200 in your mailbox. The check will happen, and probably for a lesser amount, only if the board of directors declares a dividend is to be paid out of the earnings.

† If there is preferred stock outstanding, the computation of *earnings per share* is more complicated. It then becomes, basically, net income minus preferred stock dividends divided by number of common shares outstanding. If the preferred stock is participating or convertible, it becomes more complex. Those calculations are best left to professional accountants and financial analysts.

So, it would appear that the stock in the Collapsed Tent Corporation would be a better investment—more earnings for less money invested and, *presumably,* the higher earnings would eventually result in higher dividends or a faster growing company whose stock would be worth more. Would that investing in stocks were so simple. There are many other factors, some of which we have touched on in discussing financial statements and the tools of financial management of a business. These financial tools actually form the bedrock of making decisions about investments in stocks. They are what the stock market gurus call *fundamentals*—the understanding and analysis of financial statements, ratios, etc. There are other factors that relate to the action of the stock market itself, such as estimating the future price of a stock based on previous fluctuations in its price. In App. C are suggestions as to where to look for guidance in that area.

Cash Flow Statement

This is called a financial statement, although it really is an analytical tool, so it appears in this chapter on analysis. GAAP does require it to be included in a set of financial statements if the set is to be considered complete. Most nonaccountants and some accountants (like me) would think that a cash flow statement would be simply a list of cash that came in and cash that went out, prepared just like the cash flow report we made up in Chap. 1. However, the accounting profession has attempted to make it also an analysis—a reconciliation—of the differences between the accrual basis balance sheets and income statements and the cash flow. This requires a rather complicated format, an example of which is shown in Fig. 12.7, the cash flow statements of Harry's Hardware.

For the record, let's go through the items for last year. If how this goes together and how it relates to the balance sheet and income statement does not become instantly clear, *don't worry about it.* Look at it as a list of where the money came from and where it went, and remember that all the numbers reflected in the cash flow statement are also somewhere in the balance sheet, the income statement, the statement of shareholders' equity, or in the notes to the financial statements.* Here goes (follow along with Fig. 12.4 and 12.7):

At least part of *net income,* as Harry hopes, does end up as cash in the bank, so we start with net income as a source of cash and make many adjustments to it. In this statement, sources of (increases in) cash are pos-

---

* They may be well hidden. If the other parts of the financial statements are detailed, this statement can be constructed from them. If only summary, or condensed, statements are available, such construction may not be possible.

Harry's Hardware Store, Inc.
Cash Flow Statements

For the years ended December 31,	Last year	Prior year
Net income	$53,000	$37,000
Reconciliation to net cash flow from operations:		
Add:		
Depreciation	20,000	18,000
Change in working capital:		
Accounts receivable	10,000	(15,000)
Inventory	(25,000)	(10,000)
Prepaid insurance	2,000	(2,000)
Notes payable to bank, due within one year	(10,000)	32,000
Accounts payable	12,000	(30,000)
Accrued expenses	(2,000)	7,000
Income taxes payable	(1,000)	2,000
Cash provided by operations	59,000	39,000
Cash flow from investing activities:		
Furniture and fixtures	0	(15,000)
Office equipment	(5,000)	0
Vehicles	(10,000)	0
Cash used for investing activities	(15,000)	(15,000)
Cash flow from financing activities:		
Notes payable to bank, due after one year	(24,000)	(24,000)
Cash dividend paid	(10,000)	(5,000)
Cash used for financing activities	(34,000)	(29,000)
Net increase (decrease) in cash	$10,000	($ 5,000)

Figure 12.7 Comparative cash flow statements—Harry's Hardware Store, Inc.

itive figures in this statement, and uses of (decreases in) cash are negative figures—in parentheses.

We add *depreciation* to net income, because depreciation was subtracted in arriving at net income, but depreciation is a bookkeeping entry for which no one writes a check. (See Chap. 5.)

Accounts receivable went down from $200,000 to $190,000 during the year. (See the balance sheets in Fig. 12.4.) Harry loaned $10,000 less to his customers than they paid him, so he had an extra $10,000 to put in the bank.

Inventory increased by $25,000. That was a use of, or a *decrease* in, cash.

Prepaid insurance went down, from $12,000 to $10,000. So, by the same logic as just used, that *increased* cash by $2,000.

The *current portion* (due within 12 months) of *notes payable* to the bank decreased from $92,000 to $82,000. Paying off a loan requires cash, so that *decreased* cash by $2,000.

Accounts payable increased from $45,000 to $57,000. An increase in accounts payable amounts to borrowing money from suppliers, so that *increased* cash by $12,000.

Accrued expenses and *income taxes payable* both decreased. Just like the decrease in promissory notes, the decrease in liabilities soaked up cash, or *decreased* cash by $2,000 and $1,000, respectively.

So far, this statement has analyzed the cash flow from changes in current assets and current liabilities, or in working capital. When it analyzes *equipment,* it terms the buying and selling of equipment as *investment activities.* The total of all equipment increased by $15,000. That took cash, so it *decreased* cash by that amount. Note that the increase in the *allowance for depreciation* has no effect on cash, for it is a noncash book-keeping entry. (The transaction that affects cash is the purchase of the equipment in the first place.)

Now the statement analyzes changes in long-term debt and calls it changes from *financing activities.* For the debt to go down $24,000, Harry had to write checks totaling that amount to the bank (i.e., cash *decreased* $24,000).

The last item is the dividend paid. Dividends and any change in equity, such as the sale of more stock, would show up here.

The bottom line of this statement is the resulting net increase in cash. It should agree with the change in cash from one balance sheet to the next. In this case, it does. The bottom line shows an *increase* of $10,000, which is the increase in cash from $85,000 in the prior year to $95,000 last year.

If you have followed all this so far, you should be wondering, for instance, "why an *increase* in *vehicles* would necessarily be a *decrease* in cash. The corporation could have borrowed the money." So it could have, but that borrowing would show up either as an increase in current notes or long-term notes payable to the bank. In other words, when accountants make up this statement, they view the financing of vehicles or any equip-ment as happening in two steps: (1) Harry borrows $10,000 from the bank and increases cash and (2) he immediately pays out the $10,000 for a new truck and decreases cash (i.e., when the purchase is financed, the increase and decrease in cash are listed on the statement, even though they offset).

Let me repeat, *the world will not end if you do not grasp this cash flow statement right away.* Most financial analysis can be done without it, so spend your time digesting the other parts of the financial statement package. (The cash flow statement is another of those items that, some day, will become clear at 3:00 A.M.)

Notes to the Financial Statements

Various rules of the Financial Accounting Standards Board and Generally Accepted Accounting Principles require that many items be disclosed in the financial statements or in notes that accompany them. Instead of cluttering up financial statements with a lot of detail, accountants usually put much of the required technicalities in the notes. For instance, when Alice made up the balance sheet (Fig. 12.4) for Harry's Hardware, she could have omitted the detail about equipment. She could have just put down one line, "Plant, property and equipment, net of depreciation . . . $70,000 . . . $80,000." The breakdown of equipment into "Furniture and fixtures," "Office equipment," "Vehicles," and "Accumulated depreciation" could all have been relegated to the notes to the financial statement.

Even though Alice did not condense that area, she was required to expand on some other items in the notes to the financial statements. These items include a description of long-term debt and in what years the debt would be due. There is a similar requirement that future rentals required by leases be disclosed. She did that in note 3. (See Fig. 12.8.)

Some items that have to be disclosed cannot be reduced to hard numbers, so they can only be described in the notes. A pending lawsuit is our example in Fig. 12.8.

There is often more pertinent information about the finances and operations of a company in the notes to the financial statements than there is in the balance sheet and income statement. *Be sure to read the notes whenever you read financial statements.*

Can You Trust the Financial Statements?

If Harry wanted to lie, he could add a few thousand dollars to his ending inventory. That would make his financial statements look stronger and better impress his friendly banker. (It would increase his assets, so his equity would be bigger; and it would decrease cost of goods sold, so his profit would be larger.) Although Harry is too honest to intentionally misrepresent his status, not all business owners are so honorable. For example, in Chap. 2 we talked about Frank, the boat dealer, and his misrepresentation of a large sale.

Harry's Hardware Store, Inc.
Notes to the Financial Statements
Year ended December 31, Last Year and Prior Year

1. Summary of significant accounting policies:
   Inventory is valued at the lower of cost or market, computed by the first in, first out (FIFO) method. Bad debts are anticipated by charging anticipated losses to an allowance for bad debts, which is deducted from the total of accounts receivable. Equipment is stated at cost with depreciation provided on the straight-line method over the estimated useful life of the equipment, ranging from three to ten years.

2. Long-term debt:

Note payable to bank in monthly payments of $2,000 plus interest	$120,000
Less current portion (due within 12 months)	24,000
Total long-term debt	$ 96,000

   Future maturity of long-term debt:

XXX3	$24,000
XXX4	$24,000
XXX5	$24,000
XXX6	$24,000

3. Commitments:
   The company's operations are conducted in leased premises. The lease in effect at December 31, XXX2, expires on June 30, XXX5. The future minimum rentals under the noncancellable lease are as follows:

XXX3	$51,500
XXX4	$53,000
XXX5	$27,300

4. Contingent liabilities:
   A purchaser of a painter's hat from the company has filed suit against the company, claiming damages of $3,000,000 from build-up of intense heat under the hat, causing plaintiff to go bald. In the opinion of counsel, the suit is without merit and any settlement would be substantially under the limits of coverage provided by liability insurance in force at the time of the incident.

Figure 12.8 Notes to the financial statements—Harry's Hardware Store, Inc.

How well can you rely on a financial statement? There are two people, or two groups of people, to whom you can look for assurance that the financial statements are *materially* correct.

The first is the top management of the company. Harry, for instance, has lived in the town all of his life. He went to school with Brenda, his banker, and she is convinced of Harry's honesty and believes his records are above-board. However, Harry is not an accountant, so at Brenda's recommendation, he engaged Alice to help in that area. She is a Certified Public Accountant (CPA), one of the second group of people who can provide assurance about a financial statement.

If Alice is a CPA with her own professional firm, or is associated with other CPAs in a professional firm, she is considered to be an *independent*. If she prepares the financial statements for Harry's Hardware or is involved with the statements in any way, she will attach a letter to the statements, and the letter can be one of three "flavors":

1. If she says she has *audited* the statements, Brenda knows that Alice has tested Harry's bookkeeping procedures and has confirmed that the assets on the balance sheet really exist. She has also performed some procedures to try to be certain that all of the liabilities are listed on the balance sheet. Brenda can be reasonably assured that the financial statements are materially correct.

2. If Alice's letter says she *reviewed* the financial statements, Brenda can know that Alice has at least stuck her nose into Harry's recordkeeping, so there is a good chance that the statements are materially correct.

3. If Alice says she *compiled* the financial statements, she may have done little else than take the numbers that Harry, or his bookkeeper, gave her and put them into a format that complies with Generally Accepted Accounting Principles.

However, if Alice works for Harry's corporation as an employee, she is considered to be part of the corporate management and, as such, cannot attach a letter saying she has audited or reviewed the financial statements.

If you are going to make a decision based on another company's financial statement, you need two ingredients: honest management and a competent accountant.

Summary

The financial statements of an enterprise are far more meaningful if they can be compared to some standard. Available standards include financial statements of the same enterprise for the prior year(s), industry averages, or another similar business. Converting the financial statement figures to percentages makes such comparisons easier, as does computing various ratios of one reported number to another.

Cash flow is another analysis tool, and Generally Accepted Accounting Principles require that a cash flow statement be included in a complete financial statement package.

Financial statements are only as reliable as the management of an enterprise. While the involvement of a competent accountant adds credibility, such involvement is not a 100 percent guarantee that the financial statements contain no material errors.

Review Questions

1. Comparison of income statements to prior years can be revealing, but comparison of balance sheets from year to year is relatively meaningless. T   F

2. *Common size financial statements* reduce businesses of various sizes to one set of figures that can be compared.   T   F

3. Various financial ratios are meaningful only if they can be compared to industry averages or prior years' operations.   T   F

4. A *quick ratio* involves all of the current liabilities and only cash, cash equivalents, and accounts receivable of current assets.   T   F

5. *Return-on-assets* ratio is an excellent way to compare a business that started and bought most of its equipment in 1970 to one that started last year.   T   F

6. *Notes to the Financial Statements* provide little information of value to anyone other than an accountant and can be safely ignored.   T   F

Case Study Question _____

Here are, somewhat condensed, the income statements and balance sheets of Ted's Teddy Bear Store for last year and the prior year. Your mission: Complete the table that follows the financial statement. This requires that you compute the specified ratios for both years and indicate whether they indicate an improving (I) or worsening (W) condition.

Income Statements

	Last Year	Prior Year
Sales, net of returns and allowances	$600,000	$500,000
Subtract: Cost of goods sold	330,000	280,000
Gross profit	270,000	220,000

Expenses:

Selling expenses	50,000	40,000
General expenses	165,000	150,000
Total selling and general expenses	215,000	190,000
Net operating income	55,000	30,000
Interest expense	10,000	13,000
Net income before income tax	45,000	17,000
Income tax	11,000	4,000
Net income	$ 34,000	$ 13,000

Balance Sheets

	Last Year	Prior Year
Assets		
Current assets:		
Cash	$ 10,000	$ 12,000
Accounts receivable, net of bad debt allowance	45,000	40,000
Inventory	160,000	130,000
Prepaid expenses	10,000	8,000
Total current assets	225,000	190,000
Fixtures and equipment, net of depreciation allowance	75,000	90,000
Total assets	$300,000	$280,000
Liabilities		
Current liabilities:		
Current portion, loans payable	$ 25,000	$ 25,000
Accounts payable	50,000	35,000
Taxes payable	20,000	20,000
Accrued expenses	10,000	8,000
Total current liabilities	105,000	88,000
Long-term liabilities:		
Notes payable to bank	75,000	100,000
Total liabilities	180,000	188,000
Stockholders' equity		
Common stock, 5,000 shares $10 par value authorized, 1,000 issued and outstanding	10,000	10,000
Retained earnings	110,000	82,000
Total stockholders' equity	120,000	92,000
Total liabilities and equity	$300,000	$280,000

Ratios (fill in the blanks)

	Last Year	Prior Year	I/W
Return-on-assets ratio	_____	_____	_____
Profit margin percentage	_____	_____	_____
Debt-to-equity ratio	_____	_____	_____
Current ratio	_____	_____	_____
Quick ratio	_____	_____	_____
Inventory turnover ratio	_____	_____	_____
Earnings per share	_____	_____	_____

Appendix A
Flexible Budget Computations

The following is the computation of Spouse House Company Flexible Budget (Fig. 10.5) for nine months ended September 30, second year:

Computations are for actual sales volume of:

280 houses	$420,000
Service	80,000
Total sales	500,000

Budget

Cost of goods sold: computed at usual cost of $900 per shed (280 × $900)	$252,000
Advertising: fixed at $3,000 per month	27,000
Telephone (sales, long-distance): $6 per house sold	1,680
Administrative assistant: fixed at ½ of salary of $18,000 per year	6,750
Automobile: $45 × number of houses sold	12,600
Sales commission: 5% of total sales	25,000
Warehouse rent: fixed by lease at $600 per month	5,400
Warehouse supplies: estimated at $50 per month	450
Warehouse salary: fixed by annual salary review at $24,000 per year	18,000
Delivery: contract with trucker at $100 per house	28,000
Executive salary: determined by owner at $30,000/year	22,500
Administrative salary: other ½ of $18,000 per year	6,750
Executive automobile: estimated at 2,500 miles per month at 30¢ per mile	6,750

Workers' compensation insurance: total salaries and commissions times 3%	2,370
Fire insurance: at $300 per year	225
General liability insurance: at $600 per year	450
Product liability insurance: at ½% of total sales	2,500
Professional fees: estimated at $12,000 per year	9,000
Rent, office: at contractual rate of $400 per month	3,600
Supplies, office: estimated at $50 per month	450
Telephone service, basic service: at $150 per month	1,350
Payroll taxes: at 10% of total commissions and salaries	7,900
Business license: at ½% of total sales	2,500
Property taxes: at $600 per year	450
Depreciation: computed by accountant	9,000
Total expense budget	452,675
Budgeted net operating income	$ 47,325

Appendix **B**
Sources of Industry Averages

One of the better sources of industry averages is the trade association for the type of business. Look in your public library for a directory such as *Gale's Encyclopedia of Associations,* which is a comprehensive list of trade associations with addresses; then contact the appropriate association.

Various publishers also compile and produce annual statistics on many lines of business. Among the most complete and widely used, which are probably in your public library, are *Annual Statement Studies,* Robert Morris Associates; *Industry Norms and Key Business Ratios,* Dun & Bradstreet; and the *Almanac of Business and Industrial Ratios,* Prentice-Hall.

Whatever source you use, please read the section that explains the information and how it is compiled. You will be much better equipped to evaluate the reliability of the statistics.

Appendix C

Sources of Information on Publicly Held Corporations

Want to spruce up your savings—make more than the bank will pay on your savings account? You can use the knowledge you gained from this course to help you make wise choices in common stocks. If you think a company looks strong and growing, or if your hair stylist gives you a hot tip on a stock, *do not* immediately call a stock broker and gamble the rent money. Investigate first. How?

- Obtain the latest annual report of the company in which you are interested. A postcard to the corporation, attention of the stockholders' relations department, should bring that to you. If you want to be on the corporation's mailing list to receive all its quarterly and annual reports, buy one share of stock in the corporation. (That's allowable—to buy just one share without investigation.) You will find, in the report, the financial statements in the same format we discussed earlier. They'll probably be on fancy paper, set in colorful type, but they're still the basic financial statements. The annual report also will contain pages of description, telling you how magnificent the company is. Take it with a grain of salt. It's to management's advantage to make the company sound better than it is. That will boost the price of the stock—and the value of the managers' stock options.

- The *Securities and Exchange Commission (SEC)* is the federal agency that polices the sale of stock of public corporations. The law requires that every publicly held corporation file reports with the SEC, and the SEC requires that the reports contain certain information. Unfortunately, these reports will never receive an award for ease of understanding, but you may find information in them that the management of the corporation would just as soon you did not see. You may be able to obtain a copy of the report from the corporation. If not, they are available from the SEC for a fee. Address is: Securities and Exchange Commission, 450 5th Street NW, Washington, DC 20549. Telephone 202-272-7460.

■ Use your local public library. The business sections of most libraries will have stock services on their reference shelves. These are both bound books and loose-leaf volumes that are updated frequently. They will give you a summary of financial statements over several years, a history of stock prices, and various comments. Don't be awed by the bulk of these references—only a few pages are devoted to each company. For starters, take a look at the best known references: *Standard & Poor's, Moody's,* and *Value Line.*

■ Continue your financial education if you are serious about investing. An excellent method of doing this is to join an investment club, which is a club composed of individual investors who help each other understand more about financial analysis. This is not the blind leading the blind, for the clubs use professionally prepared educational material from the national association. They pool some of their members' funds for investment (perhaps $30 a month), but the biggest benefit is the education members receive, in small, easy-to-digest, doses. Dues are nominal. To find a club near you, write the National Association of Investors Corporation, 1515 East Eleven Mile Road, Royal Oak, MI 48067.

Appendix **D**

Dates Pertinent to Dividends on Publicly Held Stock

There are several dates that are pertinent to dividends. The *declaration date* is the day on which the board of directors of a corporation declares that the stockholders should receive a dividend, and how much that dividend will be. The amount is stated as so much per share of stock. At that point, the total of the declared dividends is deducted from equity and added to the liabilities of the corporation.

The *record date* is the date on which the person who will pay the dividends looks at the list of stockholders to determine who will be paid the dividend. This is not very pertinent to a small, family-held corporation, but it is critical to the stockholders of any corporation whose stock is actively traded.

The *payment date* is the day on which the checks will be written for the dividend.

The *ex-dividend date* is the date on which the right to a declared dividend ceases to follow a stock to a new owner of the stock. (It is the date for which it will be too late to have the stock sale, or transfer, recorded before the *record date*.) Practically, this date also applies only to *publicly traded stock*.

Appendix **E**

Classes of Common Stock and Preferred Stock

In some corporations, you may find two or more *classes* of common stock. For instance, what if you and Paul, when you sold additional stock, wanted to keep 100 percent of the management control of the corporation. You could have issued a second class of common stock, which would have the same rights to dividends as the stock you and Paul owned, but would have no voting rights. Sometimes, the certificates of such nonvoting stock will state that the stock will gain voting rights if the profits fall below a certain point, the debt rises above a certain amount, or on some other condition. These classes of stock are usually referred to by letters, as "Class A Stock," "Class B Stock," etc.

This is another class of stock that, technically, also represents equity, or ownership, of the corporation. It differs from the common stock we have been discussing in that *preferred stockholders must be paid dividends before any dividends can be paid to common stockholders*. Also, while common stockholders receive whatever dividends the board of directors decides they get, preferred stockholders' dividends are set at a certain amount.

Please recall Paul's Permanent Lawns, Inc. in Chap. 8. Suppose you and Paul, instead of issuing the common stock, had decided to sell preferred stock to investors. You might have guaranteed them that each share of stock (that was sold for $1,500) would be entitled to an annual dividend of $250, and the corporation would have to pay that dividend before it could pay any dividends to the common stockholders— you and Paul. Note that if no dividends are to be paid to common stockholders, there is no requirement that any dividends be paid to the preferred stockholders. Why would you want to issue such preferred stock? First, preferred stock normally has no voting rights in electing the board of directors. Second, when the business is even more profitable, your board of directors can pay the common stockholders' dividends of $500, $1,000, or any amount per share. The preferred stockholders still receive only their $250.

There are a couple of other terms you may see in this preferred stock area. *Cumulative preferred stock* is the same as I described in the last paragraph, except that if all dividends are omitted (not paid) in any year, the preferred stock dividends for previous years must be paid before any dividends on common stock can be paid.

Convertible preferred stock is preferred stock that can be exchanged, at the option of the preferred stockholder, for common stock in the same corporation.

Participating preferred stock is stock that will not only receive its stated, or guaranteed, dividend, but will also receive some fraction of the dividends that the common shareholders will receive.

You won't see a lot of preferred stock being issued by corporations these days, because of income tax reasons. Briefly, the alternative to preferred stock is the issuance of bonds. Interest on bonds is a deductible expense for a corporation. Dividends on preferred stock are, like common dividends, a draw out of equity and do not reduce the corporation's taxable income. The main reason for issuing the preferred stock instead of bonds is that bondholders can sue for unpaid interest, while preferred stockholders just have to wait until the corporation can pay the dividends.

If your financial travels take you to some small businesses owned by wealthy individuals, you may find that preferred stock has been issued. In those instances, it is usually for estate tax reasons that are relatively complex and best left to books on taxation.

Appendix F
Goodwill

This sounds as though it is a dollar value of the reputation and good name of the company. In a way, it is, but many companies with a good reputation and faithful customers have no such item listed in their assets, while others do. Why? It has to do with the requirement that a balance sheet must balance.

After several years of operating the Spouse House Company, Rosie Rouse found that most customers wanted fancy carpet installed. She could make additional profit if she owned a carpet store, and Carl, a local carpet merchant, wanted to sell his store and retire. Carl operated as a sole proprietorship, and a summary of his balance sheet looked like this:

Total assets	$100,000
Total liabilities	$ 25,000
Equity	75,000
Total liabilities and equity	$100,000

Although the equity, based on the *book value* of assets is only $75,000, Rosie paid Carl $300,000 for his business (i.e., she would buy his assets and *assume his liabilities*). That is, she would promise to pay off his accounts payable, notes payable to the bank, etc. She bought, it would appear, his furniture, fixtures, and inventory, which had a total fair market value of $125,000. (*Fair market value* is the amount for which the assets would sell by themselves, not in a going business.) She also bought a pool of satisfied customers and the good reputation that Carl had developed. What will Rosie's balance sheet (for the carpet business only) look like right after she buys the business from Carl?

The immediate answer might be that it would look just like it did when Carl owned it the moment before Rosie handed him a check. But, that balance sheet says the equity is $75,000, and Rosie paid $300,000 for it. Maybe the balance sheet should be:

Total assets	$100,000
Total liabilities	$ 25,000
Equity	300,000
Total liabilities and equity	$325,000

Any accountant would have a genuine fit over this. It doesn't balance!

How does Jeff, Rosie's accountant, make it balance? First, he lists the assets at their fair market value, which is the cost of those assets to the Spouse House Company. Then he inserts a fudge factor,* called *goodwill*. Now the balance sheet looks like this:

Assets, as purchased from Carl	$125,000
Goodwill	200,000
Total assets	$325,000
Total liabilities	$ 25,000
Equity	300,000
Total liabilities and equity	$325,000

Voilà! It balances!

That's how goodwill comes about. For Carl's business, Rosie paid more than the equity on his balance sheet. The intangible positive attributes of his business (reputation and loyal customers) did not show up in Carl's balance sheet, because the accounting is based on cost. They do show up in Rosie's balance sheet. Those intangibles do have a cost to her—she paid $200,000 for them.

You can also look at this scenario by ignoring Carl's financial statements. The basic transaction is that Rosie paid $300,000 for net assets of $100,000, so she bought $200,000 of goodwill.[†]

Need a concise definition? *Goodwill* is the excess paid for a business over the fair market value of the assets, less the liabilities, of the business just prior to purchase.

---

* A *fudge factor* is something inserted by an accountant to correct a problem or cover up an immaterial error. Sometimes it is called a *plug*. Both terms are accountants' slang, so you won't find them in printed reports.

[†] The *net assets* figure is the market value of the assets ($125,000) less the liabilities ($25,000).

Appendix G

Nonprofit Organizations

The basics of finance, as covered in this course, can apply to nonprofit organizations such as charities, clubs, associations, religious organizations, and governments. However, there are some differences.

Years ago, most of these organizations reported on a cash basis only, but now there is a strong trend towards accrual basis reporting. Many organizations did not even prepare a balance sheet, but only a list of cash receipts and expenditures. This meant that once property and equipment had been purchased, they disappeared from future financial reports. Of course, it makes more sense to keep track of those assets by showing them, with accumulated depreciation, on a balance sheet, and showing depreciation expense on the income statement.

In some operations of a nonprofit organization, the reports may be exactly the same as for a profit-making enterprise. For instance, if a museum ran a gift shop, the reports for that shop would be essentially the same as for a hardware store. In the truly nonprofit areas, such as caring for hungry children, there will be some differences in terminology, as follows:

Equity changes to *fund balance*. This makes sense in that equity implies some ownership, and no one in particular owns a nonprofit organization. However, *fund balance* can be misinterpreted as meaning that there are funds (money) in the same amount stashed away somewhere. That is no more true than it is for equity in a for-profit business. A financial report on a complex nonprofit organization may consist of several funds, one for each activity. For instance, a community recreation organization might have separate funds for each of several activities: youth sports, health club, dramatics, and so on. Generally, the buildings and equipment of the organization are lumped into one separate fund. Although they may be in the form of several columns on one page, there will be a separate balance sheet and income statement for each fund. And, as there is a separate balance sheet for each fund, there will be a separate fund balance for each activity.

Although a nonprofit organization may have some sales (such as of memberships), most of its revenue will be described as contributions, grants, or appropriations. Otherwise, the terminology will be little different from that of a business organization. There will be expenses such as rent, salaries, office supplies, insurance, and all the expense items that challenge managers. In addition, a nonprofit organization may have a major "expense" of contributions, if one of its main purposes is to solicit money and then distribute it to other charities. (An example is a United Way organization.)

In general, the concept of financial reporting for a nonprofit organization is the same as for a business, except that the motivation is not profit for the owners, but service to the members or to the needy.

Answer Key to Review Questions and Case Studies

Chapter 1

Review Questions:

1. Language.

2. False. Numbers should be rounded off only when the error due to the rounding will not cause someone to make an erroneous decision.

3. False. Accrual basis reports reflect income earned and expenses incurred, whether or not they have been paid for.

4. True.

5. False. The Financial Accounting Standards Board makes up rules for financial reporting (Generally Accepted Accounting Principles). The Internal Revenue Service makes up its own rules for computing and reporting taxable income.

Case Study Question:

Cash Receipts and Disbursements Report for April:

Cash receipts:		
For sales (paid for) of wallpaper		$4,750
Cash disbursements:		
350 rolls of wallpaper	$1,400	
Rent	300	
Water company	175	
Payroll (March, paid in April)	300	
Total disbursements		2,175
Net increase in cash		$2,575

Income and expense, April (accrual basis):	
Sales (500 rolls of wallpaper)	$5,000
Cost of sales (500 rolls)	2,000
Gross profit	3,000

Expenses:
Rent	$300	
Telephone	120	
Water (bottle, not the deposit)	50	
Payroll expense (April)	800	
Total expenses		1,270
Net income		$1,730

Chapter 2

Review Questions:

1. Ownership (or title) passes.

2. The service is rendered.

3. The merchandise is delivered to the premises of the buyer.

4. True. See the story about Frank, the boat dealer.

5. Consignment.

6. False. In order to match bad debts with sales, an expected bad debt expense should be deducted from sales in the month in which the sales occur.

7. False. It is not income. It reduces the running balance of the *allowance for bad debts*.

8. False. Discounts for high-volume buying are generally treated as a reduction in price.

Case Study Question:

Month	Sales	Expense	Bad debts incurred	Accumulated allowance for bad debts
Beginning balance				$ 600
January	$ 4,000	$ 80		680
February	6,000	120		800
March	5,000	100		900
April	7,000	140		1,040
May	9,000	180	$ 500	720
June	5,000	100		820
July	3,000	60		880
August	4,000	80		960
September	8,000	160		1,120
October	10,000	200	800	520
November	9,000	180		700
December	2,000	40		740
Totals	$72,000	$1,440	$1,300	

Chapter 3

Review Questions:

1. True. Beginning and ending inventory, and the costs of those inventories, are also factors.

2. False. Cost of goods sold should be at *cost* prices, so it can be subtracted from sales at *retail* prices to compute gross profit.

3. True, by definition.

4. False. *Physical inventory* refers to physically eyeballing and counting the goods on hand. As for the doctor, he can't stock medical physicals on an inventory shelf, as such a physical is a service, not an item of merchandise.

5. True. If the last items bought are the first items sold, and prices are rising, the items sold will be put in *cost of goods sold* at the higher prices; and higher costs mean lower gross profit.

6. False. FIFO or LIFO may be used by a business, regardless of the actual physical flow of the product.

7. True. See the discussion of Angus' bagpipe inventory in this chapter.

8. True. It should be added to the cost of the goods that go into inventory, but it will become part of the cost of goods sold when those goods are taken out of inventory and sold.

Case Study Question:

Net sales	$5,000	
Cost of goods sold:		
Beginning inventory	300	
Purchase during September	2,450	(300 @ $4) + (250 @ $5)
Goods available for sale	2,750	
Subtract ending inventory	750	(150) rolls @ $5)
Cost of goods sold	2,000	
Gross profit	$3,000	

Chapter 4

Review Questions:

1. True, for a business. If an expenditure is not made for the purpose of increasing income, it must be for the personal benefit of the owner(s) of the business, which is not a business expense.

2. False, generally. Management reports should contain much detail for help in managing the business. Financial statements for "outsiders" report *results* of operations.

3. False. Responsibility reporting is a management tool. The IRS could care less about individual department operations. It just wants the taxes due from the operation of the entire enterprise. (Exception: foreign subsidiaries—but that's another subject.)

4. False. Dividing expenses into variable and fixed is, again, a management tool. The usual practice is to format financial statements for use by outsiders, as in Figs. 4.1, 4.2, and 4.4.

5. True, by definition.

6. False. Breakeven point can also be computed by dividing total fixed costs by the contribution margin.

7. True.

Case Study Question:

Average sale		$ 100
Variable expenses:		
Commission, sales	$ 20	
Labor, including payroll taxes	30	
Truck	5	
Soap	2	
Maintenance ($300 ÷ 100 jobs)	3	
Total variable expenses		60
Contribution margin		40
Fixed expenses:		
Rent	500	
Salaries, owners	2,250	
Salary, administrative	1,200	
Insurance	100	
Utilities	50	
Telephone	100	
Total fixed expenses		$4,200

Breakeven point = total fixed expenses ÷ total variable expenses = 105 sales/month

Chapter 5

Review Questions:

1. False. Although the cost of equipment is not an immediate expense, it does become depreciation expense as time progresses. Also, the cost of small pieces of equipment, below the capitalization level, becomes expenses immediately.

2. False. Salvage value, in this context, is an *estimate* of what the junk dealer *will* pay when the machine is worn out.

3. True. The machine may still be useful to someone else, but its *useful life* for a particular business ends when it is no longer useful to that business.

4. True. This was the major message of this chapter.

5. False. *Book value* refers to the original cost of the equipment less the accumulated depreciation.

6. True, by definition.

7. True. With the units-of-production method, the depreciation expense is dependent on the volume of production, and what that will be in the future can only be estimated.

8. False. Although "keeping two sets of books" is, for the most part, illegal, it is legal in such areas as depreciation records.

9. *b.* A $50 chair should be below the *capitalization policy* of any business. (The answer might be different if 100 chairs were bought at one time, making the cost of the *group* of chairs $5,000.)

Case Study Question:

	Annual depreciation expense*	Remaining cost of machine (book value) at end of year
Purchase		$100,000
First year	$20,000	80,000
Second year	20,000	60,000
Third year	20,000	40,000
Fourth year	20,000	20,000
Fifth year	20,000	0
Book value at end of second year		$ 60,000
Received for old machine		45,000
(Loss) on sale of equipment		$ 15,000

Chapter 6

Review Questions:

1. Cash flow.

2. True, by definition.

3. False. Depreciation is a *noncash* expense and should be ignored when computing cash flow.

*Annual depreciation expense: $100,000 ÷ 5 years = $20,000.

4. True.

5. False. It ignores interest. While it is suitable for comparing cash flows from various pieces of equipment, it should not be used to compare investment in equipment to interest-bearing investments such as bonds, certificates of deposit, etc.

6. False. The definition in the question is for *future value.*

7. True.

8. True.

Case Study Question:

Purchase price of drapery machine	$100,000
Annual saving of labor cost	40,000

Payback period $100,000 ÷ $40,000 = 2.5 years

Present value of annual cash flow from Table 6.2:

Year	Factor	Cash flow	Present value
1	0.83333	$40,000	$ 33,333
2	0.69444	40,000	27,778
3	0.57870	40,000	23,148
4	0.48225	40,000	19,290
5	0.40188	40,000	16,075
Total present value			119,624
Subtract			100,000
Net present value			$ 19,624

You also could have computed the total present value in one step, using Table 6.3 as follows:

5 years   2.99061 × $40,000 = $119,624

If you took this shortcut, give yourself a bonus point.

As for the recommendation to Sandra, the payback period is meaningless, unless we have something to compare it to, such as company policy or an alternative piece of equipment. However, the net present value, at her required 20 percent interest, is positive, so you can recommend purchase of the drapery machine (provided there are not other factors involved).

Chapter 7
Review Questions:

1. True. Examples are equipment owned and money owed.

2. True, by definition.

3. False. Property and equipment are listed at their *cost* minus depreciation.

4. False. Future interest is not a liability until the future is here.

5. False. A prepaid expense represents a payment that has been made for an expense not yet incurred—the mirror image of a liability for an expense already incurred but not yet paid for.

6. False. It arises only when a going business is purchased by a new owner.

7. True. The loan was advanced in the medium of goods and/or services, rather than money.

Case Study Question:

A.

	Current asset	Noncurrent asset	Current liability	Long-term liability
Accounts payable	—	—	X	—
Inventory	X	—	—	—
Intangible assets	—	X	—	—
Deferred income	—	—	X	—
Loan due in 90 days	—	—	X	—
Cash	X	—	—	—
Accounts receivable	X	—	—	—
Property and equipment	—	X	—	—

B.

Beginning balance of loan	$80,000
Subtract payments made	32,000
Balance	48,000
Subtract current portion	16,000
Long-term liability	$32,000

Chapter 8

Review Questions:

1. An income statement is like a video that is *running*, and a balance sheet is like a video in a *pause* status.

2. True.

3. False. The *total stockholders' equity* section is an accumulation of various activities and does not reflect the value of the underlying assets or the value of the earnings capability of the corporation.

4. False. Technically, the members of the Board of Directors are elected by the stockholders. In large, publicly held companies with self-perpetuating

management, the directors may be selected by top management. However, they still go through the formality of election by the stock-holders.

5. False. It is not "thrown in." It arises when stockholders pay cold, hard cash for newly issued shares of stock at a price higher than the par value.

6. False. After a 2-for-1 split, there is twice as much stock, but in total it still represents ownership of the same company (i.e., each share of the new stock would theoretically be worth one-half of the value of the old stock).

Case Study Question:

Book value of the corporation = $6 million, the same as *total stockholders' equity*.

Book value per share = total stockholders' equity ÷ number of shares issued and outstanding = $6 million ÷ 1 million = $6.00

Value of the corporation by capitalizing earnings = earnings ÷ desired rate of return = $1.5 million ÷ 20% = $7.5 million

Capitalized earnings value per share = $7.5 million ÷ 1 million = $7.50

Market value of the whole corporation = Market price per share × number of shares outstanding = $14.00 × 1 million = $14 million

Chapter 9

Review Questions:

1. False. Long-range planning should be reflected on current budgets, not vice versa.

2. False. If conditions change during the year, budgets should be changed to reflect conditions realistically.

3. False. While previous year's results must be considered, a drastic change in the company or the market may require a whole new set of numbers.

4. True.

5. Which answer is correct is a matter of opinion. Whatever you answered, give yourself a "correct" for this question.

6. This is another one that is a matter of opinion and depends largely on the nature of the company and the industry. Give yourself a "correct" on this one also—unless you put "wild guesses" at the top.

Case Study Question:

Item	Budget in dollars
Cost of goods sold	$12,000
Advertising	3,000
Salaries	5,000
Part-time help	1,500
Delivery expense	300
Fire insurance	100
Rent	2,000
Supplies	600
Telephone	200

Chapter 10

Review Questions:

1. *a.*

2. *c.* Divide the variance by budget.

3. False. If you checked true, re-read the chapter.

4. False. Look for the causes of the problem and take remedial action. Not preparing a cash budget and learning of the negative cash balance only on the day it happens are what can lead to bankruptcy.

5. False. Budget preparation is a responsibility of top and operating management.

6. False. Obligations do not show up as actual expenses until they are incurred (goods delivered or service performed). Exceptions: A report on obligated-but-not-incurred expenses and some government budget reports.

7.

	Operating budget only	Cash budget only	Both budgets
Advertising	——	——	X
Interest expense	——	——	X
Payment of loan principal	——	X	——
Receipt of loan from bank	——	X	——
Depreciation expense	X	——	——

Case Study Question:

	May actual	May budget	Dollar variance	Percent variance	F/U
Sales	$30,000	$30,000	0		
Cost of goods sold	17,000	18,000	(1,000)	−6%	F
Gross profit	13,000	12,000	1,000	8%	F

Expenses:					
Advertising	3,300	3,000	300	10%	U
Salaries	3,000	3,000	0		
Part-time help	1,000	1,500	(500)	−33%	F
Delivery expense	330	300	30	10%	U
Fire insurance	130	100	30	30%	U
Rent	2,000	2,000	0		
Supplies	500	600	(100)	−17%	F
Telephone	250	200	50	25%	U
Total expenses	10,510	10,700	190	2%	F
Net income before tax	$ 2,490	$ 1,300	$1,190	92%	

Chapter 11

Review Questions:

1. Raw material, work in process, finished goods.

2. True. Work in process and finished goods.

3. False. Variations in material costs, labor cost, or overhead will cause variations in inventory costs (unless a standard cost system is in place).

4. True.

5. True.

6. False. As soon as it is apparent that the contract will incur a loss on a contract, the total expected loss should be reported in the current operating report.

7. True.

Case Study Question:

Raw material (special paper):	
Inventory October 1: 100,000 sheets @ 20¢	$ 20,000
Purchased during October, 300,000 sheets @ 20¢	60,000
Total paper available	80,000
Inventory October 31: 50,000 sheets @ 20¢	10,000
Used in production _350_ sheets @ 20¢	70,000
Direct labor: 8,750 hours @ $10 per hour	87,500
Factory overhead	17,500
Total manufacturing cost	175,000
Work in process (valued at cost of 25¢ each):	
Inventory October 1, 1,000 units	$ 250
Total manufacturing cost (350,000 units)	175,000
Subtotal	175,250
Inventory October 31, 1,500 units	375
Cost of goods manufactured (finished goods)	174,750

Finished goods:

Inventory October 1, 100,000 paper airplanes @ 50¢	50,000
Goods available for sale	224,750
Inventory October 31, 40,000 airplanes @ 50¢	20,000
Cost of goods sold	$204,750

Chapter 12

Review Questions:

1. False. Changes in balance sheet numbers as ratios can be revealing (e.g., the current ratio).

2. True. It reduces the numbers to percentages (as of sales or total assets).

3. True.

4. True.

5. False. The assets are stated at cost (less depreciation). The difference in price levels between the dates the assets were purchased would make this comparison virtually meaningless.

6. False. They should be read carefully by anyone who is going to extend credit to or invest in the business.

Case Study Question:

Return on assets:		
Last year: $34,000 ÷ $300,000	11%	I
Prior year: $13,000 ÷ $280,000	5%	
Profit margin:		
Last year: $55,000 ÷ $600,000	9%	I
Prior year: $30,000 ÷ $500,000	6%	
Debt-to-equity ratio:		
Last year: $155,000 ÷ $145,000	1.1:1	I
Prior year: $163,700 ÷ $117,000	1.4:1	
Current ratio:		
Last year: $225,000 ÷ $80,000	2.8:1	W
Prior year: $190,000 ÷ $63,000	3.0:1	
Quick ratio:		
Last year: $55,000 ÷ $80,000	0.7:1	W
Prior year: $52,000 ÷ $63,000	0.8:1	
Inventory turnover:		
Last year: $330,000 ÷ $160,000	2.1:1	W
Prior year: $280,000 ÷ $130,000	2.2:1	
Earnings per share:		
Last year: $34,000 ÷ 1,000	$34.00	I
Prior year: $13,000 ÷ 1,000	$13.00	

Glossary

absorbed costs: Overhead costs that have gone into the cost of products that have been manufactured.

accelerated depreciation: Any method of depreciation that loads higher depreciation expense into the early years of an asset's useful life.

accounts payable: Money that is owed to suppliers of goods or services. It is, in effect, an interest-free loan from the suppliers.

accounts receivable: Debts owed by others to the entity, usually for goods and services.

accounts receivable turnover: How many times accounts receivable were collected during the year. (Net sales divided by accounts receivable.)

accrual accounting: The process of recording transactions when they happen (not when they are paid for) to meet the matching principle.

accumulated depreciation: The total of depreciation expense that has been listed as an expense on the income statements since the first day a piece of equipment was put into use.

allowance for bad debts: The accumulation of amounts subtracted from sales as future bad debt expense. It is reduced by amounts that become known (uncollectible) bad debts.

assets: Economic resources acquired and owned by an entity.

bad debt expense: The amount that is subtracted from sales revenue for the portion of sales that will probably become bad debts.

bad debts: Amounts owed by customers who are insolvent, bankrupt, or have disappeared. Payment will never be collected.

balance sheet: A financial report listing the assets, liabilities, and owners' equity as of a specific date.

billings in excess of costs and estimated earnings: See overbilling.

bond: One of a series of notes that are sold to investors.

book values: Values that are reflected on balance sheets. They do not necessarily represent market values.

breakeven point: That level of sales at which there is neither income nor loss.

capitalization of earnings: The computation of the investment amount that will yield, at a desired rate of return, an amount equal to the net income of a company.

251

capitalization policy: A dollar figure below which equipment cost will not be depreciated but will be considered an expense in the year the equipment is acquired.

capitalized lease: A lease that is substantially an installment sale rather than a rental arrangement.

cash basis: The method of accounting that treats cash received for products and services as income and cash disbursed as expense.

cash disbursements: All the checks written (and mailed) or cash paid out.

cash discount: An allowance granted to a customer for prompt payment of an invoice. It is an expense relative to the quick collection of money and should not be confused with a sales allowance that is granted for other reasons.

cash flow: The cash that can be generated by a business, or a particular project, over a period of time.

cash flow statement: A financial statement that shows the sources and uses of cash.

cash receipts: All the checks, money orders, and cash received in a given period of time.

cash sale: Merchandise or service that is delivered to a customer and on which payment is collected, on delivery, in cash (or equivalent, such as checks and money orders).

common size financial statement: A financial statement, expressed in percentages only, as an income statement in which the line items are expressed as percentages of net sales.

comparative financial statements: A format of financial statement that presents two (or more) years of financial statement figures presented side by side, so they can be compared.

completed-contract method of reporting income: Applicable to short-term contracts. Income is reported as earned only upon completion of the contract.

conservatism principle: Income is not shown on a report until it is earned (generally when the sale takes place), but losses are reported as soon as there is a possibility they may occur. Similarly, most assets on the balance sheet are valued at the lower of their cost or replacement cost.

consignment sale: Merchandise is shipped to someone who appears as a dealer, but is actually an agent for the shipper. The shipper retains title until the agent sells the goods and remits payment (less agent's commission) to the shipper.

consistency principle: An accounting principle that the same accounting methods should be followed year after year so that several years' financial statements can be compared.

contribution margin: That portion of the selling price of an item that remains after variable costs and expenses are paid.

controllable cost or expense: A cost or expense that can be changed by the action of a manager at a given level of management.

convertible preferred stock: Preferred stock that can be exchanged, at the option of the preferred stockholder, for common stock in the same corporation, at a rate set when the stock is originally issued.

corporation: An entity created by the state. It is a legal person, usually with unlimited life and limited liability.

cost: The amount of money or other asset paid for something. The something received can be cost of sales, expense, or it can be another asset, such as inventory. Also, a cost can be incurred by creating a liability (as an account payable).

cost of goods sold: The cost to the company of the merchandise that was sold to customers.

costs and estimated earnings in excess of billings: See **underbilling**.

credit sale (sale on account): Exchange of goods or services in exchange for a promise to pay at some date in the future.

creditor: A company or individual to whom money is owed.

cumulative preferred stock: Preferred stock on which, if dividends are omitted (not paid) in any year, the preferred stock dividends for previous years must be paid before any dividends on common stock can be paid.

current assets: Those assets that are cash or will be converted into cash within the next 12 months.

current liabilities: Those obligations that will become due within the next 12 months.

current ratio: Total current assets divided by total current liabilities.

debt-to-equity ratio: Total liabilities divided by total equity.

declaration date: The day on which the board of directors of a corporation declares that the stockholders will receive a dividend, and how much that dividend will be.

deferred income: A liability for income that has been received but not yet earned.

deferred income tax: The amount computed by subtracting the actual income tax owed from the income tax computed on net income computed by GAAP, if the result is a positive number (an additional liability). It may or may not represent an amount that will have to be paid some day.

depreciation: The spreading out, or allocation, of the cost of the equipment over the useful life of the equipment.

direct costs or expenses: Those items and labor that become part of a finished product.

direct labor cost: The cost of the people who actually do the work of putting the product together.

direct materials cost: The materials that end up being part of the finished product.

dividends: The payments of part or all of the earnings of the corporation to stockholders. Generally, dividends must be made in proportion to the number of shares of stock owned by each stockholder.

earnings: Usually means the same as net income, but in some areas (e.g., long-term contracts) can mean gross profit.

entity: An enterprise or economic unit, consisting of people, assets, and activities devoted to a specific economic purpose.

equity: The amount attached to the ownership of an enterprise, determined by subtracting liabilities from assets, or by additions and subtractions of profits, losses, investments, and withdrawals.

ex-dividend date: The date on which the right to a declared dividend ceases to follow a stock to a new owner.

expense: Costs that are matched with a time period and are deducted from the income earned during the period. Also defined as an outflow of an asset in exchange for an inflow of revenue.

FASB: See **Financial Accounting Standards Board**.

factory overhead: The costs of operating a factory that are not direct materials and direct labor.

Financial Accounting Standards Board (FASB): The rule-making body that now sets rules that define Generally Accepted Accounting Principles.

financial report: Any report that has to do with the financial status of a company or financial results of its operations. It may contain pages of explanations as well as numbers. Frequently, financial statements will be a part of a financial report.

financial statement: Financial reports in a special, prescribed format. They include balance sheet, income statement, retained earnings statement, statement of cash flows, and notes to the financial statements.

first in, first out (FIFO): A system of valuing inventory in which it is assumed that the first lot of identical goods purchased or manufactured (the oldest on hand) will be sold before goods acquired later. Compare to **last in, first out**.

fiscal year: A reporting year, the year a business or other entity adopts as the 12 months on which it will report. For instance, the federal government uses a fiscal year of October 1 to the following September 30. (Note that the correct word is *fiscal*, not *physical*.)

fixed expense: An expense that will remain the same, regardless of changes in sales volume, within a relevant range of sales volume.

flexible budget: A budget in which the budget figures for variable expenses will vary with sales volume or some other measure of activity.

floor plan sale: Used by a manufacturer or wholesaler in sales to a dealer. Similar to a secured sale, except that a bank or finance company takes the security interest in the merchandise and makes immediate payment to the seller. The dealer is expected to pay the bank or finance company at some future date.

FOB: See **free on board**.

free on board (FOB): The point, in the process of shipment, to which the shipper will pay the shipping costs.

future value: The value, in the future, of a payment today.

GAAP: See **Generally Accepted Accounting Principles**.

Generally Accepted Accounting Principles (GAAP): A broad set of rules, developed by tradition over centuries, now partially codified by the Financial Accounting Standards Board, delineating how various transactions will be reported on financial statements.

goodwill: The excess paid for a business over the fair market value of the assets, less the liabilities, of the business just prior to purchase.

gross income: This is a tax term developed by the IRS to mean about the same thing as revenue. It is sometimes used that way in discussion of financial results.

gross margin: Means the same as gross profit, although this term is more likely to be used when discussing one product rather than operational results as a whole.

gross profit: What's left after subtracting cost of goods sold from sales.

gross sales: Total sales before subtraction of returns and allowances.

income: Difficult to define unless accompanied by some additional description such as net income or net income before taxes. At one time, it could mean the same as revenue, but that is no longer in fashion.

income statement: A financial report that lists revenues, subtracts expenses, and arrives at a net income.

indirect costs or expenses: Those items and labor that assist in manufacturing the product.

indirect labor cost: The cost of the people who do work in the factory other than directly on the product.

indirect materials cost: The cost of materials that are used in the factory that do not become part of the product.

industry average figures: Average figures from financial statements of many companies in one industry. May consist of absolute numbers, percentages, and ratios.

interest coverage: The number of times interest expense will go into earnings before subtraction of interest expense and income taxes.

internal rate of return: The interest rate on an investment in a machine, or project, that would generate cash equal to the cash flow from the machine.

inventory: A stock of items. Usually refers to items for resale or raw materials or work in process that will become items to be sold.

inventory turnover: Cost of goods sold divided by inventory.

job cost: The method of allocating overhead costs in manufacturing a variety of products, few if any of which are identical to other products produced.

last in, first out (LIFO): A system of valuing inventory in which it is assumed that the last lot of identical goods purchased or manufactured (the newest on hand) will be sold before goods acquired earlier. Compare to **first in, first out**.

lease: A written agreement relative to rent of facilities such as buildings and equipment. It obligates the owner (lessor) of the facilities to rent them to the user of the facilities (lessee) over a period of time for a specified rent.

lessee: One who rents facilities from the owner (lessor) of the facilities.

lessor: One who owns facilities that he or she rents to a lessee.

leveraging: The borrowing of some of your investment needs at an interest rate below that which you will earn on the assets in which you invest.

loan: A transfer of an asset (usually cash) to some person with the expectation it will be repaid.

loss: An outgo of expenses or costs without offsetting revenue.

lower of cost or market: An application of the conservatism principle. If the replacement cost of inventory is less than the original cost, the replacement cost is used in valuing it. Also used in valuing marketable securities.

market value: The price on which a willing buyer and a willing seller agree.

markup percentage: Found by first determining the difference between the selling price and the cost price of an item and then dividing that difference by the cost price.

matching principle: An accounting principle that requires expenses to be deducted from related sales in the periods in which they occur.

materiality: A measurement of an error. A material error is one which is large enough to cause people to make a decision that is different from a decision they would make if they had the correct figures. Immaterial errors are acceptable.

net (as a verb): What is left of something after its related costs and/or expenses have been deducted.

net assets: What is left of total assets after subtracting total liabilities. In other words, the term is synonymous with **equity.**

net income: The remainder after all matching costs and expenses have been deducted from revenue.

net loss: The same as net income, except the costs and expenses are greater than revenue, so the resulting figure is negative.

net present value: The present value of future cash flows from an item or equipment (or a project) minus the cost of the equipment.

net profit: See **net income**.

net sales: Result of subtracting returns and allowances (and possibly cash discounts) from gross sales.

note: Common abbreviation of **promissory note**, a written document that describes a loan and its terms—interest, repayment, etc.

overbilling: In percentage-of-completion contracting, the difference found by subtracting revenue earned from total billings.

par value of a share of stock: The dollar amount specified in the corporate charter. Its only significance is that the original investors must pay at least that much for each share of stock. (They may pay more.) The par value has no relation to the real value of the stock.

participating preferred stock: Preferred stock that will not only receive its stated, or guaranteed, dividend, but will also receive some fraction of the dividends that the common shareholders will receive.

payback period: The time it takes to generate additional cash flow from a project such that the cash flow will be equal to the cost of the project.

payment date: The day on which the checks will be written for the dividend payable to stockholders.

percentage-of-completion method of reporting income: Applicable to long-term contracts. Income is reported as partially earned in each reporting period of the contract.

percentage variance: Variance divided by budget figures.

periodic inventory system: Method of arriving at an inventory value by physically counting and pricing merchandise on hand. Compare with **perpetual inventory system**.

perpetual inventory system: Method of determining inventory by keeping track of amounts purchased and amounts sold and adding or subtracting those figures from the beginning inventory. Compare with **periodic inventory system**.

preferred stock: A separate class of stock, the owners of which must be paid dividends before any dividends can be paid to common stockholders. Generally, dividends are at a rate that is specified when the stock is issued.

present value: The value today of a future payment.

privately held stock: Stock owned by one or a few individuals and not offered for sale to the general public.

process costs: The method of allocating overhead costs in manufacturing of a continuous stream of identical products.

profit margin percentage: Found by first determining the difference between the selling price and the cost price of an item and then dividing that difference by the selling price.

promissory note: a written document that describes a loan and its terms—interest, repayment, etc.

publicly held corporation: A corporation whose stock is publicly traded.

publicly traded stock: Stock issued and sold to the general public. It can be freely bought and sold, as through a stockbroker.

purchase: Acquisition of goods or services, either for use by the enterprise or for later resale to customers. A purchase occurs when title to goods is passed or services are rendered.

purchase discount: See **cash discount**. A purchase discount is a cash discount taken for prompt payment of a vendor's invoice.

quick ratio: Cash and accounts receivable divided by total current liabilities.

raw materials: Direct materials in their raw state, before they enter the manufacturing process.

recognize: The act of recording an event in the financial records.

record date: The date on which the person who will pay the dividends looks at the list of stockholders to determine to whom the dividends will be paid.

reserve for depreciation: An obsolete term meaning the same as **allowance for depreciation**.

retained earnings: The accumulation of additions of net income, or earnings, each year of the corporation's existence, minus any losses and the dividends that have been paid over the years.

retained earnings statement: A financial statement that displays the changes to retained earnings during a period of time.

return on assets: Income before interest and taxes divided by total assets.

revenue: The income that flows to an enterprise, before deductions for any costs or expenses. It includes sales, rents, interest, etc. For governments and nonprofit organizations, it also includes grants, taxes, fees, etc.

sale: What is charged to customers for goods or services. A sale occurs when title to goods is passed or services are rendered.

sales allowances: A reduction of price granted to a customer because of damaged merchandise, missed delivery date, etc. It is usually shown as a separate line and subtracted from sales, or it is combined with returns, so the line reads "Sales returns and allowances."

sales discount: See **cash discount**.

sales returns: Merchandise that is returned by customers after a sale. The selling price value of returns is usually shown as a separate line and subtracted from sales.

salvage value: What management guesses the equipment will be worth at the end of its useful life.

secured sale: The seller, through properly recorded documentation, retains a security interest in the merchandise (i.e., the goods the seller sold to the buyer act as collateral for the amount the buyer owes the seller until the buyer makes payment in full).

security interest: The interest that one party has in assets (collateral) owned by another party, to secure a loan. Example: The interest a mortgage company has in an individual's home, or the lien the bank has on an automobile it has financed.

semivariable cost or expense: A cost or expense that is partly variable and partly fixed.

shareholders' equity statement: A financial statement that displays the changes in all categories of the equity section of a corporate balance sheet. If this statement is produced, a retained earnings statement would be redundant and is therefore not produced.

standard costs: Budgets, based on unit costs, rather than on monthly or annual figures.

stock certificate: A document issued to each stockholder which states how many shares of the corporation he or she owns.

stockholders (shareholders): Owners of shares of a corporation.

sunk costs: Costs already incurred that cannot be changed, so they have no relevance to current decision making.

taxable income: A tax term that is similar to net income. It is what is left after all deductions have been subtracted from revenue.

time-value of money: A broad category of terms relating to the effect of interest on money over a period of time. See **present value, future value**, and **internal rate of return**.

trade discount: A discount offered by a manufacturer to a wholesaler or retailer because that entity is a wholesaler or retailer (i.e., the discount is offered to someone "in the trade" of selling the product).

turnover: The number of times an asset can be turned into sales, measured in the asset's equivalent units.

unabsorbed costs: Overhead costs that did not get included in the cost of products that have been manufactured.

uncontrollable cost or expense: A cost or expense that cannot be affected by the action of a manager at a given level of management within a given level of activity and within a given time period.

underbilling: In percentage of completion contracting, the difference found by subtracting total billings from revenue earned.

unit cost: The total cost of production divided by the number of units produced.

useful life: How long management of the company expects the equipment to be in operation (useful) for the company.

variable expense: An expense that varies with the volume of sales.

variance: The difference between actual results and budget goals.

volume discount: A discount offered to a buyer if the buyer will purchase in large quantities.

warranty: A guarantee that merchandise will perform as intended for a given period of time.

working capital: The difference found by subtracting current liabilities from current assets. It is a measure of the ability of the entity to pay its bills.

work-in-process inventory: The partially completed products that are being fabricated on the factory floor, or are being constructed.

zero-based budgeting: The process of creating a budget based on expectations for the coming year, without reference to previous years' budgets.

Index

About the Author

Robert A. Cooke is a CPA and business consultant who brings 17 years of wide-ranging experience in public accounting to the writing of this book. Among his numerous teaching and lecturing activities, he has conducted highly successful seminars—in corporate as well as public venues—on "Finance and Accounting for Non-Financial Managers and Supervisors" for Pryor Resources, Inc. His recent consulting activities have included presenting workshops and training seminars in small business management and financial management. He has also been involved personally in the ownership and management of several businesses.

Final Examination

The McGraw-Hill 36-Hour Course in Finance for Nonfinancial Managers

If you have completed your study of *The McGraw-Hill 36-Hour Course in Finance for Nonfinancial Managers,* you should be prepared to take this final examination. It is a comprehensive test, consisting of 80 questions.

Instructions

1. You may treat this as an "open book" exam by consulting this and any other textbook. Or, you can reassure yourself that you have gained superior knowledge by taking the exam without reference to any other material.

2. Answer each of the test questions on the answer sheet provided at the end of the exam. For each question, write the letter of your choice on the answer blank that corresponds to the number of the question you are answering.

3. All questions are multiple-choice, with two to four alternative answers from which to choose. Always select the answer that represents in your mind the *best* among the choices.

4. Each correct answer is worth one point. A passing grade of 70 percent (56 correct answers) entitles you to receive a Certificate of Achievement. This handsome certificate, suitable for framing, attests to your proven knowledge of the contents of this course.

5. Carefully fill in your name and address in the spaces provided at the top of the answer sheet, remove the answer sheet from the book, and send it to:

Allyson Ruiz
36-Hour Course in Finance for Nonfinancial Managers
Professional Books Group
McGraw-Hill, Inc.
11 West 19th Street
New York, NY 10011

1. Reports prepared on the accrual basis reflect:
   a. income earned and expenses incurred
   b. cash receipts and cash disbursements only
   c. income earned and cash disbursements
   d. cash receipts and expenses incurred

2. The matching principle requires that expenses be deducted from related revenue in the period in which the revenue occurs.
   a. true
   b. false

3. The Internal Revenue Service makes up the rules for preparation of financial reports.
   a. true
   b. false

4. Shirley, who has a seashell business, hires Tom to drive her truck, delivering shells to customers. During June, Tom works 150 hours, and Shirley pays him on July 5. This is an expense of which month, on an accrual basis operating report?
   a. June
   b. July
   c. not enough information given to make a determination

5. In a mercantile business (a retailer or a wholesaler), a sale occurs and is included in the sales figure on the financial report in the period in which:
   a. the customer orders the merchandise
   b. the customer pays for the merchandise
   c. the merchandise is delivered to the customer (or the customer picks it up)
   d. when the owner of the business is sure the customer will not return the merchandise

6. Pearl, who owns a jewelry store in Boston, orders merchandise from Jean, a wholesaler in San Francisco. On the way across the country, the

shipment falls into the Mississippi River and is lost. Nevertheless, Pearl has to pay Jean for the jewelry.
  a. true
  b. false
  c. depends on the shipping terms

7. Assume the same situation as in question 5, except that the shipment is not lost in the river and Jean ships the jewelry on consignment to Pearl. Jean can include the value of the shipment in her sales:
  a. when the jewelry leaves Jean's warehouse
  b. when the jewelry arrives at Pearl's store
  c. piece-by-piece, as Jean sells each piece of jewelry
  d. whenever Jean's bookkeeper decides to list it in the sales record

8. Archie owns an appliance repair business. He repairs a dishwasher for Dorothy. Archie includes the sale in his report when:
  a. Dorothy calls Archie and orders the repair service
  b. Archie repairs the dishwasher
  c. Dorothy pays Archie for the repair
  d. none of the above

9. For every expense, there was or will be a check written sometime.
  a. true
  b. false

10. On an income statement covering one year, prepared according to GAAP, a *bad debt expense* represents:
  a. the total amount owed by customers who became insolvent during the year
  b. according to estimates by management, the amount of the year's sales for which the company will never be paid in the future
  c. the total of checks written to customers who are insolvent
  d. none of the above

11. *Sales allowance* and *sales return* mean the same thing.
  a. true
  b. false

12. *Cost of goods sold* on an annual income statement should be composed of:
  a. the cost of merchandise (for resale) purchased during the year
  b. beginning inventory plus purchases minus ending inventory
  c. purchases plus ending inventory minus beginning inventory
  d. a guess as to how much the merchandise that was sold probably cost the business

13. In a time of rising prices (inflation), an enterprise can reduce its reported profits, and therefore taxes, by using which inventory system?

      a. FIFO
      b. LIFO

14. Inventory valuation must follow the physical flow of goods. That is, a coal yard must use LIFO and a grocery store must use FIFO.
      a. true
      b. false

15. A perpetual inventory system:
      a. is a system of recording every item that is added to and every item that is taken out of inventory
      b. requires a great deal of recordkeeping
      c. is feasible for many businesses only since moderately priced computers became available
      d. all of the above

16. The conservatism principle states that:
      a. accountants must wear dark suits and subdued ties
      b. income cannot be reported on an income statement until it is earned (as when a sale takes place) but losses should be reported as soon as there is a possibility they may occur
      c. assets (with the exception of property and equipment) should be reported at the lower of their cost or their current market value
      d. both *b* and *c*

17. If a mercantile business is to preserve its cash, it should:
      a. raise its selling prices when the cost of replacing merchandise in inventory is increased
      b. wait to raise prices until it starts to sell merchandise for which it paid a higher price
      c. raise its prices when the bank calls to say the bank account is overdrawn

18. A trade discount is:
      a. a discount given to a customer for prompt payment of an invoice
      b. a discount given to a customer because they are a reseller (such as a retailer) of the merchandise

19. Allocation of expenses between departments or divisions can be based upon:
      a. sales volume
      b. floor space
      c. any reasonable basis
      d. all of the above

20. If the chief executive of an enterprise can control an expense, that expense is deemed to be controllable by every manager within the enterprise.

a. true
b. false

21. *Breakeven point* can be defined as that level of sales at which:
   a. total of all expenses equals total sales
   b. total of variable expenses equals total sales
   c. total of fixed expenses equals total sales
   d. none of the above

22. *Fixed expenses* never change, no matter how big the enterprise grows.
   a. true
   b. false

23. The *contribution margin* of an item is:
   a. that portion of the selling price that management will donate to charity
   b. surplus products that will be donated to charity
   c. the difference between the sales price and the variable costs of an item
   d. the difference between the sales price and the fixed costs of an item

24. Depreciation is:
   a. a tax deduction item, for which there is no logical reason, generously allowed by the IRS
   b. the difference between what an item originally cost and its value today on the used equipment market
   c. the allocation of the cost of a piece of equipment over the useful life of that equipment
   d. accountants' mumbo jumbo that ensures their job security

25. If an asset which cost $12,000, has a salvage value of $2,000 and a five-year useful life, the annual straight-line depreciation would be $2,000.
   a. true
   b. false

26. Salvage value must be used for every asset subject to depreciation, even though it is sure to be worthless at the end of its useful life (like a well-used copy machine).
   a. true
   b. false

27. You can determine what the real estate and equipment owned by an enterprise is worth by looking at the section of the balance sheet called *property and equipment.*
   a. true
   b. false

28. Accelerated depreciation is:
    a. a method of depreciating automobiles with fast acceleration
    b. a method computing depreciation that results in a high deprecia-
       tion expense at the end of an asset's life
    c. a method of computing depreciation that results in a high depre-
       ciation expense at the beginning of an asset's life
    d. none of the above

29. Accelerated depreciation can be justified because it offsets repair
    expense that increases as equipment ages.
    a. true
    b. false

30. When a units-of-production depreciation method is used, it makes it
    easy to predict depreciation expense in future years.
    a. true
    b. false

31. The capitalization policy of an enterprise is a dollar level below which
    equipment cost will not be depreciated but will be treated as an
    expense in the year it is acquired.
    a. true
    b. false

32. An error that is not material is one that:
    a. will never be noticed by the boss, we hope
    b. can be easily covered up
    c. would not cause anyone to change a decision about operations if it
       were known and corrected

33. If a piece of equipment is sold for less than its book value, the loss
    should be ignored and omitted from the financial statements, accord-
    ing to GAAP.
    a. true
    b. false

34. If a repair to a machine is so extensive that it lengthens the useful life
    of the machine, the cost of the repair is reflected in the financial state-
    ments as:
    a. a repair expense on the income statement
    b. an addition to the cost of the machine, which is then subject to
       depreciation
    c. an intangible asset that is amortized over several years
    d. omitted from the financial statements with only a brief explanation
       in the notes to the financial statements

35. Cash flow can be defined as the cash that will be saved by replacing manual labor, an old machine, or an outside supplier by a new machine.
    a. true
    b. false

36. In computing the cash flow from a machine, depreciation has to be considered as if it were expenditure of cash.
    a. true
    b. false

37. Payback from a machine purchase is:
    a. an illegal kickback from the supplier of the machine to the folks in the purchasing department
    b. a legitimate cash bonus paid by the manufacturer of the machine to the company that bought the machine
    c. the cost of the machine divided by the annual cash flow generated by the machine
    d. a termination bonus given to the person replaced by the machine

38. A future value is how much a sum of money will be worth in a number of years if left to earn compound interest over that time.
    a. true
    b. false

39. Internal rate of return is:
    a. what can be earned by loaning money to employees
    b. the cash flow from a machine stated as a compound interest rate on the investment in the machine
    c. a method of comparing the return on an equipment purchase to other investments, such as interest-bearing securities
    d. both *b* and *c*

40. Some leases are not truly leases but are installment loans because:
    a. they are offered by commercial banks
    b. the amount and number of payments are approximately the same as they would be for an installment loan
    c. equipment leases are illegal in some states

41. An income statement can be compared to a moving picture, while a balance sheet is like a snapshot.
    a. true
    b. false

42. On a balance sheet, all assets are displayed at their market value.
    a. true
    b. false

43. Common-size financial statements express each line item as a percentage of some base line item, such as net sales or total assets.
    a. true
    b. false

44. Working capital is defined as:
    a. the amount of money an enterprise has "working," or earning interest, in an account at the bank
    b. the figure determined by subtracting current liabilities from current assets
    c. the increase in accumulated depreciation from one year to the next

45. Working capital can be a measure of an enterprise's ability to pay its bills.
    a. true
    b. false

46. Goodwill can be added as an asset to a corporate balance sheet whenever the board of directors of the corporation thinks it is appropriate to do so.
    a. true
    b. false

47. Total assets equal total liabilities plus total equity.
    a. true
    b. false

48. Equity is an accurate measure of the true value of an enterprise.
    a. true
    b. false

49. Book value of common stock should be a reflection of market value of the stock.
    a. true
    b. false

50. Net assets means the same thing as:
    a. working capital
    b. net equipment
    c. equity
    d. market value of assets

51. Division of income among partners in a partnership is inflexible, as it is determined by state law.
    a. true
    b. false

52. If you are a stockholder in a corporation, the number of votes you have at a stockholders' meeting is determined by:
    a. how much you paid for your stock
    b. whether or not you are an original stockholder
    c. the number of shares of stock you own
    d. the political clout of your stockbroker

53. Dividends are one of many expenses that are subtracted from sales to arrive at net income.
    a. true
    b. false

54. Budgeting is too complicated for mere mortals. The preparation of budgets is best left to the accountants.
    a. true
    b. false

55. Long-range and short-range goal-setting and planning should precede the preparation of budgets.
    a. true
    b. false

56. Sales budgets should be prepared by:
    a. the sales manager
    b. the sales people in the field
    c. the chief accountant
    d. both *a* and *b*

57. There is no need to budget balance sheet items, such as inventory levels.
    a. true
    b. false

58. Zero-based budgeting, in essence, consists of:
    a. adding some percentage to last year's budget numbers
    b. asking for more expense budget than you will need, so you will have what you want after your request is cut by management
    c. computing your needs from scratch, as if there were no numbers from prior years

59. Flexible budgeting can be defined as:
    a. a budget in which the budget for variable expenses will vary with the actual sales volume or some other measure of activity
    b. a budget that will let department managers change their budget if they spend more than they expected to spend
    c. a budget that top management changes every week
    d. a budget printed on flimsy (flexible) paper

60. Budget variance percentages are usually computed as follows:
    a. (actual results minus the budget number) ÷ the budget number
    b. (actual results minus the budget number) ÷ actual results

61. Budgets should be compared with actual results:
    a. at the end of the year
    b. at least monthly
    c. whenever the managers have some extra free time
    d. never (it is of interest to the accounting department only)

62. A cash flow budget should take into consideration:
    a. the operating budget
    b. available bank credit
    c. equipment acquisition budget
    d. all of the above

63. Much confusion over operating and budget reports is caused by department managers considering an amount as spent when the funds are obligated, while accountants do not consider the expense as incurred until delivery of the product or service takes place.
    a. true
    b. false

64. In manufacturing, direct labor usually consists of:
    a. the wages and salaries of everyone who works in the factory or is connected with the production department(s)
    b. the salaries of managers—those who direct others
    c. the wages of those who actually work on the fabrication or assembly of the product
    d. the wages of all hourly employees

65. In manufacturing, direct material usually refers to the materials that become part of the finished products, as opposed to incidental items and supplies.
    a. true
    b. false

66. Factory overhead generally refers to:
    a. the cost of a new roof on the factory
    b. all the costs of production except for direct materials and direct labor
    c. all the costs of operating the enterprise (including sales, accounting, etc.) except for direct materials and direct labor
    d. all the costs of production except for depreciation on machinery, direct materials, and direct labor

67. Probably the most common method of allocating overhead costs to various products is to base the allocation on direct-labor hours.

a. true

b. false

68. In the long-term contract method of reporting gross profit:
    a. gross profit is assumed to be earned only when the contract is 100 percent completed
    b. gross profit is assumed to be earned when the contract is signed
    c. gross profit is assumed to be earned equally over the years the contract is in progress
    d. gross profit is assumed to be earned according to the percentage of completion at the end of each year

Questions 69 to 79 relate to the following financial statements of Claude's clothing store:

Claude's Classy Clothing
Income Statements
December 31

	Last year	Prior year
Sales, net of returns and allowances	$500,000	$400,000
Subtract: Cost of goods sold	300,000	250,000
Gross profit	200,000	150,000
Expenses:		
Selling expenses	100,000	80,000
General expenses	50,000	45,000
Total selling and general expenses	150,000	125,000
Net operating income	50,000	25,000
Interest expense	9,000	10,000
Net income before income tax	41,000	15,000
Income tax	10,000	4,000
Net income	$ 31,000	$ 11,000

Claude's Classy Clothing
Balance Sheets

	Last year	Prior year
Assets		
Current assets:		
Cash	$ 12,000	$ 10,000
Accounts receivable, net of bad debt allowance	36,000	32,000
Inventory	100,000	82,000
Prepaid expenses	2,000	1,000
Total current assets	150,000	125,000
Fixtures and equipment, net of depreciation allowance	50,000	55,000
Total assets	$200,000	$180,000

Liabilities
Current liabilities:

Current portion, loans payable	$ 30,000	$ 25,000
Accounts payable	40,000	35,000
Taxes payable	4,000	3,000
Accrued expenses	1,000	2,000
Total current liabilities	75,000	65,000

Long-term liabilities:

Notes payable to bank	60,000	75,000
Total liabilities	135,000	140,000

Stockholders' equity
Common stock: $10 par value per share:
15,000 shares authorized; 1,000 issued

and outstanding	10,000	10,000
Retained earnings	55,000	30,000
Total stockholders' equity	65,000	40,000
Total liabilities and equity	$200,000	$180,000

69. Working capital of this corporation, at Dec. 31 last year, is:
    a. $150,000
    b. $200,000
    c. $48,000
    d. $75,000

70. The corporation borrows $20,000 from the bank, repayable in 90 days, and puts the money in its checking account. The working capital will have:
    a. increased
    b. decreased
    c. stayed the same

71. The book value of this corporation, at Dec. 31 last year, is:
    a. $200,000
    b. $65,000
    c. $55,000
    d. cannot be determined from the information given

72. The liquidation value of this corporation, at Dec. 31 last year, is:
    a. $65,000
    b. $200,000
    c. $55,000
    d. cannot be determined from the information given

73. If you decided to buy this corporation from Claude at a capitalization rate of 25 percent (based on the numbers from last year), you would pay:

    a. $124,000
    b. $775,000
    c. $65,000
    d. $7,750

74. The current ratio of this corporation, at Dec. 31 last year, is:
    a. 1.2 to 1
    b. 1.5 to 1
    c. 2.0 to 1
    d. none of the above

75. Compute the current ratio for this corporation at Dec. 31 of the prior year and determine whether the ratio, from the prior year to last year is:
    a. improving
    b. worsening

76. The inventory turnover ratio of this corporation, at Dec. 31 last year, is:
    a. 3.0 to 1
    b. 5.0 to 1
    c. 0.3 to 1
    d. 2.0 to 1

77. The earnings per share of this corporation, at Dec. 31 last year, are:
    a. $2.07
    b. $13.33
    c. $31.00
    d. some other number

78. The debt-to-equity ratio of this corporation, at Dec. 31 last year, is:
    a. 13.5 to 1
    b. 2.5 to 1
    c. 2.1 to 1
    d. 7.5 to 1

79. Receivable turnover, in number of days, of this corporation, at Dec. 31 last year, is 26.3 days.
    a. true
    b. false

80. Finance is an easy subject that can be mastered with very little study and concentration.
    a. true
    b. false
    c. both true and false

Name_____

Address_____

City_____State____Zip_____

Final Examination
Answer Sheet:
The McGraw-Hill 36-Hour
Course in Finance
for Nonfinancial Managers

See instructions on page 1 of the Final Examination.

1. _____	17. _____	33. _____	49. _____	65. _____
2. _____	18. _____	34. _____	50. _____	66. _____
3. _____	19. _____	35. _____	51. _____	67. _____
4. _____	20. _____	36. _____	52. _____	68. _____
5. _____	21. _____	37. _____	53. _____	69. _____
6. _____	22. _____	38. _____	54. _____	70. _____
7. _____	23. _____	39. _____	55. _____	71. _____
8. _____	24. _____	40. _____	56. _____	72. _____
9. _____	25. _____	41. _____	57. _____	73. _____
10. _____	26. _____	42. _____	58. _____	74. _____
11. _____	27. _____	43. _____	59. _____	75. _____
12. _____	28. _____	44. _____	60. _____	76. _____
13. _____	29. _____	45. _____	61. _____	77. _____
14. _____	30. _____	46. _____	62. _____	78. _____
15. _____	31. _____	47. _____	63. _____	79. _____
16. _____	32. _____	48. _____	64. _____	80. _____